NARRATIVES

OF

TOURS IN INDIA

NARRATIVES

OF

TOURS IN INDIA

MADE BY

HIS EXCELLENCY LORD CONNEMARA, G.C.I.E.,

GOVERNOR OF MADRAS.

1886-1890.

BY

J. D. REES

GYAN

Published by

Gyan Publishing House
5, Ansari Road
Daryaganj, New Delhi-110002
Phone: 011-47034999, 9811692060
E-mail: books@gyanbooks.com

Distribution Network
gyanbooks.com
India, USA, Canada, UK, Australia

ISBN: 978-93-6208-277-0 (HB)
First Published, 1892

2nd Impression 2024

Printed at: Gyan Press, Delhi.

NARRATIVE OF TOURS IN INDIA
Author: J. D. REES

TOURS IN INDIA.

NARRATIVES

OF

TOURS IN INDIA

MADE BY

HIS EXCELLENCY LORD CONNEMARA, G.C.I.E.,

GOVERNOR OF MADRAS.

1886—1890.

BY

J. D. REES,

Companion of the Most Eminent Order of the Indian Empire; Collector and Magistrate, Nilgiris; Persian and Hindustani Translator to the Madras Government; Fellow of the University of Madras; Fellow of the Royal Geographical Society; Member of the Royal Asiatic Society and of the Geographical Society of Paris; some time Translator to the Government of Madras in Tamil and Telugu.

MADRAS:

PUBLISHED BY THE SUPERINTENDENT,
GOVERNMENT PRESS.

1891.

PREFACE.

THE first of the following Narratives of Tours, made in India between the years 1886 and 1890, was written for private circulation, that friends at home might know what Lord Connemara and his staff were doing in India. A copy of the first narrative, how I know not, was communicated to the English Press and was very favourably reviewed. The Editors of certain Indian newspapers then asked that they might be supplied with copies; and, as there was nothing confidential in the narratives, their requests were granted. In this way these papers, which were originally meant to be private, and were intended for home consumption, have been made public, and they are now reprinted in a book form in accordance with suggestions made by many literary, official, and journalistic friends. The eighth and ninth, and a portion of the tenth narratives were written by Mr. Claude Vincent, who performed my duties, during my absence in England last year. The rest are my own composition, and I am responsible for the accuracy of the information they contain, and for the opinions which are expressed in them.

MADRAS, J. D. REES.
7th Dec. 1890.

CONTENTS.

CHAPTER I.

NORTH ARCOT, SALEM, COIMBATORE.

CHAPTER II.

BELLARY, ANANTAPUR, KURNOOL.

CHAPTER III.

WYNAAD, MALABAR, COCHIN, TRAVANCORE, TINNEVELLY, MADURA, TRICHINOPOLY, TANJORE.

CHAPTER IV.

CALCUTTA.

CHAPTER V.

SALEM.

CHAPTER VI.

MYSORE, SERINGAPATAM, BANGALORE, OOSOOR, KOLAR.

CHAPTER VII.

MALABAR, SOUTH CANARA, GOA, BELLARY, CUDDAPAH, NORTH ARCOT AND NELLORE.

CHAPTER VIII.

GANJAM.

BY MR. CLAUDE VINCENT.

CHAPTER IX.

TANJORE AND SOUTH ARCOT.

BY MR. CLAUDE VINCENT.

CHAPTER X.

CALCUTTA, DARJEELING, ALLAHABAD, SIMLA, QUETTA, KURRACHEE AND BOMBAY.

CHAPTER XII.

THE EURASIAN SETTLEMENTS OF WHITEFIELD AND SAUSMOND.

CHAPTER XIII.

TANJORE, TRIVALUR, CHINGLEPUT, CONJEEVERAM, BEZWADA AND CUMBUM, SOUTH ARCOT.

MAYAVERAM-MUTTUPETT AND EAST COAST RAILWAYS.

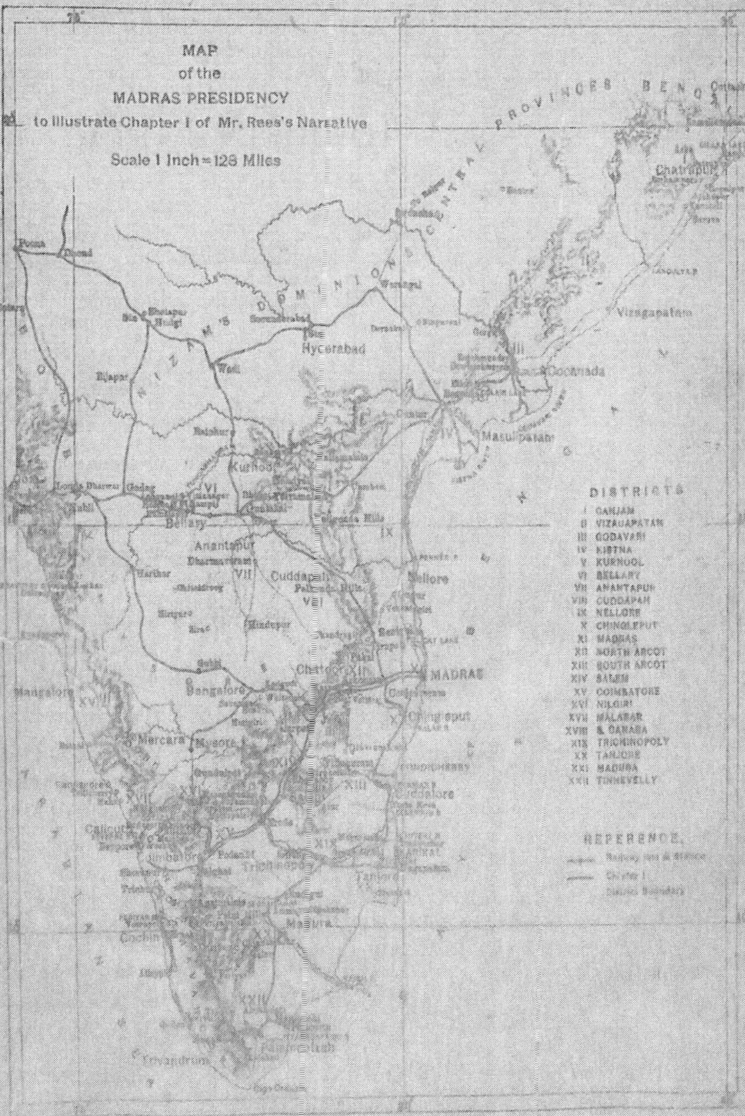
MAP
of the
MADRAS PRESIDENCY
to illustrate Chapter I of Mr. Rees's Narrative
Scale 1 Inch = 128 Miles
DISTRICTS
I GANJAM
II VIZAGAPATAM
III GODAVARI
IV KISTNA
V KURNOOL
VI BELLARY
VII ANANTAPUR
VIII CUDDAPAH
IX NELLORE
X CHINGLEPUT
XI MADRAS
XII NORTH ARCOT
XIII SOUTH ARCOT
XIV SALEM
XV COIMBATORE
XVI NILGIRI
XVII MALABAR
XVIII S. CANARA
XIX TRICHINOPOLY
XX TANJORE
XXI MADURA
XXII TINNEVELLY
REFERENCE.
Chapter I
District Boundary
Vizagapatam
Hyderabad
Cocanada
Masulipatam
Kurnool
Bellary
Anantapur
Cuddapah
Nellore
MADRAS
Chingleput
Bangalore
Mangalore
Mercara
Mysore
Cuddalore
Calicut
Trichinopoly
Tanjore
Madura
Cochin
Trivandrum
Palamcotah
Chatrapur
Wadi
Poona

TOURS IN INDIA.

CHAPTER I.

NORTH ARCOT, SALEM, COIMBATORE.

Departure from Madras—Our party—Gathering at Railway Station—Maharajah of Vizianagram—"Sakuntala"—Forest fires—Address from Hindu Brethren of Wallajnagar—Arrival at Katpadi—Vellore jail—Lingam Lakshmaji—Fort—Kalyanamantapam—Ex-zemindar of Palcondah—Mission school—Tombs of Tippoo Sultan's relatives—Musulman Stipendiaries—Reception at Salem—Rev. Mr. Foulkes—Salem riots—Curious mottoes—More addresses—Shevapett mosque—Condition of town—Native entertainment—Central jail—Prisoner's petition—Local dispensary—Weaving industry—A busy afternoon—Arrival at Coimbatore—Visits to local institutions—Sir Thomas Munro—Village Munsiffs' bill—Horse-breeding establishment—At Mettapolliem—*En route* to Hills—Burliar gardens—Mr. Lawson—Colonel Jago—Mr. Burrows—Municipal address at Charing Cross—Arrival at Ootacamund.

ON March 30th, 1887, we* left Madras for the first time since the Governor's arrival on the 8th of December 1886 from England. A very large assembly of gentlemen, European and Native, and of European ladies were present on the platform at 5-30 P.M. to see us start. Members of Council, Maharajas, ex-Dewans of Native States, Military officers, Civil officers, representatives of the Press, all seemed to express a feeling of genuine regret that the Governor was leaving. The presence of the Body Guard of

* His Excellency the Lord Connemara.
Mr. Rees, Private Secretary.
The Viscount Marsham, A.D.C.

Lancers in scarlet tunics, well-mounted and well-dressed, a general feature of such departures from Madras, was not absent on this occasion. Of the chiefs present on the platform, perhaps the Maharaja of Vizianagram looked the most distinguished. The night before starting we had sat up till past midnight seeing his theatrical company perform in Sanskrit the well-known drama of Sakuntala, or the missing Ring, in which we have such charming pictures of early Indian womanhood.

The Agent of the Railway came with us to Arkónam, where we dined extremely well in the Refreshment Room of the Railway Company. The Superintendent of Police met us here, and after leaving the station, the train moved on through the night towards Vellore our destination, and on the way forest-fires, raging in the hills on our left, made the line of march one grand illumination. The outline of the hills was marked in fire. This is one of the evils which we hope the new Forest Rules will prevent.

As we passed Arcot, the "Hindu Bréthren of Wallajahnaggar" presented a comprehensive address on the platform, which there was no time to answer. At 10 o'clock we got to Kátpádi, the station whence Vellore and Chittoor, the chief towns of the North Arcot District, are reached. Here we were met by Mr. Crole, the Judge, and Mr. Glenny, the Collector, who kindly entertained us for the night in a little camp near the railway station.

To those, who have not visited India, it will be necessary to explain that the Collector is the administrator of a district and the agent of Government, and Chief Magistrate within a charge, which may run in Madras Presidency from 2,000 to 10,000 square miles. His somewhat misleading designation is derived from the fact, that he is responsible for the revenue of his district, which may amount to as much as half a million sterling, the largest portion of which is paid as land assessment. Actual collections are made by native officers in every village. A certain number of such village officers pay in their collections to another functionary, who again deposits them in the treasury of a superior official, having authority over a large number of villages, whose subordinate he is. A certain number of these superior native officers are in turn under the authority of an officer in charge of a division of a district, and the last named officer, and all others in charge of such divisions are subordinate to the Collector, who is personally responsible to the Government.

Next morning at 6 o'clock we rode to Vellore and visited first the Central Jail, one of the most important in the Presidency. Colonel McLeod, the Superintendent, and the Medical Officer met us here. We had some conversation with a State prisoner, and with the notorious convict Lingam Lakshmaji, once Agent to the Maharaja of Jeypore in Vizagapatam, once Deputy Inspector of Schools, Author, Pandit, Patron of the drama, Sanskritist, writer of Latin essays, and now undergoing a sentence of imprisonment for forgery. Under the orders of Government this individual is allowed special privileges during his imprisonment. He is employed on literary work. The solitary wards, the industrial section where admirable carpets are made, the gunny bag weaving, and the purdah-making were all inspected.

To the prolonged visit to this very interesting jail, succeeded a visit to the not less interesting fort,—the old fort of Vellore,—built of massive granite stone, and surrounded by a broad wet ditch, up to which gently slopes the grassy *glacis*. Inside the fort the most beautiful specimen of architecture is the Kalyana-mantapam, or marriage-porch, the carvings of which are very remarkable. There are also large mansions in which State prisoners used to be kept, and here the ex-Zemindar of Palcondah, whose case has more than once been before Parliament, lived for many years. The Governor conversed with him for some time and promised to consider a petition he is about to present to Government. He expressed himself very much pleased with his reception. He speaks no English, and is an infirm, but not undignified old gentleman. All that Government can do to alleviate his lot has been done for him. It is hopeless now to consider whether or not he should have been otherwise treated when a child.

We lunched with the Sub-Collector, and there met the District Engineer, the Head Assistant Collector, and others. After luncheon the school of the Free Church of Scotland had to be visited, and the tombs of the relatives of Tippu Sultan to be seen. There is a large Mussulman population in Vellore, many of whom draw stipends from Government in consideration of their relationship to, or dependence upon, the ex-royal family of Mysore.

After dining again in the little camp with Mr. Glenny, we got into our railway carriages, and, during the night, were carried on to Salem, which we reached in the early morning. Nothing at Vellore gave more pleasure than the condition of the Central Jail, which is attributable chiefly to Colonel McLeod, its Superintendent, who has been in charge for many years.

On the morning of the 1st of April, Mr. McWatters, the Collector, the Judge, the Superintendent of Police, Mr. Cavendish, the Superintendent of Jail, and others met the Governor on the platform, and we soon started for Salem, which is about as far from the station as are Vellore, and most other populous places, along the Madras Railway. Arches of flowers were erected across the road, and inscriptions in various languages put up. At the gateway of the town the Rev. Mr. Foulkes, whose wife is one of the few European Zemindars, together with a deputation of citizens, stopped Lord Connemara to present him with an address. The streets were crowded to overflowing with people. Flowers, garlands, bags of scent were thrown on to the carriages. No one would have thought that as lately as 1882 the Hindus and Mussulmans of this town had been at daggers-drawn, and that a riot had ensued which called for the intervention of the Military before it was put down. Some of the mottoes on the arches were rather curious. At the hospital an archway bore the inscription "Never say die;" at the Collector's house there was another, *Mens sana in corpore sano.* French, Latin,

Tamil, Sanskrit and English proved insufficient to express all the feelings of the good people of Salem, who gave His Excellency a very handsome and very hearty reception.

At 5 o'clock in the evening a Hindu address and a Mussulman address were presented, to both of which a reply was of course given. Next we went to see the mosque at Shevapett, the proximate cause of the riots referred to above. The afternoon was occupied in acquiring information concerning the industrial and sanitary condition of the town, the various aspects of the railway question, the water-supply and other matters, which it will take much time and much money to bring to a satisfactory conclusion. Several matters of detail, which were referred to in the various addresses presented, were also noted and an opportunity was taken to express an earnest hope that the Mussulman community, here and elsewhere, would improve in education and advance in enterprise.

At night a native entertainment was given at the Collector's office, where the usual dances, and songs were performed, and sung.

Next morning early the Central Jail was inspected. One of the prisoners had a petition to present. He said he had often been in jail, in fact, could not keep out of it. No sooner was he released than he again got into mischief, he felt that he was a great expense to Government, and gave a great deal of trouble, and he could see nothing for it, but that he should be provided with an appointment, and so settled for life.

At the Dispensary little was elicited except the complaint of the Doctor, that the instruments supplied by the Store Department of the India Office were not so good as they might be. Enquiry has shown, however, that such complaints seldom bear examination.

One of the chief industries of Salem is weaving, which, it is feared, is rather in a depressed condition.

In the afternoon the Governor, accompanied by the Collector, visited the weavers' quarter, next inspected the Collector's and Forest Offices, gave away prizes at the Salem College, and visited the London Mission School.

After this fairly busy day, we dined at 7 o'clock and drove to the station, halting at a very fine archway erected by the late Station Master, and left at 9 o'clock for Coimbatore, where we arrived in the early morning on the 3rd of April, and where we were met by the Collector Mr. Willock, the Judge, Mr. Stokes, and many others.

No time was lost in commencing business, and after a drive around the town, we visited the Normal School, the Taluk Office, and the Municipal market, where an address was presented by the Municipality, and where the leading natives of the town were introduced to His Excellency. In replying to this address, the Governor took the opportunity to say that though heads of villages might not, when acting in a judicial capacity, give universal satisfaction, the existing state of things was brought about by no less distinguished an authority than Sir Thomas Munro, and that he would have to consider the subject in all its bearings, and could not promise at present that any changes should be made. He thought, however, that it was probable that greater powers of supervision over the

Village Munsifs might be conceded to superior courts. A Bill to bring this about and to remedy other defects in the existing state of affairs will shortly be before the Legislative Council. In fact where there is a competent Village Head, in whom the people have confidence, he does a great deal of useful work. In a village in Tinnevelly, in which I resided, the sole European inhabitant, for upwards of a year, the Munsif, had a capital court-house, sat on a bench covered with green baize, conducted business with much dignity, did substantial justice, and always had his hands full.

The jail was visited and various points were noted for communication to the Secretariat, more particularly concerning the treatment of juvenile criminals. The Government horse-breeding establishment received attention, six stallions were inspected, and a dinner party concluded a long day.

We slept in the train and awoke next morning at Mettupálaiyam at the foot of the Hills. On the way up the ghaut the Governor inspected the Burliar Gardens, where we were met by Mr. Lawson, and afterwards proceeded to Coonoor, where the General Commanding the Division and his Staff, Colonel Jago, Master of the Nílgiri Hounds, Mr. Burrows, the Collector, and many others received us. After a brief halt for breakfast, we rode into Ootacamund, where an address of welcome was read by the Municipality at Charing Cross, who hoped that His Excellency would like the place, and were assured, in return, that he looked forward with great confidence to find a happy summer home among them on the Nílgiris.

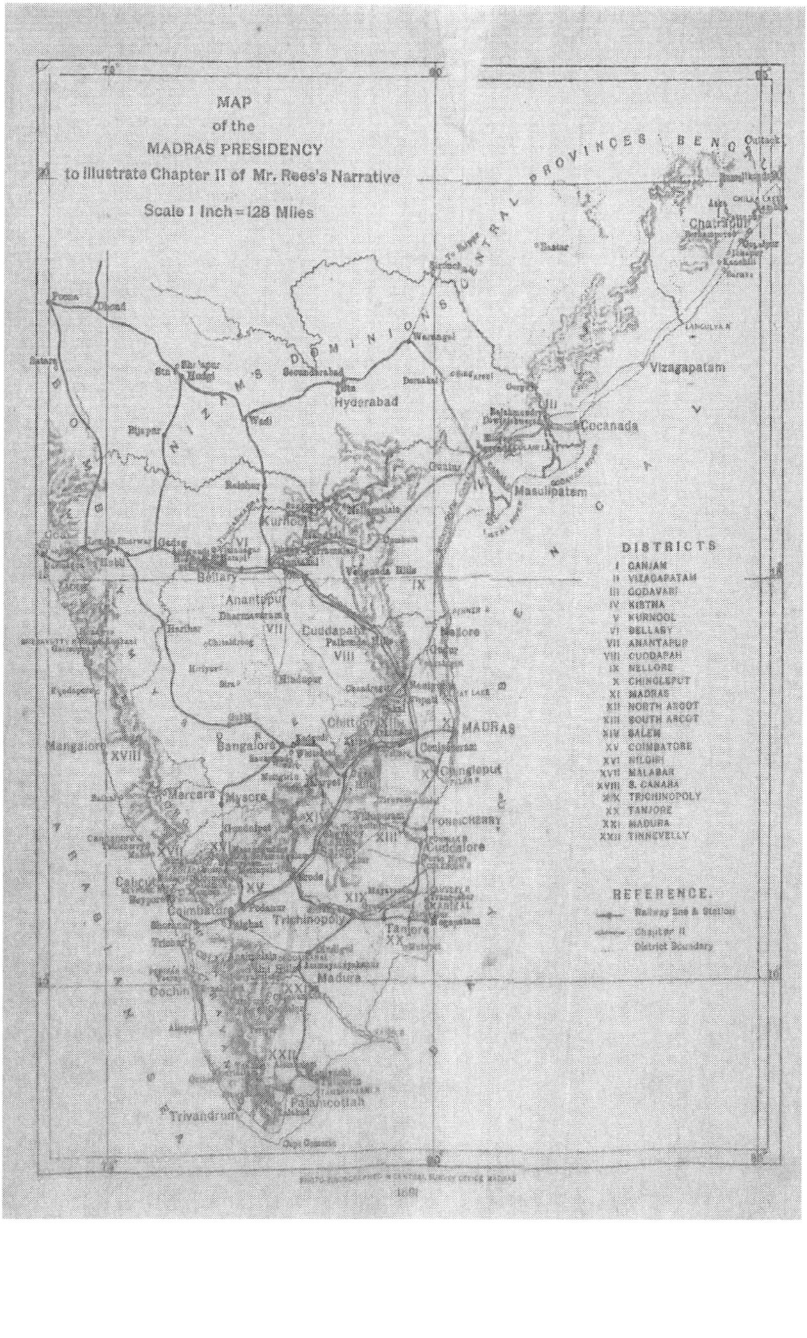
MAP
of the
MADRAS PRESIDENCY
to illustrate Chapter II of Mr. Rees's Narrative
Scale 1 Inch = 128 Miles
DISTRICTS
I GANJAM
II VIZAGAPATAM
III GODAVARI
IV KISTNA
V KURNOOL
VI BELLARY
VII ANANTAPUR
VIII CUDDAPAH
IX NELLORE
X CHINGLEPUT
XI MADRAS
XII NORTH ARCOT
XIII SOUTH ARCOT
XIV SALEM
XV COIMBATORE
XVI NILGIRI
XVII MALABAR
XVIII S. CANARA
XIX TRICHINOPOLY
XX TANJORE
XXI MADURA
XXII TINNEVELLY
REFERENCE.
Railway line & Station
Chapter II
District Boundary
CENTRAL PROVINCES
NIZAM'S DOMINIONS
Hyderabad
Secunderabad
Vizagapatam
Cocanada
Masulipatam
Bellary
Anantapur
Cuddapah
Nellore
MADRAS
Chingleput
Bangalore
Mysore
Mangalore
Mercara
Calicut
Coimbatore
Trichinopoly
Tanjore
Madura
Cochin
Trivandrum
Palamcottah
Cuddalore
Chatrapur
Kurnool
Chittoor
Conjeeveram
Warangal
Wadi
Raichur
Hubli
Poona

CHAPTER II.

BELLARY, ANANTAPUR, KURNOOL.

Departure from Ootacamund—Our party—At Mettapolliem—Anamalai Hills—Salem—Renigunta—Sacred Tirupati—Nellore State Railway—Kodur and Mamandur Reserves—Sir Dietrich Brandis—Cuddapah—Guntakal—Southern Mahratta Railway—Bellary—Raja of Sandur—His State—Levée—Military Hospital—Fort Church—Madras Cavalry Lines—Messrs. Sabapathy and Company's mills—Sir Ramasawmy's Lying-in Hospital—Thugs—*En route* to Hospett—Darojee tank—Our party—From Hospett to Vijianagar—An accident—A panther at large—Humpi ruins—Duarte Barbosa—Old Vizianagar—Pampatiswami temple—Picturesque sights—Vigneswara Swami—Mantapams—Nizam's frontier—Fallen temples—Elephant stables—Deserted zenanas—Ryots' indifference—Megasthenes on India—Vittalswami's pagoda—Indian squirrels—Legend from Ramayana—Bathing ghaut—Torii-like monoliths—Anagundi—Coracles—Jain temples—Native club—London Mission schools Sisters of the Convent of Good Shepherd—Entertainment at Prince of Wales' choultry—People's Association address—Technical education—Sanscrit address—Sham fight—Burmese dacoits—Gooty—Sir Thomas Munro's tomb—Anantapur—Addresses at Munro's cutcherry—Replies—Buckacherla project—Pamedy cloths—Dharmavaram silks—Address at High school—Sir M. E. Grant Duff—Jubilee Park—People's Association address—Gooty fortress—Ascent of hill—A Mahratta General—Dhone—*Tooma* trees—Hindry—Sir Arthur Cotton's canal—Kurnool—Sunkesala—Canal journey—Nawab of Banganapalle—His brother-in-law—Addresses—Local water-supply—Native entertainment—Nandyal—Yerramalais—Viaduct—Visit to Cuddapah postponed—Ascent of ghaut—Results of Tour.

AT 8 o'clock on the morning of Tuesday, the 26th July 1887, we* left Ootacamund and proceeded out of a raincloud to the sunshine of Coonoor, ten miles, whence we descended into the heat of the lower regions of Coimbatore.

* H.E. the Lord Connemara.
Mr. J. D. Rees, Private Secretary.
Major Stewart-Mackenzie, 9th Lancers, Military Secretary.
Captain Wyndham Quin, 16th Lancers, A.D.C.

Next morning, at 4 o'clock, the English mail was delivered at Arkonam, where we breakfasted. At 10 o'clock we proceeded by the ordinary train, through Karvetnagar Zemindari, to Renigunta, the station for the sacred town of Tirupati, which has recently become the junction for the State Railway to Nellore, which, it is hoped, will enable the Government of Madras to grapple more effectually with famine, should it unhappily again attack us, and which opens out a tract of country hitherto cut off from the district served by the railway. The Engineers employed on the railway, here explained the progress of the line over which at present goods are being carried, and which, in a month or two hence, will, it is hoped, be open for passenger traffic. Mr. Higgens, the Forest Officer, had come hither to accompany us to Cuddapah, and, on the way through the Kodur and Mamandur Reserves, he described the operations now in progress in connection with forest preservation in those and other adjoining localities, of which he has special knowledge, having served in the Cuddapah district for some ten years, and having himself been in charge of the forest operations in the district for five years. Like myself, he had sat at the feet of Sir Dietrich Brandis, under the spell of whose energy and ability, a love of forest business sinks deep into the soul.

Arrived at Cuddapah, we were met by the Collector, Mr. Gabriel Stokes, the Judge, Superintendent of Police, and others. Mr. Stokes then took us for a drive when we saw the new office being built for the Collector, and the chief sights of the town, in which cholera in a mild form was present. The large tank adjoining the Collector's house was quite dry, though there were signs of rain along the line as it passed over fields cultivated with cholum, indigo, raggi, and other crops. After dining at the Collector's and learning that cholera was on the decrease, we went to our carriages, which were shunted off into a siding on the railway, until 1-30 A.M., when the mail train from Madras took us on to Guntakal. At Guntakal junction, whence the branch line to Bellary leaves the main Madras line, we were met by Messrs. Wilkinson and McClouhin, of the Southern Mahratta Railway Company, who gave us much information concerning the proposed extension of that railway to join the Mysore line, which has since been completed, and concerning the traffic on the section thereof which extends from Gadag to Hudgi, which, he said, was satisfactory and increasing. It will be remembered that the line from Guntakal to Bellary has quite recently been made over to the Southern Mahratta Railway, the broad-gauge line having been taken up and the rail laid down on the Indian metre gauge—the gauge on which the whole of Southern Mahratta system is constructed.

After passing through a plain of black cotton soil, relieved by little droogs, or rocky hills, at intervals, we reached Bellary at 10-45, where the Collector, Mr. Winterbotham, the Judge, Mr. Goldingham, the officers commanding the different regiments and batteries stationed at Bellary, and a large number of persons were assembled. A guard of honour of the Bedfordshire Regiment was drawn up on the platform, where the Municipal Commissioners presented an address, which was briefly acknowledged.

After this the party drove to the Collector's house with an escort of the 2nd Madras Lancers. At 4 P.M., the Raja of the tiny valley of Sandur came to pay his respects and present his gift or nazzar. The State of Sandur is an interesting survival of the Mahratta dominion. Within his 160 square miles, the Raja has plenary powers extending to life and death, subject to the approval of the Madras Government. He is a comely, frank, and well-mannered young man, speaking Hindustani well, and a very little English. With him were two of his relations and his Dewan or Minister, Mr. Firth. Lord Connemara told the Raja that he was glad to hear that things were going on well in his little State, and that it would be the constant aim of the British Government to afford every protection to Native States, which represent the old families and past history of the country. To this the Raja replied that he not only dwelt secure under the shadow of the British Raj, but was, in fact, British himself, and was not to be spoken of as separate. His Excellency said he hoped to welcome the Raja one day at Madras, and then he and his relatives departed, after presenting a number of trays of flowers, sweetmeats, betel, raisins, and the like, all of which were touched by the Governor.

To this function succeeded a levée, at which all the chief European and native inhabitants of the town and district were presented to the Governor, who spoke a few words, in almost every case, to those introduced. The native officers of the regiments quartered at Bellary also filed past. The business and pleasures of the day were not yet over, and at ½ past 5 came a garden party at which the ladies of the station were presented. The country around Bellary, which not long since had presented an arid and burnt-up appearance, was now fairly green and not unpleasant to look at.

Next morning, the 29th, at ½ past 6, there was a parade of the troops of the garrison. The 2nd Madras Lancers, Field Batteries S/I and G/II, Royal Artillery, the 6th Madras Native Infantry, and a wing of the Bedfordshire Regiment, the other wing of which is in Madras, were on parade. Afterwards His Excellency, in company with Colonel Parsons, Officiating Brigadier-General, inspected the Military hospital—a fine building adjacent to the Parade Ground. The Fort Church was next visited, in company with Mr. Williams, the Chaplain, and, lastly, before returning home for breakfast, the lines of the Madras Cavalry Regiment. Colonels Parsons and Galloway explained the internal economy of the regiment, and the Veterinary Surgeon, who was present, testified to the healthiness of Bellary, as a station for horses. At 1 o'clock, the Mills of Messrs. Sabapathy and Co. were visited, and Mr. Sabapathy and some of his partners showed Lord Connemara over the extensive works and explained the uses of the elaborate machinery. Up till now spinning only was effected in these mills, but, of late, cloths have been woven which are in large demand for local use. At 4 P.M., the Civil Hospital and the District Jail claimed attention. His Excellency was much interested by his visit to the former institution, and suggested the addition of a Lying-in Hospital similar to that attached to the Monegar Choultry at Madras by the bounty of Sir Ramaswami Moodelliar. One of the patients at the hospital had endeavoured to burn himself by drinking kerosine oil and then setting fire to his clothes. A sad case was that of a pilgrim on his return from Ramesvaram to Benares, whose strength failed him by the way. Such cases are by no means uncommon in this district. The poorer pilgrims succumb, on the road, to disease and fatigue, and their miseries are frequently alleviated in institutions such as these. At the Jail, two venerable-looking prisoners, who had been convicted as Thugs and had spent 30 years in prison, seemed, at first sight, to be fitting subjects for mercy, as did a State prisoner from Malabar; but here, as in the case of Lord Lytton's Frontier petitioner, the constituted authorities have first to be consulted. After a brief visit to the European Club, there was only just time to keep an engagement to dine with the Bedfordshire Regiment, to which succeeded a very enjoyable dance given by the residents of the station at the Masonic Hall. The Governor replied briefly to the kindly words of welcome uttered, on behalf of the hosts, by Mr. Goldingham, the District Judge. Distances are very great in Bellary, and, at 2 A.M., when the party retired to bed, all its members thought they had done a pretty good day's work.

Next morning, at 11, a start was made for Hospet by the Southern Mahratta Railway, and the greater part of the three and-a-half hours occupied in accomplishing the 40 miles that intervened were spent in getting through arrears of papers which had accumulated in the hands of the Private Secretary in the last two days. There was time, however, to observe the country as we passed through it, and the most noticeable features were the Darojee tank, and the flourishing little forest reserve abutting on its waterspread. Besides the members of the Governor's staff, Mr. and Mrs. Winterbotham, Mr. and Mrs. Campbell, and Major Vernon accompanied the party. On either side of the railway were fields of young cholum all the way. After lunching at the station, we drove in our own carriages the seven miles intervening between Hospet and Kamalapur, one of the two little villages which now mark the site of the once famous city of Vijianagur. On the way one of our carriages broke down, the axle giving way. This damage was speedily repaired, in a temporary fashion, by the resourceful natives of the place. On the way we got news of the presence of a panther in the rocks hard by, and most of our party went off with rifles and police carbines to shoot it. The animal, frightened by this war-like demonstration, and even more so by the crowd of natives who surrounded the cave in which he had been seen to take refuge, declined to leave it, though efforts were made to smoke him out, and worry and frighten him out in every conceivable way.

On the morning of the 31st, soon after daybreak, we drove to Pampapatiswami temple at Hampi, the other of the two villages in the ruins of Vijianagur. Duarte Barbosa, a traveller of the 16th century, whose works have been published by the Hakluyt Society, gives a most interesting account of the glories of Vijianagur before it was sacked by the king of Beejapore, the ruins of whose capital are briefly referred to at the end of chapter XIII. Amongst other things, he says that the king was always waited upon by women, and that the fairest ladies in the kingdom followed the camp in war, so that the brave who distinguished themselves in battle might at once receive their reward. The editor of the volume in the Hakluyt series above referred to, has pointed out that Plato provided in his Republic, that the bravest men might kiss, and be kissed by the loveliest women, without stint or reserve.

A good road wound round the rocky hills, on which, and between which, and around which, the great city once extended. A channel from the Tungabhadra, on the banks of which river the city stood, irrigates the deserted site. Hence it is that, unlike the ruins of most of the cities of old times, those of Vijianagur present a pleasing and attractive aspect to the traveller. After passing ruined temples and many-pillared hostelries, the ruins of a columned hall stand close by the road, and here the rice-cultivation presses up to the deserted dwelling. Next, a long and regular street of ruined pavilions is reached, between which lies a green cluster of cocoanut trees which glisten in the morning sun. The ground is everywhere uneven, and on most of the little hills are gigantic boulders with tiny temples perched upon the upper stones, and below cavern dwellings, partly natural and partly carved. At one point on the road-side is a colossal image of Vignesvaraswami, the god who removes obstacles; and a little beyond this is the main street, at one end of which is the Sivite temple of Pampapatiswami, whose hearth is still warm and to whose festival tens of thousands of natives still flock in the spring. In a broad and handsome street, flanked on either side, as everywhere in this historic city, by pillared halls or *mantapams*, are crowded together the few native huts that make up the modern village of Hampi. To the west of this street flows the Tungabhadra, and, at the lower end thereof, a flight of steps leads over a saddle, on the other side of which is a valley between the rocky hills, leading again to the river, through a street like that just described, and with the usual temple at the end remote from the water. Above this rises a hill of greater height and of easier access than most of those around. By the roughest of stone steps you may ascend to the little temple that crowns its summit, whence a fine view can be obtained of the ruined city, as a whole. On every side you see fallen temples and pavilions, and rocky hills covered with huge boulders, and little valleys below them marked like chessboards with small square fields of rice divided by little green banks. At one point the remains of an ancient bridge may be seen leading across to the dominions of the Nizam of Hyderabad, between whose territories and ours the river is the boundary. Woods, or, as one would say in India, gardens, of cocoanut trees relieve the monotony of cultivation, and across the river in the Nizam's country nothing meets the eye but a tangle of rocky hills and stony valleys between. On almost every hill were huge rocking stones—or stones that looked as if they might have rocked—poised across larger horizontal rocks. Such stones exist nowhere else, unless it be in the fabulous city of Kor, of which we have lately heard so much. On many of these rocks are little kiosques, three pillars and a hood, light and airy structures that a breath of wind might, you would say, almost lift into river or valley below. Elephant stables, zenanas, where squirrels and bloodsuckers revel in the former home of beauty and intrigue, concert hall and council chamber, make up a vision of the past, while around it the patient and contented ryot cultivates his rice and cocoanuts, thinks little of the past, and, notwithstanding his supposed passion for representative government, absolutely nothing of the future. His indifference is sublime. Is it not recorded that, when Mussulman and Hindu were fighting for supremacy in the south of India, he went on with his cultivation and barely took the trouble to ask who had gained the day, and did not Megasthenes take note of a similar phenomenon upwards of 2,000 years ago?

The finest of the temples lies in one of the most solitary of the clefts in the hills of heaped-up boulders of gneiss. The carving and the architecture of Vittalswami's pagoda are not surpassed in the south of India. Three large white monkeys were in possession, and they made way with reluctance for two Europeans. There are no boys about here, and, if there were, Hindu boys do not throw stones at animals. Monkeys and squirrels therefore walk about with the confidence begotten of experience. Not the English squirrel, but a small and pretty beast with three gold marks down his back. These are the marks of the fingers of Rama, who once stroked his ancestor, in token of appreciation, since which day all squirrels wear a coat of the same pattern. On the path leading from this temple to the steps of the bathing ghât is a stone arch, one transverse and two upright monoliths, curiously like the Torii found in front of every Shinto temple in Japan, but here said to have been used as scales on which to weigh rich pilgrims, who had to give to the god their own weight in gold. In all these ruins the sacred banyan (*Ficus religiosa*) hurries on the work of destruction. It sprouts in the clefts of the temples, and twines around the stones to the ultimate destruction of the edifice it adorns. The mango and the tamarind, less sacred and destructive, beautify the precincts of the holy places.

Our camp here as elsewhere was most comfortable, thanks to the excellent arrangements made by the servants under the direction of the Military Secretary. Captain Wyndham-Quin, when he awoke every morning, would send his servant to "see if Polliam butler was there, and if so, to ask him where we are, and where we are going next." Such confidence had we in our native retainers.

At Anagundi, on the other side of the Tungabhadra, dwell some representatives of the fallen house of Vijianagur. Across the river is a ferry; the transit is accomplished in coracles, round bamboo-baskets made water-tight by buffalo hides. You would find little difference between them and the coracle of the Severn, or the gouffa of the Tigris, each of which appears, at first sight, in its own way, unique.

I pass over the Jain temples and a modern Hindu temple, on the sloping steps of which you may see the graceful Brahmin woman emerging like a Hindu Venus from the river with all her dripping garments clinging round her shapely form. Two pleasant days have been spent in visiting these ruins, but two pages of description may prove too much. Midday on the third day, the 1st of August, we started back for Bellary, driving to Hospet, where, as at Kamalapur, cholera, now, as in the palmy days of Vijianagur, one of the scourges of the country, had made its dreaded appearance. At Hospet an Assistant to the Magistrate of the Bellary district, with his wife, lives in a Mussalman tomb which has been converted into a dwelling-house. Nothing can be less sepulchral, nevertheless, than the air of the place or the appearance of its inhabitants.

Arrived at Bellary, room was just found for a little rest, and next day, on the 2nd, the usual round commenced of functions, inspections, and interviews. The People's Association, by their chosen delegates, had something to say about irrigation projects, the conduct of public affairs, and what not; the native officials, who desired interviews, had also to be received.

In the afternoon, the first place to visit was the Native Club, where lawyers, merchants, Government officials, and other native gentlemen of Bellary town, play billiards, read the papers, and abuse the Government, just like Englishmen. Next came the London Mission Schools, where some hundreds of Canarese and Telugu boys are educated Englishwise. The Bible is taught in the school; but there is no effort made to convert the pupils. One of the senior boys read an address, in which he said that all the boys were His Excellency's children. Lord Connemara, in reply, said it was true that, in one sense, he was the father of a very large family of over thirty millions; that, in any case, he hoped that all his children who were studying in that school would pass the examinations for which they might go up, and, if they failed, would try again. The Convent of the Good Shepherd proved a most interesting institution, and the Sisters, clad in white serge and black hoods, had made their surroundings, in the hideous cantonment of Bellary, as charming as spotless cleanliness and good taste could make them. A pleasant dinner with the 2nd Madras Lancers, which regiment had recently returned from Burma, was not the last event of the day, for, to it succeeded an entertainment at the Native Hostelry, or Choultry, built to commemorate the visit of the Prince of Wales. Here a long address was read by the People's Association, dealing with irrigation, the alleged corruption of native officials, and other subjects. To this the Governor replied promising to look further into the Tungabhadra project, with which he was already acquainted, and, with reference to what was said about the native officials, to consider the rules relating to the length of the tenure of their appointments in one locality. His Excellency expressed himself strongly averse to frequent changes.

We went to bed with songs in Canarese, Telugu, and Hindustani ringing in our ears, and, after a short night, got up early on the 3rd of August to visit the Protestant Orphanage and the High School, and to breakfast with the 6th Madras Infantry. At the Orphanage, occasion was taken to express satisfaction at the practical turn that education took in that institution, where a carpentry class for boys is maintained. At the High School, a Sanscrit address, composed in honour of the Governor, was read by one of the masters.

In the afternoon, a native officer of the 2nd Madras Lancers gave an entertainment, to which all our party were bidden. The most interesting event in the programme was a realistic representation of the capture of a village of Burmese dacoits by a squadron of the regiment, which has recently returned from that country. With leaves and palms a sham village was made, from behind which the dacoits fusilladed the advancing Lancers, who came on, nevertheless, accompanied by their interpreter, in the national costume, mounted on a Pegu pony. The dacoits were speedily routed, and, as they ran away, when caught, threw themselves on the ground before the horses' fore legs, and cried for mercy. The chief of the dacoits, the Boh, was finally tried for his life, found guilty, and executed on the spot with summary military justice. After which he got up, and walked home, and we went to dress for dinner. The interpreter on the Pegu pony was a great feature of the show, and no one could be shot or even aimed at, till this functionary declared him to be the right man.

Next morning, Thursday, 4th, at 5 o'clock, a large assembly of Bellary people and not a few ladies got up to see His Excellency leave and bid him good-bye, and, before 10 o'clock, the train drew up at Gooty within sight of the high and precipitous rock, the abandoned fort on the top of which has, in its day, played no unimportant a part in the history of the Ceded Districts. In the cemetery at the foot of the hill is the cenotaph of Sir Thomas Munro, whose remains were transferred to Madras, and who died at a village 15 miles away, while taking a last fond look at the people of this part of the country, for whose welfare he had, long before he became Governor of Madras, laboured so wisely and so well.

It is a hot drive of 32 miles, between fields of young cholum and castor-oil, along a road bordered with acacias, which, at one point, crosses the now dry bed of the Pennér, to Anantapur, the capital of a new district lately created out of a portion of Bellary. Everything here is quite new, and you step out of the house door into a wilderness. However, there was much to be learnt about the condition of the people, the incidence of the extra taxation recently introduced under Lord Ripon's self-government scheme, about the Forest Department, the new buildings which Government is erecting at large expense, and many other subjects of the like and of a different nature.

The district, though till lately only a piece of Bellary, is 5,000 odd very dry square miles in extent. The Governor spent the greater part of the day in going through railway and irrigation schemes with Colonel Hasted, and Mr. Nicholson, officers who know the district well, and have its welfare much at heart. In the afternoon, no less than four addresses were presented on the classic ground of Munro's office. In reply to these addresses, His Excellency said what pleasure it gave him to visit the scenes of the earlier career of that distinguished administrator, whose example he thought every one in high office in India would do well to imitate. He promised that the Bukacherla Irrigation Project should be reconsidered in the light of the new suggestions now made; and the various points touched in the different addresses were replied to in the guarded manner necessary, as great care has to be taken not to raise false hopes, or to accept too readily statements which, however plausible and made in perfect good faith, are merely *ex parte* statements. The cloths of Pamidy and the silks of Dharmavaram were hung around the room. The native gentlemen present were introduced to His Excellency, who next proceeded to the High School, where, as usual, an address was received and answered. Lord Connemara took the opportunity to say that the establishment of the school was due to the visit of his distinguished predecessor Sir M. E. Grant Duff. The Jubilee Park, in which, as in other good works, Mr. Nicholson is so much interested, the hospital, the new Collector's office, which seems at present all too grand for the place, were next inspected. The Assistant Commissioner of Salt Revenue had waited on His Excellency, in the course of the day, for the purpose of discussing the rise in the price of salt, which was referred to in the addresses, and which, it is to be hoped, is due, as the Governor trusted, "to local and temporary causes only." In the big tank, there was unfortunately not a drop of water; but on the way back to Gooty, next morning, signs of rain were manifest, and when we got to our camp, the tents were wet through and through.

In the afternoon the People's Association presented an address of an ordinary character with the usual references to irrigation works, and to the grateful recollection in which Sir Thomas Munro lives in the memory of the inhabitants, and not less Robertson, whose memory is as green as are the trees which he planted all over the country. Within sight of the fortress of Gooty, the central point around which Mahratta, Mussulman and Hindu have often fought, and which, though frequently attacked, has never actually been taken, His Excellency admonished the members of the deputation to remember that taxation was certainly not less light in the days of rapine and of plunder, than it is now when life and property are secure. During dinner the blessed rain, for which we were all wishing, came down in torrents, testing the power of our tents to a considerable extent. The lights attracted innumerable animals, things creeping and things flying, and by the time coffee arrived very little of the table cloth could be seen. The most prominent animals were flying ants, which shed their wings, and seemed to get on quite as well without them, but thousands of these appendages strewed the table; and they say that the natives collect them and make them into curry. By-and-by frogs came to eat the insects, and other animals to eat the frogs, reminding one of Edwin Arnold's lines in the "Light of Asia":

> "How lizard fed on ant, and snake on him,
> And kite on both; and how the fish-hawk robbed
> The fish-tiger of that which it had seized;
> The shrike chasing the bulbul, which did chase
> The jewelled butterflies; till everywhere
> Each slew a slayer and in turn was slain,—
> Life living upon death."

The rain made the ascent of the hill next morning all the cooler. A fair road ascends to the ruins of the barracks, where quite lately Mr. Smith, sergeant of the Royal Engineers, came "on duty for the purpose of blowing up guns, and Mrs. Smith," for so he describes his mission in the book at the travellers' rest-house. The roughly-paved road is made of quartz, and of a purple-tinted stone like Egyptian porphyry. There are deep reservoirs and wells in every available place, and springs, if you may believe the people here, in the castellated top of the rocky precipice that forms the top of the hill. Here, on a little platform hanging over a sheer rock, a Mahratta General, according to tradition, played for their lives with his captives, and hurled them over the precipice if they lost. The rest of the day was spent in writing English letters, in disposing of office-papers, and in getting ready for a start.

Next morning, August 8th, soon after 6 o'clock, Mr. Nicholson and Colonel and Mrs. Stuart saw us start for Kurnool. At Guntakal we had to change again to the new Bellary-Kistna State Railway, and proceed along the single metre gauge line 43 miles to Dhone, where the Collector of Kurnool, Mr. Kough, and the Superintendent of Police met us. After lunching at Dhone we proceeded to drive the 33 miles that intervene between the railway and the capital of the district. The country was green and the crops of cholum and castor-oil looked much more advanced than they had in Anantapur and Bellary. There were the numerous little forests of *tooma* trees in the beds of the tanks. A herd of antelope ran alongside the carriage, at a distance of a few hundred yards, for perhaps a mile, and along the road, at intervals, all the way to Kurnool, were stationed men holding red flags, and at the villages were triumphal arches with inscriptions. A mile or two before the town was reached, throngs of natives, in their holiday clothing, began to line the roads, and from the gateway to the Collector's house was one continuous well-dressed, good-tempered crowd, which proved more demonstrative in its welcome than is usual with Asiatics.

The Hindry is crossed by a fine bridge, and the

aqueduct of the Kurnool canal—an ill-fated work, which, initiated by Sir Arthur Cotton, was begun in 1863, and in 1882 was transferred, under a decree of the Court of Chancery, to the Secretary of State, the works being purchased by Government for over a million pounds sterling. The Secretary of State paid the Company £1,779,000 for the canal, the amount actually spent on it, and it now costs some £15,000 a-year to keep up, and yields a return of about £6,000. Irrigation is not practised much in the country through which the canal flows, and food-grains grow therein in ordinary years without other help than that of the rains from heaven; hence the failure of this great engineering work, which Government is sparing no efforts to convert into a moderate success. The first thing to be done in Kurnool was to inspect the head-works of the canal at Sunkesala, 17 miles up the river, and the Governor, accompanied by the Chief Engineer, accordingly started for this purpose next morning (9th).

The journey up the canal was uneventful, but for the slaughter of a crocodile, who, as he sunned himself on the bank, was shot from the boat. The 10th was a busy day, beginning with the reception of the Nawab of Banganapalle, who, like the Raja of Sandur, is the Liliputian king of 160 square miles of country. He is a fine-looking man, who drives himself about in a mail phaeton, and whose chief object in life is to obtain a salute. His brother-in-law was a more interesting person, and when the Governor asked him if he was a sportsman, which he looked all over, replied that he preferred shooting to anything except fighting. His Excellency observed that these were the times of peace, and that it was necessary to find some other occupation, but the Nawab's brother-in-law replied that that was true, but if occasion should offer he was quite ready, for he much preferred fighting to anything else. So saying, he held up his curved scimitar with damascened handle and crimson velvet sheath, and said that this weapon was always at Her Majesty's disposal. Lord Connemara said he was sure of it, and asked the Nawab if it had been long in the family, to which he replied that it had been his father's and his grandfather's, and had often been unsheathed in battle. This fire-eater looked the character he assumed. His moustaches were fiercely brushed upwards, and bristled all around his mouth. He was very tall and very big and enveloped in innumerable white muslin petticoats. All these he tucked about him with solicitude, when he rode off on a white horse as bravely caparisoned, as he himself was dressed. Around him were spearmen and pikemen and bannermen, a motley and barbarous crew.

After him came many other less interesting personages, among whom, however, we must not reckon the representative of the family which, as lately as 1840, ruled in this district. He is in feeble health, and said he feared he should not live much longer to enjoy his pension. Indeed, he doubted if ever he should be able to pay a visit to the Governor again.

Then came addresses from the Municipality and from various Associations. These, though important and interesting from an administrative point of view, are all very much alike, and do not bear repetition in a general account of a journey.

The drive around the town in the evening was full of interest. The streets were very prettily decorated, and the flat-roofed houses were thronged with interested spectators. Here and there the ruined palaces of Nawabs, and the fallen bastions of the ruined fort spoke of the past. At present one of the most important questions in Kurnool is that of the water-supply. The Tungabhadra water is brought in a channel from the river and distributed about the town. It is not, however, protected by pipes from contamination by subsoil drainage, and the municipality has a scheme, hitherto not fully matured or developed, for its protection and its improvement. Another allegation is that leakage from these channels has increased the fever, for which, and for cholera at different times, the place has had an unenviable reputation. It is curious to note that, while everywhere else the cry is for water, in Kurnool, where there is enough and to spare, complaints are made of the effects of too much of it. Some of the cisterns were inspected by the Governor, in company with the Chief Engineer for Irrigation and the local medical officer. In the evening there was a native entertainment given by a rich cotton merchant of the place. A native band played the *Roast Beef of Old England*, and various other English tunes, in very good time.

Rain had fallen during the previous day, and there was some doubt as to whether we should be able to cross the river and get back to the railway. The journey, however, was successfully accomplished, and then we travelled up the Bellary-Kistna State Railway, as far as it is opened, to Nandyal, a large place which is desirous of being made the capital of the district. The line passes through the Yerramalais, by many a picturesque curve, through low scrub jungle, to reach the plain in which Nandyal is situated. At all stations along the road, crowds of natives were assembled to receive the Governor, with music and dancing and other demonstrations. Arrived at Nandyal, the Engineers took possession of the party, and, after the receipt of an address in a very handsomely decorated waiting-room at the railway, they ran the train down to their own quarters, and here the day's march of 80 miles came to an end, but not the day's business, for a native entertainment was to take place in the evening, at which all were present. On the morning of August 12th, at 4 A.M., the Governor with Colonel Hasted and Mr. La Touche, after a run of two hours, arrived in the middle of the jungle, and at the end of the line. They then got out and went about five miles in a trolly, out of which Lord Connemara was once upset, down to the village, which has sprung up since the works on the viaduct and tunnel have been commenced. The viaduct will be a large iron girder supported upon masonry about 200 feet down the valley. There was no time to visit the tunnel which is a mile further on. On the summit of the ghaut nothing could be more beautiful than the vast wooded hills, but there is no population, as the district is pestilential from fever. The scenery recalls, in some features, the hilly country of New Brunswick.

Unhappily the jungle which makes it beautiful, makes it unhealthy. Generally 50 and occasionally 75 per cent. of the men working on the line are down with fever.

The programme had included a visit to Cuddapah, where a question of interest concerning the water-supply to the town is under discussion; but a serious outbreak of cholera having occurred there just when we were due, it was considered, by the Collector, the medical authorities, and the Government, unsafe for any travellers to halt there. Objections that apply to individual travellers apply a thousandfold in the case of the Governor, with whom and about whom Europeans collect by tens or hundreds, and natives by thousands.

It was with great regret that this portion of the tour was perforce postponed, but not abandoned, and a return made to the Nílgiris. We chanced upon a perfect day to ascend the ghaut. White fleecy clouds lay here and there on the green woods that clothe the slopes of the mountains, and the bamboos across the valley looked like gigantic green feathers, glistening with dew in the morning sun, as a slight breeze swayed them now and again. The country between Arkonam and Salem on the way back to the Hills is very interesting. Groves of mango and tamarind trees afford frequent shade to those who wish to camp out, and raggi and other crops were green and flourishing. The number of Mussulmans seen at the stations along the way is accounted for by the fact that the tanning of skins is largely carried on in the adjacent villages.

However, in the course of the three weeks that had elapsed since we left the seat of Government, three districts had been visited exclusive of Cuddapah, a short halt at the capital town of which district had also been made, on the way to Bellary.

The new district of Anantapur and its new buildings had been seen; the large and important military and civil station of Bellary had been thoroughly inspected; Kurnool, with its canal, had been visited, and the progress of the all-important Bellary-Kistna State Railway had been noted on the spot.

Add to these results the information acquired on an infinite variety of subjects connected with general administration, and the acquaintance made of many district officers, some of whom seemed to justify the recent description in the *Times* of the Indian Civil Service as "unique in the history of human government," and you have the record of three weeks pleasantly and, it is hoped, profitably spent.

CHAPTER III.

WYNAAD, MALABAR, COCHIN, TRAVANCORE, TINNEVELLY, MADURA, TRICHINOPOLY, TANJORE.

Indian monsoons—Departure from Ootacamund—Our party—Naduvatam Cinchona plantations—Cheap febrifuge—Anecdote—At Nadghani—Indian Gold Mining Company—Corumburs—*En route* to Malabar—Poon-spar tree—Eddacurra village—Government teak plantations—Mahogany—India rubber—Keddah operations—Tirumalpad—Nilambur camp—Mambat—A mishap—Snake-boats—Reception at Calicut—Novel address—Zamorin's visit—Addresses—Mappilla Act—Mappillas—Levée—Lunatic Asylum—King of the World—Basel German Mission—District Jail—Calicut city—Port Trust—Deputation of evicted tenants—Ireland of Madras Presidency—Mr. Logan—Prize-giving at Government College—Kerala Vidyasala—Departure—Beypore—Calicut extension—Mr. Hanna—Kallai bridge—Ferookh bridge—Anecdote of Tippoo Sultan—Reminiscence of Lord Mayo—From Shoranur—At Trichur—Illuminations *en route*—Mr. Hannyngton—General Sir Harry Prendergast—Drive around town—Nairs—Their marriage system—Pagoda—*Pradakshanams*—Jail—Desperate character—Cathedral of Syro-Chaldean Christians—Bishop Mar Elias John Mellus—*Kor Episcopos*—Condition of Chaldeans—Eccentric procession—Houses of Nairs—Start for Cochin—At Bolghatty—"Punchbowl"—British Cochin—Raja's visit—Archbishop of Veerapoly—Durbar—White and Black Jews—Jews' synagogues—Women of White Jews—State banquet—Toasts—Periar project—Viceroy—First Prince—Vasco da Gama's tomb—Jesuits' College—Local Chamber of Commerce—Departure for Trevandrum—Backwater illuminations—At Quilon—Dewan of Travancore—Workali tunnels—Town *en fete*—Maharaja's visit to Governor—Malayali Sabha address—False impression—Minister's post—Wise administration—Virtue of sea-sand—Prize-giving at Maharaja's College—State banquet—"Model State"—Ride to Courtallum—Camp Gorge bungalow—Romantic valley—At Courtallum—Addresses—Tenkasi temple—Departure—At Tinnevelly—Palamcottah—Bishop Caldwell—Bishop Sargent's schools—Levée—Addresses—Tuticorin—Tamraparni irrigation—Working of Agricultural department—Mr. Varada Row—At Madura—Tumkum—Queen Mangammall—Montrose heart—Lord Napier and Ettrick—Meenatchiumman temple—High priest—Periyar project—Lord Dufferin—American Mission school—Tirumal Naick's palace—Mr. Hutchins—Local water-works—Albert bridge—Local self-government—Levée—Addresses Departure—*En route* to Periyar—Cumbum valley—Nature of project—

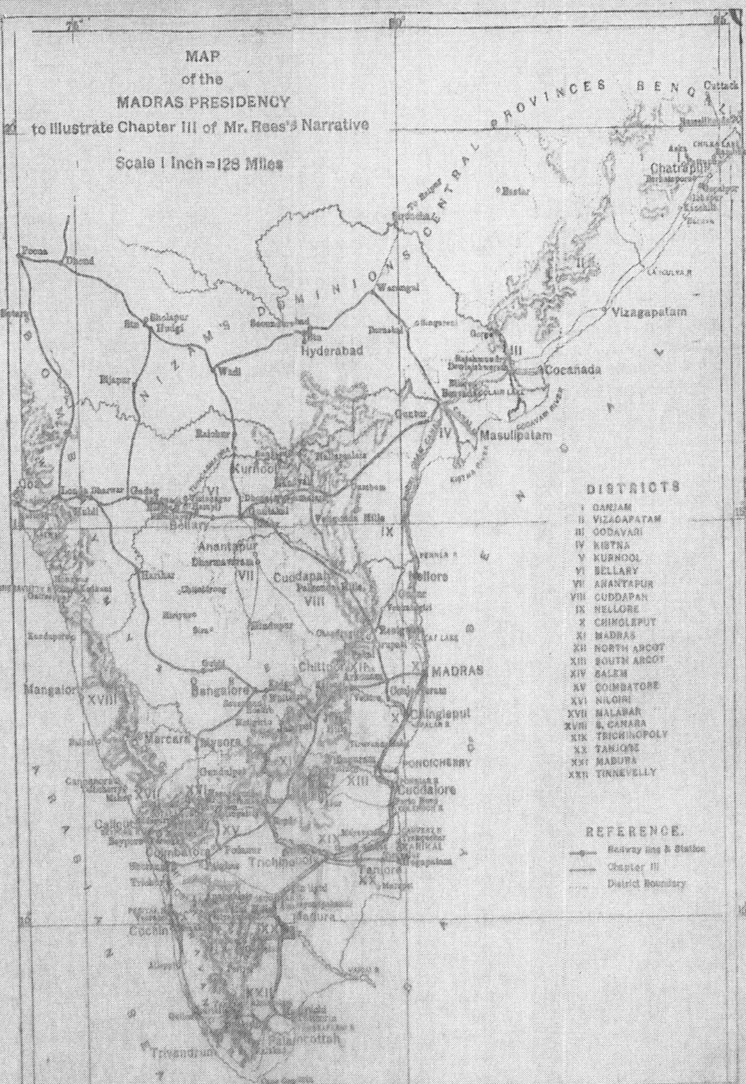

MAP
of the
MADRAS PRESIDENCY
to Illustrate Chapter III of Mr. Rees's Narrative
Scale 1 Inch = 128 Miles
CENTRAL PROVINCES
NIZAM'S DOMINIONS
Chatrapur
Vizagapatam
Hyderabad
Cocanada
Masulipatam
Kurnool
Bellary
Anantapur
Cuddapah
Nellore
MADRAS
Chingleput
Bangalore
Mangalore
Mysore
Marcara
PONDICHERRY
Cuddalore
Calicut
Coimbatore
Trichinopoly
Tanjore
Madura
Cochin
Palamcottah
Trivandrum
DISTRICTS
I GANJAM
II VIZAGAPATAM
III GODAVARI
IV KISTNA
V KURNOOL
VI BELLARY
VII ANANTAPUR
VIII CUDDAPAH
IX NELLORE
X CHINGLEPUT
XI MADRAS
XII NORTH ARCOT
XIII SOUTH ARCOT
XIV SALEM
XV COIMBATORE
XVI NILGIRI
XVII MALABAR
XVIII S. CANARA
XIX TRICHINOPOLY
XX TANJORE
XXI MADURA
XXII TINNEVELLY
REFERENCE.
Railway line & Station
Chapter III
District Boundary

Brahmin Surveyor's adventures—Murder—Remarkable incident—Agricultural labourers—Captain and Lady Eva Wyndham Quin—Shower of rose-water—Return from Periyar—Departure—Dindigul water-works and cigar manufactory—Mr. Heimpel—German enterprize—At Trichinopoly—Srirangam—Central jail—Health of convicts—Raja of Pudukottah—Mr. Seshayya Sastryar, C.S.I.—Grand anicut—Addresses—Entertainment at Jesuits' College—Lords Dalhousie and Mayo—At Tanjore—Palace—Jail—Palace library—Late Dr. Burnell, C.I.E.—Subjects of addresses—Arrival at Madras.

A RECENT arrival at Ootacamund from England said, after weeks of rain, that as soon as one monsoon was finished, another was waiting around the corner. To weeks of south-west monsoon succeeded a few fine days, and on the night of the 2nd and early morning of the 3rd October, the first burst of the north-east monsoon came on, and it appeared at one time as if we could hardly start according to our programme.

At noon, however, on the 3rd October 1887 we* left Ootacamund for the last time this year for Naduvatam *en route* for the Wynâd. The Commander-in-Chief and all the Civil and Military officers of Government assembled to wish the Governor good-bye, and many ladies were present. Lady Connemara took His Excellency for the first few miles in her carriage, and then a ride of 17 miles over rolling downs, between which nestle the little woods called *sholas*, brought us to the great Cinchona estates of the Madras Government at Naduvatam. These had already been inspected by the Governor on a previous occasion, and no more need be said here than that this enterprise of the Government has been chiefly instrumental in demonstrating the fitness of the soil and

* His Excellency the Lord Connemara.
Mr. Rees, Private Secretary.
Captain Wingfield, 7th Hussars, A.D.C.

climate of the Nílgiris for the cultivation of Cinchona. Experiments with new and valuable varieties are constantly being tried, and at present the Director, Mr. Lawson, late Professor of Botany at Oxford, is engaged in manufacturing a febrifuge, in which, it is hoped, the poor, who suffer terribly from fever in the neighbouring coffee and mining districts, will be able to purchase a cheap and effective medicine. They cannot afford to buy sulphate of quinine, and most of the alkaloids hitherto manufactured have proved nauseous and distasteful.

The view from the Director's house in the Cinchona estate is most beautiful. Some 3,000 or 4,000 feet below extend, as far as the eye can reach, well-wooded uplands, broken by frequent hills and hidden here and there by white clouds, which only veil one portion, to throw that uncovered into stronger relief. The dark green of the forest is here and there varied by patches of light green rice. On the left tower the grand peaks of the Nílgiris, and far away on the right the red outline of the table-land of Mysore melts into the horizon.

We rode down through these clouds and into the uplands and the forest, along a steep bridle-path, leaving our baggage to come by road. Cinchona and coffee covered the hill-side, and one village (Gudalur) was passed before we reached the level of our camp (Nadghani). The vegetation was most luxurious, and everything suggested fertility and prosperity. The roads were empty in the early morning but for an occasional Inspector of Police who would hurriedly draw himself up, generally *across* the road, on our approach. It is recorded of one of these that his horse, drawn up across the path, kicked out at his superior officer, whereon he apologised, saying it was meant by way of respect.

Arrived at the little village of Nadghani, 20 miles from Naduvatam, at half-past 8 A.M., we found our host Mr. Burrows about to start to meet us, and as we had far out-paced our baggage, we bathed, dried our clothes in the sun, put them on again and breakfasted.

The first thing to be done after breakfast was to visit the works of the Indian Gold Mining Company. To do this we drove up and down the little green hills, characteristic of the Wynâd country for a few miles, and on nearing the mine, as we were driving along the roughest of roads cut in the steep hill-side, a salute of 17 guns was fired a few yards off, by dynamite cartridges. The managers of the various mining and planting companies in this part of the Wynâd were assembled to meet His Excellency at luncheon at the house of Mr. Coward, the manager, and afterwards we proceeded, each with a candle in his hand, to penetrate Coward's and the Skull Reefs, occasionally knocking our heads against the roof of the tunnel, and everywhere wading through running water. Into the latter reef a shaft, some 200 feet deep, had been sunk to enable the miners to pump out the water which threatens to make working impracticable.

At the end of the Skull tunnel we saw the auriferous reef of quartz from which fair results are being obtained, and, as His Excellency said, in reply to the toast of his health at luncheon, there is some hope apparently that things may pay here if only strict economy is observed in working. The enormous prices paid for mining rights, and for land, when the Wynâd gold mania was at its height were sufficient to swamp any prospects, however bright and promising. At present, so far as we could learn, this mine may be considered as likely to pay as any other in the Wynâd, and to be, on the whole, a fairly representative one.

We saw, amongst other things, an ancient working of the Corumburs, who are said to have been engaged in gold mining here two thousand years ago. Not improbably the ancestors of this curious hill-tribe dug out the gold that went to adorn the temple of king Solomon.

Next morning, at half-past 6, with Messrs. Burrows and DeWinton and Colonel Jago, we started in rain to ride down the Karkoor Ghaut to the Ernâd Taluk of the Malabar District below. It is hardly possible to conceive a ride more beautiful than this. For 15 miles the road passes through the densest of jungle. Enormous trees tower above an under-growth of evergreen shrubs, tree-ferns, creepers and palms of every sort and kind. The tall standards of the poon-spar were perhaps the most conspicuous, as this useful tree is one of the most valuable, of the timber trees we saw.

At the foot of the ghaut is the village of Eddacurra, and here the Collector of Malabar, Mr. Logan, his Assistant, Mr. Wedderburn, the Superintendent of Police, and the Forest Officer met us and accompanied

His Excellency through the Government Teak Plantations, through a section of which the road passes. This great plantation, which has almost repaid already the total amount of money expended upon it, will, it is calculated, in 12 years be worth nearly one million sterling.

The road passes through a section occupied by young giants, aged 20 and 30 years. Even in its babyhood, the Teak tree displays a leaf of enormous size, giving proof of future greatness. From its size and bright light-green colour, it can be distinguished in the forest at a great distance. The standards through which we passed travel all over the Western Coast of India and right away to the Persian Gulf, and are in great demand for house-building, just as the poon-spar to which reference is made above is much favoured for ship-building.

Besides the cultivation of Teak, that of Mahogany and India-rubber is vigorously carried on in Nilambur under the supervision of Mr. Hadfield, the intelligent and energetic officer in charge, who also performs khedda operations on a small scale, and had a few amusing baby-elephants to show us.

In the evening the Tirumalpad of Nilambur came to pay his visit. He is not a very great man, but acquired a great property, or rather his grandfather did, from the Zamorin whose agent he was. He is, in fact, a rich landlord, whose possessions are of recent date.

Our camp at Nilambur was made of forest-produce. The walls of the dining room were of split Bamboo with lattice windows; the roof was interlaced with the beautiful *Cycas*, and adjoining it was a Bamboo room, which contained one article of furniture, if it can be so called, a unique carpet made of the shreds and petals and blossoms of many-coloured flowers, arranged with great skill, taste, and care, upon the ground, worked out in patterns with geometrical precision, and as pleasing to the eye of the observer as it was suggestive of laborious solicitude on the part of the maker. For days before the Governor's arrival children had been sent out with baskets, each with instructions to collect bells and flowerets of a single hue, from which their parents might cunningly fashion this beauteous work.

After dinner we drove 5 miles in the dark through a green lane, lighted by torches, to Mambat, where a tiger had killed two people in the bazaar a few days before, but which we passed with safety, and where we embarked at a pretty *impromptu* pier in snake-boats, which were to take us down the Beypore river till 4 o'clock in the morning, when we were to strike into a little canal leading to Calicut. These snake-boats have high curved sterns like Cleopatra's barge, with a blend of the Venetian gondola. They are very narrow, so crank that you cannot take off your boots in them, and propelled by eight or ten, nearly naked, boatmen, each flourishing a one-bladed paddle, very much like a garden spade, and yelling at the top of his voice. In spite of all this, we slipped down the river, and at 7 o'clock in the morning arrived at the Karaparamba pier at Calicut, where the Municipal authorities were ready with the inevitable address, which, however, as the Governor remarked, was in one respect novel, for it referred to no grievance, and preferred no request.

After a drive to the beautiful house in which the Collector of Malabar lives, we had breakfast, and disposed of the office papers of the last two days. Then the Zamorin of Calicut came to visit the Governor. His procession of elephants with shields on their heads, of fantastic red-coated soldiers, and of half-naked Nairs with red-lacquered shields and truculent-looking swords is, in its way, quite unique, as indeed is the Maharaja Bahadur himself. His jewelled tiara-like hat struck into the tassels of his palanquin. He had borrowed his elephants. He looked unhappy in his gold brocade, yet he was not without dignity. He appeared broken in health, and, in all respects, the shade of a great name.

Then came two addresses, one from the Native Christians which was mostly historical, and one from "Young Malabar." The latter address referred to one of the three subjects to which most of the petitions received here relate, namely, the disarmament of four taluks in this district under the Mappilla Act, consequent on the commission of outrages by those religious fanatics. The Mappillas are the descendants of Arab fathers, by Hindu mothers, and they are more devotedly attached to Islam, than most of those whose parents on both sides have always professed that faith. His Excellency replied that he would be very glad if the public safety would allow the Government to look upon this disarmament as a temporary measure. Doubtless, it is hard upon the Hindus that they should be deprived of their arms, which, as they urge, they require, in some measure, for protection against wild beasts,—for their crops, more than for themselves,—because Mappillas will use them to shoot the red coats and the white men, but if the Hindus have arms, the Mappillas will get them, and there is the difficulty. The Collector, Mr. Logan, as the Governor remarked, would be the last man to advocate the introduction of a harsh or unnecessary measure into the district, to the people of which he is so sincerely attached. This address referred also to the revenue settlement of the district,—a thorny question which is under the consideration of Government, and cannot, with advantage, be discussed in this paper. A *levée*, which was very well attended, concluded the work of the day.

Next morning the 7th of October, at half-past 6, the round of inspections recommenced with a visit to the Lunatic Asylum, which was marvellously clean and very well ordered. There were many murderers; amongst them, several Mappillas, and one old Mussulman who exhibited a paper appointing him King of the World. The King of the World wears very clean clothing, and keeps himself very much aloof from his fellow-lunatics.

The Basel German Mission here is a great industrial as well as religious institution. We went to see its tile-manufactory. The tiles are admirable, and cost about 65 shillings a thousand. They are grooved laterally and transversely, so as to carry off, without leakage, the heavy rainfall of the Western Coast, and it is small wonder that such good work pays well, and that the tiles travel so far as they do. The Mission makes also excellent towels, linen, and cloth, in the weaving establishment, which we visited.

A drive thence, through a deep cutting, the banks of which were covered with small ferns and green grass, brought us to the District Jail, which, under the superintendence of Dr. Cook, who also has the Lunatic Asylum, like that institution, presented the same appearance of discipline, cleanliness and order. The Superintendent told us that prisoners generally go down in weight during the first months of their captivity, owing to sorrow, remorse, or some such feeling, but soon recover. If this be established, it is an interesting fact.

On the way home we passed a pond, the water of which was almost hidden by the lovely red lotus, now in flower. The city of Calicut, which contains 57,000 inhabitants, is scattered about amongst groves of cocoanut trees, interspersed with patches of green cultivation, traversed in all directions by green lanes, and consists of neat detached tiled houses, inhabited, for the most part, by a well-to-do and good-looking population. It is, in every way, a most striking contrast to the ordinary eastern town with its mud-built houses, close streets, and crowded highways and by-ways, as are its people in manners, customs and appearance, to those of other parts of India.

In the afternoon there were many addresses to receive and answer; the first was that of the mercantile community, which desired that a Port Trust might be created, and complained that the revenues of their ports went to swell the general Port Fund balance of the Presidency. The Wynâd Planters had a great deal to say about cattle-trespass, which they desired might be remedied by the levy of inordinate fines on the owners of errant cattle, and they complained that the Settlement, now being carried out in the South-East Wynâd, was inequitable. Lord Connemara had some conversation with the members of both of these deputations, and assured them that he would consider the important and technical subjects referred to in consultation with his colleagues, but could not entertain the proposals regarding cattle-trespass.

To this succeeded a deputation of a rather unusual character, consisting of evicted tenants. Malabar is just now the Ireland of the Presidency, and various changes have been, and are being, made in the law to secure greater compensation for improvements, and to limit the right of the proprietor so as to provide for greater permanency of occupation. This deputation consisted chiefly of Mappillas, who had been evicted, for the most part by Hindu landlords, and they came to press their side of the question, which has an earnest advocate in the Collector, Mr. Logan, who has made a long and attentive study of Malabar tenures and the incidents connected therewith.

At 5 o'clock in the afternoon, prizes were distributed to the pupils at the Government college, and one of the boys read an original poem composed in honour of the Governor, in which, whether a true poet or not, he freely availed himself, as His Excellency remarked in his speech, of a poet's license, not more however, in ascribing to the Governor superhuman virtues, than in diction and metre.

The college maintained by the Zamorin for the education of the youths of the nobility, and the head-quarter reserve of Police were next inspected, and after this there was nothing to be done but to eat dinner and sleep till 7 o'clock next morning, when we drove to the Calicut station of the new Beypore-Calicut extension of the Madras Railway, which we left in the first train that has ever travelled over this portion of the line. Mr. Hanna was in charge of the train, and first of all a halt was called at the Kallai bridge, above and below which the river is covered with huge logs of timber, which have been floated down from the forests we have ridden through in the last two or three days,—their first stage on a long journey, probably to Bombay, Arabia or the Persian Gulf. There was a question, which had been discussed with the deputation of the mercantile community, of clearing the bar of the river of the sand which now silts it up, and a reference to the Public Works Secretary was at once made upon the subject.

After leaving the Kallai bridge, the line diverged through rice-fields, leaving on the right hand the railway embankment, which a little while before had suddenly subsided a dozen feet or so, and then we came to the Ferookh bridge, which is to span the Beypore river near the point where Tippu Sultan is said to have forcibly converted thousands of Hindus to the faith of the Prophet. The works in progress here were inspected, and the scene was visited of the recent trifling accident which was speedily repaired by the energy of Mr. Hanna, who designed the bridge. We crossed the river in boat which Lord Mayo used on his visit for the same purpose, and then proceeded by rail to Beypore, till now the terminus of the railway.

From Shoranur on the Madras Railway to Trichur in the Native State of Cochin is a most beautiful drive of 20 miles. The road is protected from the rays of the sun, for nearly the whole of the distance, by the arched boughs of Banyan trees, and alongside run banks hidden by caladiums and arums, and fringed by a green edge covered with the sensitive plant which abounds all over the country. Now and again, neat homesteads appear, situated in the middle of rice-fields of an emerald green, surrounded by gardens or orchards of cocoanut or other palm trees, while not far off successive hills or ranges of hills lead up to the dark blue contours of the Western Ghauts. From time to time, neat villages are passed whence the prosperous and good-looking inhabitants came out to give the Governor a welcome.

Before we had got half-way it grew dark, and for 10 miles, at intervals of perhaps 50 yards, men holding flaring torches were stationed along the way. After the carriages had passed, they would forsake their stations and run behind till tired, others taking their places when they failed, and so looking back, the spectacle was like a crowd of gigantic fire-flies flitting about in the dark receding avenue of trees. The illuminations in Trichur were also quite beautiful, and here we were met by Mr. Hannyngton the Resident, who had the day before returned from England and relieved General Sir Harry Prendergast.

The morning of Sunday the 9th was occupied by a drive around Trichur, a most remarkable town, chiefly inhabited by Nairs, the land-holding class of the coast. They are commonly described as polyandrous, but they are not. The fact is rather that marriages are easily made and as easily unmade. The Nair lady is a very independent person. Some one offers a cloth, that is the proposal. If she accepts it, that is the marriage. If she gets tired of her husband, she gets rid of him and takes up with another, and is not held to have behaved disgracefully in so doing. To give a cloth as a present is a very common thing in India. By cloth is meant the garment worn by women in the East, and it may be very plain or cheap, or very rich and costly. But here whatever kind of cloth it be, to give one is very significant, as a distinguished visitor to Trichur found when he offered one to a Nair lady in whose house he had received some civility. Whatever opinion may be held from a moral point of view of these marriage relations, they result in manly males and for the most part comely and very often beautiful females, as also it may be noted, do those of the polygamous Mormons in Utah. I refer to these relations as "marriages," for such in fact they are. The Courts of Law, however, in view of the legal incidents flowing from a union of so different a character to that which is commonly known as marriage, deny it the name. A proposal has been made to provide the Nairs with a form of marriage corresponding with that in force amongst most other civilized communities. It is to be hoped that in spite of the difficulty of the subject some means will simultaneously be adopted of declaring the existing sexual relations to amount to a legal marriage, for that is what is really required.

The curious resemblance of the customs of the Western Coast to those of Plato's ideal Republic has already attracted the attention of Lord Stanley of Alderley, and need not be dwelt on here.

The geographical and social centre of the town is the temple which occupies a large green square, and is surrounded by a high green wall covered with moss and little ferns. You enter, or would if permitted, by two gateways of three stories with green roofs,—in fact, everything is green. If the corners of the roofs of the successive stories of these gateways were up-tilted at the edges, they would be extremely like the gateways of a Lamassery or of a Mongolian town; and as it is, the appearance of the edifice is quite Buddhistic, and wholly unlike that of the conventional Hindu temple. In front are two tall and sacred Banyan trees, around which platforms are built. Here every morning you may see the townsfolk performing the *pradakshana*, or circumambulation, muttering prayers the while, and will not fail to note the fair Nair lady in spotless white linen cloth, her ears distended by large round wheels of solid gold, holding in her hand a palmyra leaf umbrella, or the Brahmin fresh from her bath in the neighbouring tank with dripping cloth clinging to her limbs. Monkeys hop about unconcernedly amongst the worshippers. Some of the women carry babies athwart their hips as they walk around, saying their prayers. The whole scene recalls the following lines from Edwin Arnold's "Light of Asia":

> "The housewives bearing water from the well
> With balanced chatties and athwart their hips
> The black-eyed babes . . . .
> . . . . Here a wife
> Stealing with cakes and garlands to the god
> To pray her husband's safe return from trade
> Or beg a boy next birth."

Everything reminds the visitor that he is in a Native State, and that Native customs and manners are followed and preserved. Yet you hear a little English. Passing a school on the way back to the Residency, a small boy said to me "Ride-the-horse-at-a-full-gallop."

In the afternoon we visited the Jail, the condition of which, though not unsatisfactory, could not be compared with that of similar institutions in British India. We saw many desperate characters,—a Brahmin who murdered his wife, another who had murdered his servant, and protested "that he did not kill that man, but that he had suicided himself of his own accord." One convict had not spoken for three years. His Excellency spoke to the Dewan suggesting the release of some of the prisoners. After service at the Protestant church, conducted by the Archdeacon of the newly-formed Missionary Diocese of Travancore, we visited the cathedral of the Syro-Chaldean Christians, who are under the Patriarch of Babylon, and whose affairs are administered by a Bishop Mar Elias John Mellus. This functionary, however, is generally absent in Mesopotamia and a *Kor Episcopos* from Mosul (Nineveh) acts for him. There was a great procession through the church, fireworks and rockets, a kind of Durbar, an address,—altogether a grand function. The Christians of this Coast do not neglect those outward and visible signs which produce so much effect on the impressionable peoples of India.

In Kurdistan and the neighbouring vilayet of Bagdad, the Chaldeans, as a people, are not recognisable. Here they are spoken of as a nationality, but the *Kor Episcopos* looks quite an Arab,—a curious contrast to the Native of Malabar, who interpreted his Chaldean tongue and the Governor's English. The address and answer over, gigantic candles, according to custom, were given, the largest to the Governor, the next largest to the Resident, and so on; and we all marched down the middle of the church in uniform, each holding a candle in one hand and a sword in the other,—a most eccentric procession.

The Governor, with the Resident, visited one or two of the Nairs' houses. These are little detached tiled dwellings, each standing in its own garden, surrounded by foliage and garden trees, and superlatively clean within and without. Brazen vessels shining like mirrors, wood-work polished to the last degree, and beds hanging from the ceiling, were among the characteristic features of the menage. After dinner we started in torrents of rain in big house-boats for Cochin, and awaking in the morning near the Island of Bolghatty in the backwaters on which the Residency is situated, we found our little convoy surrounded by snake-boats, each containing about 30 paddlers. These are boats of honour attending on the Governor's barge, and how they get so many men into boats so crank and narrow is astonishing.

We breakfasted at the Residency,—a fine house in a unique situation, looking out on water all round, the vision being bounded on every side by cocoanut palms, at once a source of beauty and of wealth to the country. Cochin and its neighbourhood might be described as a rural Venice. In the deep embrasures of the windows of the house which is now the Residency, the Dutchmen of Cochin used in old times to drink deep draughts on holidays, and hence the house was known as "the Punchbowl." So the legend runs.

The town and harbour of British Cochin lie across the water on the right, and the native town of Ernakulam on the left. His Highness the Raja of Cochin came after breakfast in his State barge to visit His Excellency, and the Dewan interpreted during the interview. The conversation related to the satisfactory financial and agricultural condition of the State, to His Highness' health, to the kind preparations he had made for His Excellency, to the Imperial Institute and other topics.

Afterwards several of the princes came, and the Archbishop of Veerapoly, the head of the Roman

Catholic Christians in these parts, where every known kind of Christian is found.

In the afternoon, the Raja of Cochin held a Durbar in his palace across the water to give His Excellency the opportunity of returning his visit of the morning. The Raja is a kindly and courteous gentleman, much respected by his subjects and by Europeans who know him, as, indeed, are the heir-apparent and all the younger princes.

The White and Black Jews of Cochin, who pretend to have settled here since the destruction of the temple at Jerusalem, were now holding the feast of Tabernacles. The Governor, by request, visited the Synagogue of the White Jews, where a prayer in Hebrew was offered up for the welfare of Her Majesty the Queen, and her representative. The same ceremony was repeated at the two Synagogues of the Black Jews. These are converts of many generations. The women of the White Jews are extremely fair, and their skins look dazzlingly white by contrast with the black and bamboo-coloured population around them. They dress in fantastic robes with gay cloths about their heads and golden coins about their necks. These Jews keep up some sort of connection with Jerusalem. Two men from the holy city sat close beside us while the sacred books of Moses were being unwound from the interior of silver cylinders, capped by erections like Imperial crowns. The walls of the small Synagogue were hung with yellow satin and hundreds of cocoanut-oil lights burnt within, intensifying a thousandfold the hot, steamy and oppressive atmosphere with which the Malabar Coast pays for "the fatal gift of beauty."

At night there was a State banquet, and the heir-apparent and the First Prince dined to represent the Raja. The former proposed Lord Connemara's health in a short but eloquent speech, extremely well delivered; and he ascribed to His Excellency what he, in turn, disclaimed, the sole merit for the sanction recently accorded to the execution of the Periyar Project. The Governor pointed out that a share of the credit was due to Sir M. Grant Duff and others, and to none more than to the Viceroy, who had the interests of this part of India much at heart. The First Prince is a great Sanskrit scholar, and has never left Cochin in his life, for the reason, I believe, that one of the princes once travelled and died away from home. He speaks English very well, is anything but narrow-minded, speculates vaguely on the world beyond, and meanwhile enjoys himself in his leisure hours by reading Sanskrit and playing foot-ball. The members of the Cochin family, who are very numerous, are remarkable for the unanimity and concord in which they all live together, and the State is so laudably economical that the Government had, in their last review of its administration report, to urge on it a more liberal expenditure on such services as education and public works.

Next day, the 11th, was a day of uninterrupted inspections. British Cochin is a little town, which has shrunk out of all recollection of its former greatness. We saw the supposed tombstone of Vasco da

Gama in the old Portuguese church, and inspected the light-house, the harbour, the schools and manufactures of the place. A dispute about cutting down a tree which had convulsed this ancient city was explained at length to the Governor, who, after listening with much patience, said he thought that the side which gave way on such a trifle was the side which was right, whatever the merits of the case might be. It is to be hoped that the disputants will take this to heart, for the tree episode well illustrates the spirit of the place.

At the Jesuits' college, a grateful reference was made in the address to the efforts that Lady Connemara has made to improve the condition of her Indian sisters. The Cochin Chamber of Commerce, the Reform Association and many other individuals were after this received, and the afternoon was spent in a visit to the Ernakulam High School.

In the evening, as we left the Residency in boats, the shores of the backwater for miles around were beautifully illuminated with continuous rows of torches and lamps, and next morning (12th) we awoke in the territories of the Maharaja of Travancore, with whose representative at Aleppey we breakfasted, and then proceeded to Quilon, sometimes passing through narrow artificial canals, and sometimes through broad natural lakes. On the banks of the canals oleander trees, screw-pines and caladiums pressed down to the water's edge, and in many places the trees formed a bower for long distances above the waterway. At intervals toy-pagodas and towers made of bamboo, covered with coloured cloth, put off from the bank to join our convoy, and rafts on which were standing rows of gigantic cows, similarly constructed. As we neared Quilon the illuminations began, and when we got to the Residency the Dewan of Travancore and other high officials met us.

Next morning (13th) we went again through a similar country in boats to Trivandrum, after passing near Quilon through the Wurkali tunnels,—two very considerable engineering works,—which, by means of an under-ground canal, connect the backwaters north and south of it. One of these tunnels is a mile long.

The country through which we passed by water for the last 180 miles is always liable to be submerged for miles around, and it is a fact that cattle can be seen here putting their heads under water to graze, and that crops are harvested at times by gathering the heads of stalks from boats.

At the landing place of Trivandrum, His Excellency was met by the Maharaja, a fair complexioned prince, 38 years of age, of medium height, and clad in gold brocade and wearing a jewelled aigrette and feather in his cap. A Guard of Honour of the Nair Brigade in red and a few troopers of the Body Guard, a line of elephants, a crowd of officials, and dense masses of fair-skinned natives were assembled at the pier. The Governor and the Maharaja drove off together, and both left their carriage on the way to inspect a gigantic pandal or shed in which 2,000 school-children, many of whom wore a quantity of jewels, were packed tier above tier to view the procession. The streets up to the Residency were gaily decorated with arches, flags and the like, and it is a new sensation, whenever you come to this Coast, to see ladies walking about the streets and looking out of the windows, just as if they were, what here they really are, the most independent half of the population.

Early the next morning the 14th, His Highness the Maharaja paid a private visit to the Governor, and conversed with him for a long period about affairs of State, as did the Dewan who came afterwards. Then followed an address from the Malayali Sabha or Association, which may be described as the party of progress in these parts The address stated that the Sabha owed its origin to the endeavours of a few Malayali students of the Maharaja's college to remove the prevailing impression as to physical exercise being derogatory to the dignity of manhood! The Sabha is, however, an Association of some importance, and the Governor took the opportunity in replying to say that he was glad to find that the party of progress was patronised by the Maharaja, and was inspired, itself with most loyal feelings towards His Highness. There was more significance in this than might appear at first sight, because certain persons are at present busily engaged in decrying the local administration in the Madras Press.

The post of Minister in a Native State is not a bed of roses, and here we have a few discontented servants of the State assisted by the party which cries "Travancore for the Travancoreans," just as, on the rendition of Mysore, we heard so much of "Mysore for the Mysoreans." In fact, no opportunity is lost of appointing competent Natives of the State to the public service; but it will be long ere the stranger Brahmin can be dispensed with here or elsewhere. Good men must be entertained when they can be found, from whatever part of India they may come. It was abundantly evident to the Governor that the affairs of the State are, on the whole, efficiently and wisely conducted.

The rest of the morning was spent in receiving different addresses and high officials, and in the afternoon the Maharaja paid a State visit. The road from his palace to the Residency was covered with sea-sand, which, it seems, has some peculiar virtue, for on the rare occasions when the king of Travancore has to walk in public,—of course on this occasion he drove, —it is always laid down for him to tread on. A file of twelve enormous elephants, with shields on their heads, formed a part of his procession.

On the 15th October the Governor gave away prizes at the Maharaja's college, and commended to the boys the importance of physical exercise for proficiency in which, as well as in intellectual studies, some of the prizes were devoted. He also said a few words deprecating breathless and ill-considered changes, and commending the gradual adoption of such reforms as experience had shown to be indisputably necessary.

A State banquet is an inevitable feature of a visit such as this, and in reply to the Maharaja's toast of his health, Lord Connemara said that His Highness was endeavouring to follow in the footsteps of his enlightened predecessors who had ruled in "the model Native State," and so long as he did so, might count on the support of himself and his Government.

None of the characteristics of an Oriental Court are absent here. There are family differences and jealousies, intrigues and counter-intrigues, good intentions and more or less successful or unsuccessful efforts to bring them to fruition. Yet it may be asserted that such unpopularity as the Maharaja and his Minister have achieved, with some sections or factions in the State, is as much due to a determination in making appointments to choose the best men without fear and favour, as to any other cause. It is not only the Chinaman who in these days is hated for his virtues.

On Sunday we left to ride across the Western Ghauts to Courtallam in our own territory. The first 25 miles pass through beautiful forest scenery where wild elephants abound. A report had come in that two of the native grooms taking out posted horses had been killed by these animals, whose tracks we frequently saw along the road. This turned out to be untrue; but the effect produced was such that matchlockmen in numbers were collected at the temporary stables and little rest-houses in which we camped, around which elephant trenches are always, as a matter of course, dug and maintained.

The bungalow at Camp Gorge is most beautifully situated in a romantic valley that runs through from one side to another of the Western Ghauts. The hills on either side of the defile are densely wooded, and on the top of one of these, some miles away, fireworks were let off after dinner, and torches, thrown down from a precipitous rock on the summit of the mountain, had a curious effect in the dark night. We rode before breakfast the last 25 of the 70 miles which separate Trevandrum from Courtallam, a little village at the foot of the hills near a waterfall, which is said to wash away the sins of those that bathe in it, whence the place derives its name. The climate here is artificial owing to the presence of clouds which hang around the Western Ghauts, which reduce the temperature ten degrees below that of the surrounding plains.

There is little to do in Courtallam but bathe in the waterfall and admire the scenery; but three miles off there is the large town of Tenkasi, or the Southern Benares, the inhabitants of which presented an address, as did also the people of Kalakad, who desired that one of their old native irrigation works on the water-shed of the Western Ghauts might be repaired. A visit to the Tenkasi temple brought together a dense and demonstrative crowd.

On the morning of the 20th we left Courtallam and rode to Alankulam, a distance of 18 miles, where we breakfasted in the roadside bungalow before going the remaining 18 miles to Tinnevelly, where, in spite of the rain which in an hour made either side of the road a torrent of red-sand stained water, the people turned out in enthusiastic crowds. The ride from fertile and well-wooded Courtallam through a sandy plain covered with palmyrahs, to the richly-irrigated rice-lands on either side of the Tamraparni, on which Tinnevelly is situated, well illustrate the diversified character of the soil and the scenery of this district. The people are well educated, public-spirited, and exceedingly litigious, and the number of Christians is far larger here than in any other part of India.

On the other bank across the Tamraparni lies the town of Palamcottah, once a military cantonment, but now merely a large native town, the regiment having been removed in accordance with the wise policy that now concentrates troops in fewer centres where emulation and *amour propre* prevent them from deteriorating, as it was found they did, when left long in solitary stations.

Tinnevelly is the head-quarters of the Church Mission Society, presided over by Bishop Sargent. The head of the other great Society,—the Society for the Propagation of the Gospel, which is of equal importance,—is the veteran Bishop Caldwell, a scholar and philologist of high reputation. He told us a story which illustrates the ignorance of some classes, even in this enlightened district. The King of the South of India, seven or eight hundred years ago, was called the Pandyan, and a descendant of his, a petty landholder, lives at Singampatti, not far from Courtallam. The Bishop met some of the hillmen one day, and asked them who governed the country in these times, and they said "The Pandyan." "And where does he live?" "At Singampatti." "And what about the white men?" said Bishop Caldwell, "have they nothing to do with the Government of the country?"

"Oh, dear, no," said the hillmen, "they often come here but only to shoot. They have nothing to do with the government of the country."

The Governor visited Bishop Sargent's schools and highly commended the good work which the Reverend Bishops and their assistants had been carrying on for the past fifty years in the district, and assured his hearers that the Government were anxious that a just proportion of the educated of all classes of the community should be employed in the public service, and that no one class or religion should be preferred to another.

In the afternoon there was the usual levée at which the Zemindars of the district mustered in full force, most of whom are the descendants of the Polygars who gave such trouble before they were subdued, and in whom the spirit of the Naick dynasty was fully developed, and was with difficulty extinguished. Then followed addresses from the three Municipal towns of the district, which contained the usual remarks about local self-government, and the need of a better water-supply, and to which the usual reply only could be made.

Of these Municipalities, Tuticorin, once a renowned sea-port, is still famed for its pearl-fisheries. Captain Phipps, the Port Officer and Superintendent of Pearl-fisheries, came up to see the Governor about certain questions concerning the fishery arrangements.

On the 22nd there were more girls' schools to inspect and more addresses to receive, and the inhabitants of Tinnevelly had various objections to make to the present distribution of water for irrigation from the Tamraparni River, to regulate which is such a difficult task that it is possible, the Governor remarked, that legislation may be required before the officers of the Public Works Department can satisfactorily deal with it. His Excellency, in answer to their address, deprecated the creation of permanent appointments in connection with the Agricultural Department, though he approved the holding of exhibitions. Enquiries made into the working of the Agricultural Department at head-quarters suggest some doubt as to whether the results have been commensurate with the expenditure, and engender a disposition to view with a critical eye specious proposals for further development.

At Tinnevelly one of the Assistants to the Collector is Mr. Varada Row, a young Brahmin of good family, who has been appointed a Statutory Civilian. He dresses like a European, and rides well. He is a curious product of the times we live in. He continues to observe his caste customs, and yet so far as one can judge from outward appearances they prove no obstacle to the performance of his duties. It must be observed, however, that he is an unusually favourable specimen of the Statutory Civilian, and takes a liberal view of most things, including caste.

On Sunday the 23rd, after hearing a sermon preached in Tamil by Bishop Sargent, we left by special train for Madura, passing through a country cultivated with dry crops, chiefly cotton and cholum, and keeping the line of the Western Ghauts in sight on the left hand.

Arrived at Madura, we drove across the river Vigay to the Collector's house known as the Tumkum, a curious and lofty structure built, it is said, by the great Tirumal Naick, from whose time the celebrated Palace and Temple date. On the way the first inscription met with was "Welcome to Hospital!" The Tumkum is said to have been a species of Grand Stand, whence the king and courtiers viewed elephant fights and exhibitions of the like nature; and it is also recorded that Queen Mungammal was here walled up and starved to death, like an erring Vestal, having been discovered in an intrigue with her Brahmin Minister. The name of Mungammal is still gratefully remembered, because she planted all over the country, for hundreds of miles, avenues under which the wayfarer, at the present day, can travel in shade from sunrise to sunset.

This interesting house possesses another association of a far different kind. One of the Collectors of Madura, of the Johnstone family, brought here the heart of Montrose, which was stolen by thieves of the Maraver or robber caste for the sake of the silver casket in which it was enshrined. My authority for this is the *Pall Mall Gazette*, which published a very interesting article on the Montrose heart, while yet it was a Conservative organ in the hands of Mr. Greenwood. But enquiries made of Mr. Campbell Johnston, Lady Greville and others of the family, entirely confirm the story. The circumstances are narrated in an interesting letter from a member of the Johnston family, who was Chief Justice of Ceylon, to a member of the family of Lord Napier and Ettrick, late Governor of Madras, who published a history of Montrose, with whose family that of Napier of Merchistoun is closely connected.

The great temple of Madura Meenatchi has been so frequently described that it need only be noted here how completely the shrine is the social and religious centre of a community with which Hinduism is a living and actual fact. Those who hold that Hinduism has approached the stage of "proud decrepitude" and "shivers to decay," should travel through the holy places of the South of India and see the towers of the temples constantly repainted and the temples themselves extended, and repaired, and filled with a never-ending stream of worshippers, sincere, if their conformity be but conventional. They should hear, too, the addresses presented to the Governor, not one of which does not beg for the improvement of the law relating to the vast religious endowments of the Presidency, so as to make malversation less easy and the upkeep of the religious services more certain and satisfactory.

The chief priest of the temple showed us around. His tall and upright figure was clad in a shining cloth of gold, and he wore twisted around his shaven crown a fillet of sacred beads and a band of gold. Thus apparelled, he looked the incarnation of priestly pomp, but was withal a most courteous old gentleman, and made an excellent speech in Tamil referring with gratitude to the recent visit of the present Viceroy, to the former visit of Lord Napier to whose action the restoration of Tirumal Naick's palace was due, and to the present visit of Lord Connemara, which, he said, was connected with the most momentous event that had ever happened in the history of Madura,—the commencement of the great Periyar Project. He told us with pride that Lord Dufferin had presented him with his photograph.

Thence we proceeded,—abrupt transition,—to the school of the American Mission, and next to Tirumal Naick's palace, which has been restored at a cost of £30,000, and is used for the accommodation of all the public offices of the city. In the king's bed-room,—an enormous apartment,—the District Judge holds his Court, and behind his chair is hung the picture,—the only one which the palace contains,—of one who long occupied, with unusual distinction, the post of District Judge, the present Member of Council, Mr. Hutchins, C.S.I.

The morning of the 25th was devoted to inspecting the Madura water-works and the new bridge across the Vigay, which is being built in part from funds subscribed for the visit of His Royal Highness the Prince of Wales, in commemoration of which it is to be called the Albert bridge. A slight fresh had come down the river in the night, and to get to the Mantapam or little temple on the island on which is situated the pumping station, we had to ride through several feet of water.

Madura is prominent amongst the towns of the Madras Presidency for an enlightened interest in public works, and it has taken more kindly to the new local self-government scheme than any other important centre.

A not uncommon incident of life in India cut us off from our work on the 25th. The river came down and the causeway was impassable. The resourceful railway ran special trains backwards and forwards to our side across the railway bridge, and except that, everything was a little later, the afternoon's programme of levée, inspections, addresses and speeches was adhered to in its entirety.

On the 26th we travelled by train to Ammayanaikanur, a small place in spite of its long name, and thence a difficult march of 80 miles took us to the site of the Periyar Project. We halted, of course, *en route*, first at Periakulam at the foot of the Pulney Hills and just under the station of Kodaikanal, and next at the foot of the Periyar Hills, as the road up can only be traversed in broad day-light owing to the wild elephants and tigers which abound in this locality. Before getting to the foot of the hills, the road, often almost impassable, runs down the fertile Cumbum Valley, on either side of which are mountains, the tops of which, seen above the low-lying monsoon clouds, looked prodigiously high. The valley ends in a complete *cul-de-sac*, but in an almost invisible fold in the hill-side, a good road leads to the summit and across to Travancore, passing by a newly-cut path to the camp now occupied by the Engineers engaged on the Periyar Project.

The nature of this really great scheme may be explained in a few words. Parallel to the water-shed of the Western Ghauts, for perhaps 40 miles, runs a stream called the Periyar, which consequently at the point where it commences to descend from the hills, is already a considerable river. It happens providentially that close to the water-shed at this point is a tract of country not, indeed, level, but intersected by low valleys, which admits of being converted into a huge lake. It is intended to obstruct the course of the river by a gigantic dam, 165 feet high, to store 200,000 million gallons of water, which now flow unneeded to fertile Travancore, in the artificial lake; to bore a tunnel 1¼ miles long through solid rock on the side of the lake remote from the river; and to precipitate such portion of the water as lies above the level of this tunnel, down into the valley below, where it will join a tributary of the Madura river and convert 100,000 arid acres of that thirsty district into fields of rice. It will at once be apparent that the scheme is a very bold one, and presents entirely novel features. It is an effort to give to the dry East Coast a share of the superabundant rainfall of the West.

At present a channel is being cut through a portion of the site of the proposed lake, which will be utilized for floating materials to the works, and a road has already been made, along which we rode for 7½ miles through dense forest, all of which will, it is hoped, in six years be submerged by the waters of the diverted river.

The difficulties of starting work in a remote and almost impenetrable jungle are considerable. Wild elephants give a great deal of trouble. One of them visited our camp in the night. They not only frighten the native workmen, but they destroy their work and knock down their houses. A herd will come along the newly-made road, and, reaching a temporary bridge, will send the lightest member across to test it. Being made to support bipeds only, it will generally give way, whereon the herd will express its disapproval of such workmanship by promptly demolishing it.

A Brahmin Surveyor, a Bachelor of Arts and of Civil Engineering, employed on the works, has been living in terror of wild beasts ever since he came up. He hears elephants "growling all night, which sends his heart down to zero point of courage." He has, he says, been "chased by a blue-eyed bison" and flying "with a great velocity" dropped his theodolite. The instrument broke and he tried to replace the cobweb with one of his own hairs,—a wire cable to a silver thread. When remonstrated with, he said he dropped the theodolite "in order to save life" (his own). On another occasion, he fell down a precipice and "would have been killed, had not gravity come his aid." Nor is this the full tale of his adventures. One day, while carrying a big stick, he met a bear, or thought he did, and fled leaving all his work-people to face the animal. Mr. Taylor, the Executive Engineer, told him he should not have left his men, but he explained that on seeing the bear he immediately made a mental calculation of his stick's powers of resistance by "Hodgkinson's Tables," and found them insufficient. As for the work-people, he left them, "because they could not run as fast as he could."

His brother actually did get into trouble one day, and this Bachelor of Arts and Engineering thanked God it was his brother and not himself, "because he drew less pay, and would consequently be less missed by the family." Altogether he is a source of much amusement, and hopes great things for himself, saying that since he came up, he has already been made "half a man." It is quite a new thing for a young and educated Brahmin, the heir of all the (Hindu) ages, to take to jungle work at all.

On the way, however, we heard of a case which suggests another view of the India of to-day,—a case of murder which recently came before the Courts. A woman on the Western Coast gave birth to a child which, for some reason or other, was decided to be a Rakshasa or demon. It was accordingly killed, and its slayers were in the Court of First Instance acquitted on the ground that they had not intentionally killed a human being, but what they believed to be a monster. The Court above found, of course, that as they had killed a human being, the crime was murder. Again, one of the district officers in Madura said that a highly-educated native doctor came to him to ask whether if he cut off an old woman's leg, and she died in consequence of the operation, he would be guilty of murder, and whether if he did not, he would be guilty of the same offence, believing as he did that she would certainly die if he did not amputate the limb. These incidents,—and they might be identified indefinitely,—only show how many and what divergent forces are at work in modern India, and how the march of progress synchronises with the existence of abysmal ignorance and superstition. The agricultural labourers (chiefly women) who crowded along the road to greet the Governor with shrill cries of welcome, leaving their infants hanging in cloths from the boughs of the banyan trees, have not advanced one step in one thousand years, while the Brahmin B.A. and B.C.E. is saturated with the learning of modern schools.

On the way down the Cumbum Valley, we had proof that the complaints made on all hands that cattle starve owing to forest reservation is at least an overstatement of a case, which doubtless has some small foundation in fact.

Captain and Lady Eva Wyndham-Quin, who have been in Travancore for the last month, passed down the valley a day in advance. Lady Eva has, we hear, ridden very long distances, and he has shot two bison, six ibex, one bear, two alligators, and two sambur in the hills just above us.

Meanwhile, we get back to the railway in constant fear of the rain, lest we fail to get across the rivers. In fact, however, travelling through the monsoon we have escaped miraculously, and the heaviest shower we have been out in was of *rose-water* projected too generously from a silver sprinkler on our unprotected heads.

Hardly had the above been written, when we rode 30 miles partly through a deluge of rain. The sides of the road were converted into torrents, and we had to ride against time to get over the rivers before they came down in full fresh from the hills above us.

We were glad to meet the Military Secretary, Major Stewart-Mackenzie at Ammayanaikanur, where we took the train for Trichinopoly, halting for an hour at Dindigul to see the new water-works and to visit Mr. Heimpel's manufactory, at which the well-known Trichinopoly cigars are made. Mr. Heimpel told us that he exported to England every month upwards of half a million cigars, which are chiefly re-exported to Russia and Germany, and some of which actually go to Havanna. Here, as at Calicut, we had proofs of that enterprise of the great German nation, the competition of which in trade has been felt of late years by the British manufacturer all over the world.

On the last day of October we rode out from Trichinopoly to Srirangam, a town of temples on the banks of the sacred Cauvery, which, like the Vigay and the Tamraparni, we found in fresh and flush from bank to bank. There is nothing remarkable about these temples but their size and wealth in lands and precious stones. The table service of the God consists of a quantity of huge golden bowls.

In the Central Jail we saw, among a population of upwards of 800, some of the Burmese dacoits who have given so much trouble, and a Hindu convict who protested in English that the case against him was a "concoculation." "Likewise," said he, as we passed on, "I have passed Criminal Higher." This is one of the tests which candidates for employment in the public service have to pass. In another sense the test is also passed by those who are candidates for a home in jail.

All was satisfactory in this, the Jail, it will be remembered, in which the health of the prisoners was so unsatisfactory a few years back, that its condition and management formed the subject of repeated questions in Parliament, and of an exhaustive inquiry by the Madras Government. Careful inquiries were made as to the food and water supplied to the convicts.

The Tondiman or Raja of Puthucotta, whose territory lies near Trichinopoly, came in to visit His Excellency. He is a boy of 13, and speaks English well, and the affairs of the little State are in the competent hands of the Dewan Regent, Mr. Sheshaya Shastri, a very able administrator, subject to the control of the Collector of Trichinopoly, who is also Political Agent for Puthucotta.

The morning of the 2nd November was devoted to a visit to the Grand Anicut, an old native work, about 13 miles from Trichinopoly, designed to regulate the supply of water between the Caveri and Vennar rivers, which irrigate the Tanjore District, on the one side, and the Coleroon, which carries away the surplus water, on the other. Immediately below the anicut, regulating sluices have lately been constructed across the Caveri and Vennar at a cost of about £55,000, which will enable the supply, when the river is low, to be divided in proper proportion between these rivers, and in high floods prevent the admission of more water than the rivers are capable of carrying, thereby preventing the occurrence of disastrous inundations in the Tanjore District.

The afternoon was devoted to receiving addresses,

visiting schools and returning the visit of the Raja of Puthucotta. The entertainment provided at the Jesuit College was of a most novel and original character. Among the subjects on the programme was a representation, by small boys of about 10 and 12, of a class being examined in Indian History by the master, a preternaturally sharp boy who was the smallest of all. It was agreed by master and pupils that Lord Dalhousie was the greatest of Indian Viceroys, and Lord Mayo the most popular, and that a Governor, who was at once the son-in-law of one and the brother of the other, possessed special claims on their regard and consideration. These small people performed their respective parts with infinite *aplomb* and the little master of the class was quite a prodigy of self-possession. He spoke before an audience composed of many hundreds of his school-fellows and of strangers, with a voice and delivery that very few English public schoolboys could command on their last speech-day. It is the peculiar gift of small boys in this country to be pleasantly and unpretentiously precocious.

Next morning we moved along the delta of the Cauvery to Tanjore, where the great Temple, the Palace and its occupants, and the new and admirable Raja Mirasidar Hospital, raised by local subscriptions in this wealthy district, claimed attention. The Jail, too, built on the far more expensive and possibly somewhat more satisfactory cellular system, received a visit, and the presence of some 20 or 30 civil debtors suggested an inquiry, which is now being made, as to the alleged greater severity of the law of civil debt in this, as compared with other parts of India.

The Palace of the last Raja of Tanjore, now occupied by his ten surviving widows and their relations, is a large rambling succession of shady courtyards, lofty halls, and dark passages ornamented throughout in the striking but meretricious style of Hindu art. All was gold and red and blue, and monstrous gods and demons figured on every wall.

The building contains some very interesting arms, and pictures,—some of the Rajas, in what Bishop Heber happily calls, " the king of spades " style, others portraying the crimes and punishment of the Marquise de Brinvilliers,—but the glory of the Palace is its library containing a vast store of Sanscrit manuscripts, many of them of great value, which have been catalogued and classified by the late Dr. Burnell. The evidence of that most distinguished Orientalist and Sanscritist will carry much weight in deciding, should the question still be deemed open, the relative value of Eastern and Western literature. After his retirement from the Madras Civil Service, he passed some time in the libraries of Rome in the congenial study of their contents ; and writing to Tanjore, said how much he regretted he had spent the leisure of a busy official life on Sanscrit and connected subjects, which were, he said, mere garbage compared with the literature of the West.

Lord Connemara alone was admitted inside the purdah, behind which the Ranis and their children were seated, and the rest of us sat outside the golden curtain, though a narrow net-work ran along the purdah, on the eye-line, through which curious faces kept peering. The scene behind the purdah was not of an unusual character. All the ladies talked at once as the principal male member of the family introduced Rani after Rani to the Governor's notice.

The subjects referred to in the addresses and petitions presented in this, one of the wealthiest districts in India, did not differ materially from those received elsewhere. They chiefly referred to the severity of the Salt and Forest laws, the injustice of the house-tax, on the imposition of which the extension of local self-government in rural districts depends, to the difficulty of settling disputes as to irrigation, and so on.

A pleasing feature of addresses throughout was their constant and grateful mention of former Governors, Lord Napier, Lord Hobart,—particularly by the Mahomedans,—the Duke of Buckingham and Sir M. E. Grant Duff. It was not less pleasant to note the constant recognition of Lady Connemara's efforts to promote the good works begun by Lady Dufferin's National Indian Association, and Lady Grant Duff's Madras Gosha Hospital.

The executive officer in Tanjore, immediately below the Collector and Magistrate in rank, is Mr. Manavedan Raja, the Senior Statutory Civilian serving in this Presidency. This gentleman, who belongs to the family of the Zamorin of Calicut, discharges his important duties in a very satisfactory manner.

We left Tanjore at 10 P.M. on the night of the 4th November and joined Lady Connemara, who had come down from Ootacamund with Lord Marsham and Mr. Wisely two days before, at Madras at 10 A.M. on the morning of the 5th, after visiting two Native States and five British districts and travelling 1,030 miles in all, of which we rode 212, drove 114 and were carried by rail 488. The remaining 216 miles we did by water in house-boats on the Western Coast.

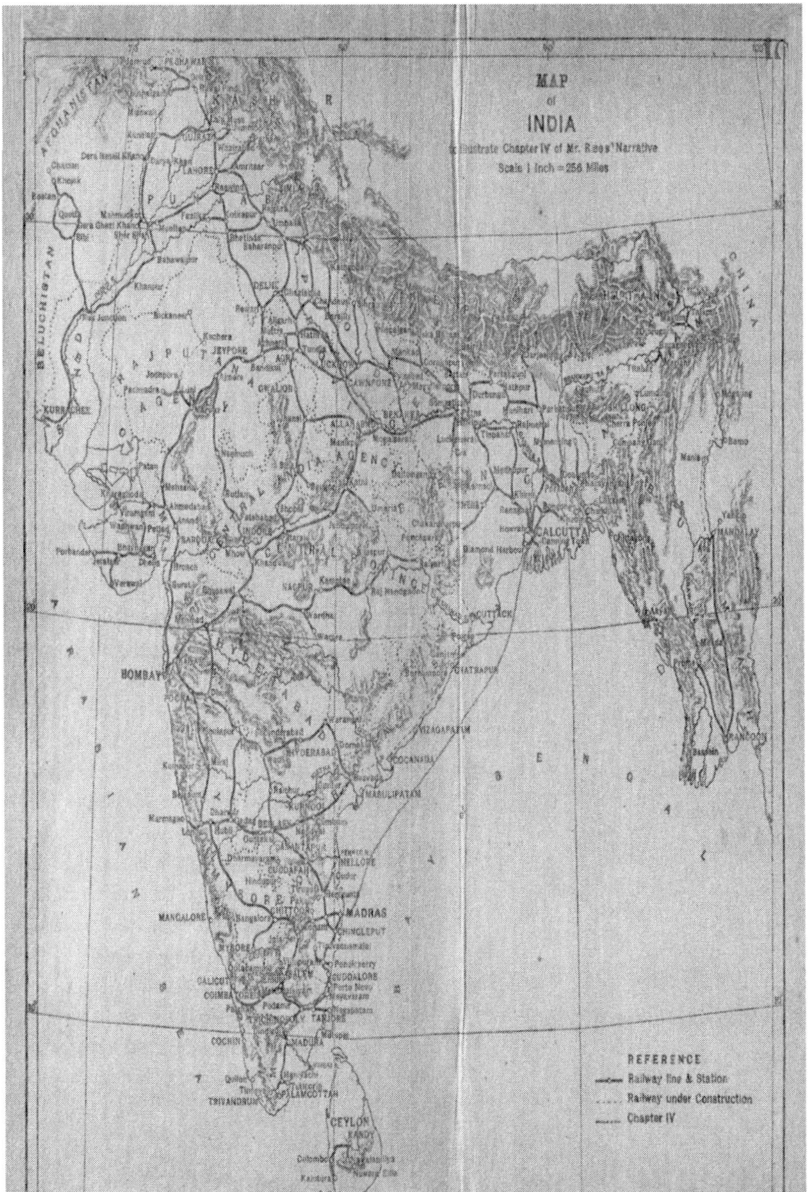

MAP
of
INDIA
Chapter IV of Mr. Rees' Narrative
Scale 1 Inch = 256 Miles
AFGHANISTAN
BELUCHISTAN
CHINA
PESHAWAR
LAHORE
Amritsar
DELHI
JEYPORE
KURRACHEE
CAWNPORE
BENARES
CALCUTTA
Diamond Harbour
MANDALAY
RANGOON
BOMBAY
POONA
NAGPUR
INDORE
BARODA
CUTTACK
VIZAGAPATAM
COCANADA
MASULIPATAM
HYDERABAD
KURNOOL
BELLARY
NELLORE
CUDDAPAH
MADRAS
CHINGLEPUT
MANGALORE
Bangalore
MYSORE
CALICUT
COIMBATORE
CUDDALORE
TANJORE
COCHIN
MADURA
PALAMCOTTAH
TRIVANDRUM
CEYLON
KANDY
Colombo
Nuwara Eliya
Galle
REFERENCE
Railway line & Station
Railway under Construction
Chapter IV

CHAPTER IV.

CALCUTTA.

Voyage to Calcutta—"River of ruined capitals"—"James and Mary"—Our party—Landing at Prinsep's ghaut—Marquess of Dalhousie—At Government House—Legislative Council—Council chamber—Debate—Pacification of Burma—Sir Dinshaw Manikjee Petit—Story of salt tax—Fancy fair—Nepaul Minister—Ceremony of Investiture—Memorials of Lord Mayo—Visit to Barrackpore—Lady Ripon's avenue—grave—Religious Endowments' Bill—Evening party—Representative Indian men—Meeting of Countess of Dufferin's fund—Viceroy's acknowledgment of Lady Connemara's services—Lady Dufferin's efforts—Lords Mayo and Dalhousie—More speeches—Visits—Sports at Body Guard lines—To Diamond Harbour—On board *Rewa*—Incidents of voyage—Eclipse ceremony—Arrival at Madras.

A JOURNEY from Madras to Calcutta by a P. and O. Steamship is of such an ordinary character as to call for no description. In fine weather it is a mere yachting journey of three nights and three days, the last day being spent partly in waiting for the tide, and partly in hastening up "the river of ruined capitals" after crossing one bar to get over the other two with the tide.

Near the junction of the main channel of the Ganges with the Hoogly are the two moving quicksands named "James and Mary," the passage of which, always difficult, was rendered more exciting by the recent loss thereon of two steamers. The river-bed changes more or less from day to day, and its condition is almost hourly recorded and telegraphed to Calcutta, whence news is transmitted to stations down the coast, in order to give the pilots the latest information. The charts are, owing to these frequent changes, of very little use.

Arrived at Garden Reach, where a black flag was flying over the palace of the recently deceased king of Oudh, we * found Lord William Beresford and Captain Currie in the Viceroy's launch, ready to take on to Government House Lord and Lady Connemara and party, and Lord Eustace Cecil and Mr. Cecil, who had come up from Madras with us. We landed at Prinsep's ghaut, whence Lady Connemara had embarked with her father, the Marquess of Dalhousie, when last she was at Calcutta, when the parting cheer to the Viceroy died away into a sob of regret. Here a guard of honour of the 7th Bengal Native Infantry was drawn up, and, after the Governor had inspected it, we drove to Government House. At the foot of the grand staircase, Sir Steuart Bayley, Lieutenant-Governor of Bengal, and Sir Donald Mackenzie Wallace, Private Secretary to the Viceroy, met the Governor and Lady Connemara, and escorted them to the top of the steps, where the Viceroy and Lady Dufferin, and the members of their family awaited their arrival.

* His Excellency The Lord Connemara, G.C.I.E.
Her Excellency The Lady Connemara, C.I.
Lady Eva Wyndham-Quin.
Mr. Rees.
Captain Wyndham-Quin, A.D.C.
The Viscount Marsham, A.D.C.
Surgeon-Major Briggs.

The climate at Calcutta seemed cold to visitors from the far south of the Peninsula, but there was warmth enough in our welcome to neutralise its effect.

Next morning, Friday the 3rd February 1888, was

entered in the thoughtful programme, drawn up under the Viceroy's orders by Lord William Beresford, as a "free day," but there were many visitors, and at 12 o'clock a meeting of the Legislative Council at Government House. Above the Viceroy's chair in the Council Chamber is the picture of Warren Hastings, to which Macaulay refers in his celebrated Essay; but Lord Dufferin who sat below had no need to preserve a *mens æqua in arduis*. Every member of the Council who spoke approved of the measures His Excellency was taking to meet a small deficit, namely, an increase in the salt tax, and the imposition of a duty on paraffin oil. At the close of the debate, however, the Viceroy had occasion to refer to the satisfactory progress of the pacification of Burma,—a subject that recalls the sessions in that Chamber of less united Councils in more stirring times. The debate was of an unusually interesting character, and showed that the official and non-official members were of one mind as to the financial measures proposed. The Parsee Member, Sir Dinshaw Manikjee Petit, did not think that the extra 8 annas tax on salt would press hardly, or indeed be appreciably felt by the people.

Apropos of the salt tax, room may perhaps be found for a story said to be true and certainly amusing: An old woman, who would neither explain nor plead, was being tried by a Magistrate in the Madras Presidency for being in possession of illicit salt, or salt privately manufactured from saline earth. She was about to be fined one rupee, when the Magistrate said, "I may as well satisfy myself that it is salt," and proceeded to taste some of the dubiously white powder found on the old woman's person. Before he had raised it to his lips, she cried aloud, "Not only do they fine me one rupee, but they eat the ashes of my dead husband."

In the afternoon there was a great fair for the benefit of "the little sisters of the poor" at St. Xavier's College, in the success of which Lady Dufferin and her daughters took a kindly and energetic interest. Lady Bayley at her stall had collected curios from Tibet, brazen feet of Buddha, Buddhistic blotting books and the like. Lord Connemara was not able to be present, as he had gone to see the Maharaja Minister of Nepaul, the nephew of Jung Bahadur, who was on a visit to Calcutta.

The event of the next day was the Investiture of the Most Eminent Order of the Indian Empire. In the grounds in front of Government House an enormous Durbar tent had been put up, and tickets had been issued to about 1,500 spectators. On either side of this central tent stood two assembling tents, and at 12 o'clock in one of these, His Excellency the Viceroy joined the Companions and the Secretary of the Order, who had previously arrived. In the other tent the only Knight Grand Commander, who was to be invested, Lord Connemara, with his staff, awaited the summons of the Secretary to appear before the Grand Master, who preceded by the Secretary in a white silk robe, and followed by the Companions of the Order, had slowly marched down the lane between the spectators to the throne at the end of the tent. The summons came directly after the proceedings had been formally opened. First came the Under-Secretary in the Foreign Department bearing the insignia of the Order on a velvet cushion; next came the Secretary and then Sir Steuart Bayley, Lieutenant-Governor of Bengal, and Sir Charles Aitchison, late Lieutenant-Governor of the Punjab. Between these two Companions of the Order and followed by his personal staff, Mr. Rees, Captains Wyndham-Quin and Lord Marsham, the Governor of Madras proceeded to the *dais*, whereupon Lord William Beresford drew his sword and handed it to the Viceroy, who first of all conferred upon Lord Connemara the dignity of a Knight Bachelor of the United Kingdom, after which Sir Steuart Bayley and Sir Charles Aitchison invested the new Knight Grand Commander with the ample robe of the Order and affixed its Star to the left breast of his coat. Then they conducted His Excellency to the throne, where he made obeisance to the Viceroy, who invested him with the Collar and pronounced the formal admonition. A salute of 17 guns was next fired, and His Excellency was then conducted to his seat on the right of the Grand Master by the Secretary of the Order.

The new Knights were next invested with ceremonies of the like nature, but of less circumstance and detail. Among them were Sir Donald Mackenzie Wallace, the Viceroy's Private Secretary, the Maharaja of Durbungha and the Maharaja of Vizianagram, whose handsome appearance and graceful bearing did credit to the Presidency whence he comes. The investiture of the Companions did not take long, and at one o'clock the Viceroy marched out in State, surrounded by his staff, and followed by Lord Connemara. Then came the Knights and Companions, and so ended the chapter. It was a brilliant ceremony, well designed, and well executed in every particular.

In the afternoon "the little sisters of the poor" again claimed our attention, and a most varied and admirable programme, under the patronage of their Excellencies the Viceroy and Lady Dufferin, resulted, it is hoped, in large and well-deserved profits.

On Sunday we drove past Lord Mayo's statue to the Cathedral, within which is a handsome stained glass window, another memorial of that much-beloved and well-remembered Viceroy.

To this succeeded a most enjoyable visit to the Viceroy's country-house at Barrackpore. We went up by water in the Viceroy's launch, His Excellency himself steering the greater part of the way. We admired the broad river and the temples on its bank, and were charmed by Lady Ripon's beautiful avenue of bamboos, which completely excluded the midday sun. The turf was green, the kites were bold; luncheon under the trees was perfect; a walk to Lady Canning's grave was peaceful and pleasant; a ride next morning cool and exhilarating, breakfast in the bower-like verandah behind the bongainvilliers and the Bignonia, most grateful, and a morning journey back to Calcutta in the steam launch an enjoyable ending, to a most delightful little visit.

In the afternoon at a small tennis-party were

collected together all that was eminent in the official, and much that was charming in the social, world of the Indian capital. There were present the Members of the Viceroy's Council, some of the Secretaries to the Government of India, and others with whom the Governor and his Chief Secretary, Mr. Stokes, had already held consultations concerning certain matters of business of importance to the Southern Presidency, which can only be settled with the concurrence and approval of the Government of India. Such informal discussions, though most salutary and fruitful in results, cannot conveniently be here recorded.

The morning of Tuesday 7th was devoted to conferences with Sir Charles Eliott, Public Works Member of the Government of India, and Sir Charles Aitchison. With the latter and with Mr. Scoble the Governor fully discussed the question of amending the law relating to religious endowments. There has been an agitation in Madras, which is presumed to represent the feeling of the Native community, in favour of radical alterations in the law, so as to empower District Committees to exercise effectual control over the trustees of religious institutions, who, it is alleged, at present mismanage the funds of the institutions committed to their charge. It was felt, however, that a Central Committee controlling the District Committees, which had been proposed in Madras, would partake of the nature of a Government institution, or would, at any rate, bear that complexion in the eyes of the natives. It also seemed that the powers which District Committees possess already are much more extensive than is generally supposed. It is a pity that these powers were not set out, as enumerated in the old regulations, instead of being merely referred to in Act XX of 1863, as being conferred by such regulations. The chief difficulty no doubt is to provide funds for the initial expenses of suits brought against trustees who embezzle or waste temple funds; and it was thought that such expenses in *bonâ fide* cases might be charged to the institutions concerned, whether or not the suit was ultimately successful. To the conference it seemed expedient to amend the existing Act XX of 1863, to define the powers possessed by District Committees, to re-appoint such Committees, which have, with few exceptions, ceased to exist, and to provide greater facilities to those interested in bringing malpractices to light.

The afternoon was devoted to a visit to the Botanical Gardens, and after dinner a large evening party took place at Government House. The appearance of the crowd of visitors was very striking. There was the Maharaja Minister of Nepaul clothed in black satin and gold, with a white cap like that of a Russian cavalry officer. Around him were the members of his staff in red coats, turbans and aigrettes of bird of paradise feathers, and diamonds. Conspicuous among the bravely-dressed people, *simplex munditiis*, was the Parsee millionaire Sir Dinshaw Manikjee Petit, clad in plain white linen and wearing the high glazed hat which alone recalls the origin of his co-religionists. The Ameer of Afghanistan was represented by his agent, a tall and burly Afghan, wearing a fur cap; the nobles of Madras were represented by the Maharaja of Vizianagram ; the foreign Consuls, in uniform and *bien decorés*, mustered in full force. The Bengalis were most numerous, but nearly all parts of India were represented. Among the guests was Prince Furruk Shah, the great grandson of Tippu Sultan, and many other friends of the late Lord Mayo,—all anxious to be presented to his brother. Among the ladies were three Burmese clothed in their graceful national costumes. English ladies, and English Hussars and Lancers, the red of the line, the blue of the Political Department, the shawls of the Baboos, and the black coats of the Civilians, Mussulmans, Bengalis, Madrassees, Parsees, Afghans, Burmans, Punjabees and Nepaulese combined to make up a varied and striking scene.

On Wednesday afternoon the annual meeting of the Countess of Dufferin's Fund was held in the Town Hall. The Viceroy was in the chair, and the proceedings were opened by Mr. (now Sir Andrew) Scoble, Legislative Member of the Supreme Council, who in moving that the annual report be accepted, gratefully acknowledged the services rendered by Lady Connemara and her Branch Committee in having led the way in enlisting the services of Local and Municipal Boards, and having thereby helped, in a great measure, to nationalise the objects of the Association. He paid a high tribute to the energy and industry of the Countess of Dufferin, who was, he said, not only the patroness, but also the working head and the working heart of the Association. Lord Connemara, who followed, thanked Mr. Scoble for the kind reference made to Lady Connemara's efforts, and also commended the Madras Committee and its Secretary, Mr. Rees, for their exertions. The Viceroy in like manner thanked those who had spoken for the tribute they had paid to Lady Dufferin's successful and laborious efforts, and said that it gave him great pleasure to preside on the occasion, not only because the incorporation of the Association would now establish it upon a firm and lasting basis, but also because "he had received the assistance that night of the brother of one of the noblest Viceroys that ever presided over the destinies of India, who sacrified his life in the discharge of his duty, and to whose memory the affectionate reminiscences of the people of India still clung with undying fidelity." His Excellency also found an additional pleasure in presiding when he remembered that beside him sat Lady Connemara, "the daughter of the most illustrious statesman that ever left the shores of England, in order to devote his great talents and his undaunted energies to the service of his country, the memory of whose achievements will last as long as history itself, and who secured once for all the safety of British India." Lord Dufferin reminded his hearers that Lord Dalhousie, "though he left these shores alive, soon afterwards succumbed to those unparalleled labours which signalised his Viceroyalty." Speeches were also made by the Maharaja of Durbhanga, the Sheriff of Calcutta, Mr. Evans and others. The Sheriff in his speech having referred to the custom of seclusion of women as being a bad one and inimical to all progress, as well as to the spread of female education and the adoption of female medical aid by the women of India, Mr. Evans pointed out that the Countess of Dufferin's Fund in no wise took this view and merely wished to diffuse medical aid amongst the women of India without regard to any social or religious distinction whatsoever. The Lieutenant-Governor of Bengal, Sir Steuart Bayley, in his speech took the ground taken in the reports of the Central Committee and of the Madras Branch, that the provision of practitioners of the Hospital Assistant Grade was, in fact, what was most wanted, and that the choice did not lie between such, and between highly-educated practitioners, but between such and no practitioners at all. It was gratifying to us to find that the lines upon which we are working were not only approved by the Central Committee, but were emphatically declared to be those best calculated to nationalize the movement, and to give it a permanent footing in the land.

On Thursday the morning was occupied as usual with visits, amongst others from the Maharaja of Vizianagram, and in the afternoon rain interfered with the programme, but was powerless to keep away the visitors who had been bidden to the most enjoyable ball which took place in the evening.

The next day, Friday, we went in the afternoon to the Body Guard Lines to see tall troopers in their long scarlet tunics tent-peg and wrestle on horse-back. Besides this, there was a tug-of-war; the competitors on either side being Hindus and Muhammadans, all mounted. The result showed that the horses had very little to do with it, and that their weight could not be brought to tell at all. I think the victory was on the side of the co-religionists of Sir Syed Ahmed, who has lately been protesting that numbers cannot count for everything, and that between Muhammadans and Hindus, the less than half is more than the whole.

In the evening Lord and Lady Connemara dined with the Lieutenant-Governor of Bengal, and next morning, with great regret to have come to the end of so pleasant a programme, and to leave such kind hosts, we despatched our things by the steamship *Rewa*, and started ourselves by special train, after luncheon, to embark at Diamond Harbour. On the way down we passed through fields of rice now covered with stubble, which, in the rainy season, are under water, and through which now and again you could see a cultivator paddling himself in a dug out, even at this time of the year. A steam launch took us across to the *Rewa*, which we learnt had had a fratricidal collision with another steamer of the same Company in the river. Her voyage up and down was eventful. On the way up she had halted for three hours in mid-sea, to allow a Hindu Raja to bathe and cast gold and silver into the water and pray in the eclipse. We said "good-bye" to Captain Currie of the Viceroy's staff, who had accompanied us, slept on board the ship and next morning steamed away to Madras,—all regretting that one of the pleasantest visits of our life was done and ended.

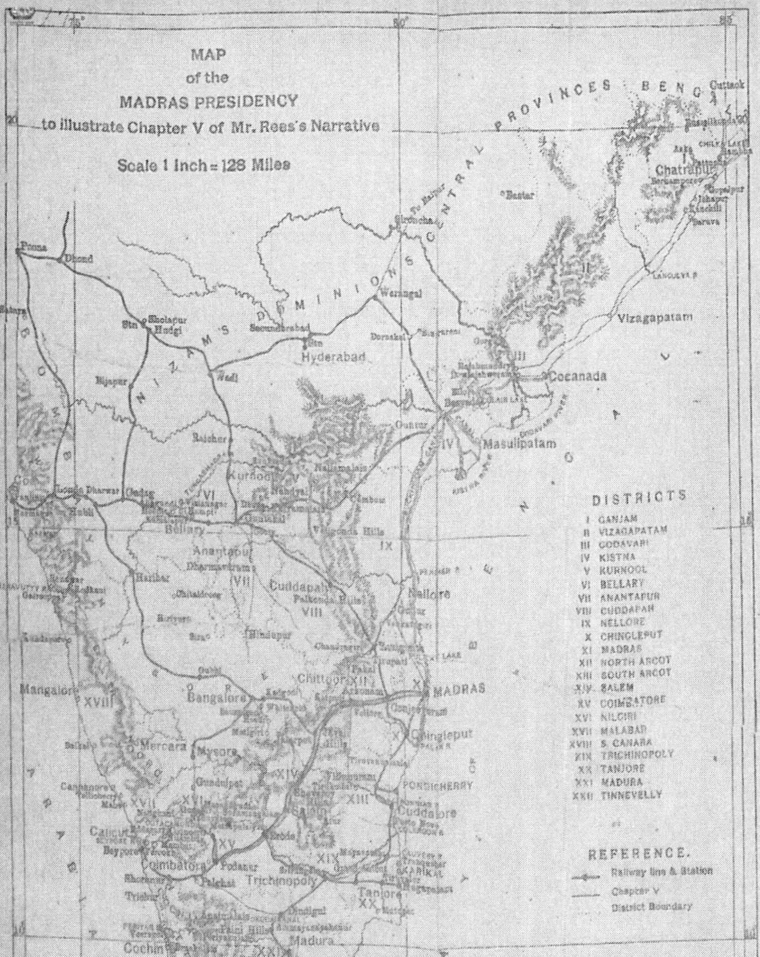

PHOTO-ZINCOGRAPHED IN CENTRAL SURVEY OFFICE MADRAS

1891

CHAPTER V.

SALEM.

Departure from Madras—Reception at Salem—Opening of Agricultural Exhibition—Mr. Nicholson—Mr. Dykes—Cattle shows—Former exhibitions—Municipal address—Governor's reply—Sections of show—Alambadi bulls—Kangyam bulls—Nilgai—Pegus and Arabs—"Parfait Amour"—Government stallions—Arabs and Persians—Pony-breeding operations on hills—Agricultural implements—Native and Swedish ploughs—Native harrow—Persian wheel—Native picottah—Vegetable products—Specimens of fibres—Iron-smelting—Spear heads—Animal products—Native manufactures—Palampores—Bricks—Lacquerwares—Native saddles—Shermadevi mats—Garden party—Mr. Sturrock—Proposed transfer of Coorg to Madras Presidency—Prize-giving at Agricultural exhibition—Departure for hills—Eucalyptus plantations—Sim's Park—Welcome at Charing Cross.

On the evening of the 22nd of March 1888, we * left Madras for the second annual visit to the Hills. A very large number of Europeans and natives came to the station to bid His Excellency good-bye.

* His Excellency The Lord Connemara, G.C.I.E.
Mr. J. D. Rees, Private Secretary.
Captain Wyndham-Quin, 16th Lancers, A.D.C.

Next morning arrived at Salem, we were met by the Collector, Mr. McWatters, the Judge, the Superintendent of Police, and many other District officials, now all of them well known to the Governor.

The reason for this visit was the opening of the Salem Agricultural Exhibition. It had been decided by the Madras Government to hold periodical exhibitions at different central stations in the Presidency, and occasionally at Madras itself. Before arriving at these conclusions this important subject received the fullest consideration. Mr. Nicholson, whom we saw at Anantapur last year, contributed several valuable and interesting papers to the discussion. He considers that it is in regard to agricultural *implements* that the case for Agricultural shows is strongest. He presided over a fairly successful exhibition held at Gooty last year, and his opinion is quoted as being that of a well-informed and earnest officer, with whom many others of experience and ability thoroughly agree.

It has to be urged also that the cattle shows held for many years in the Nellore District, and originated by Mr. Dykes, who is yet well remembered there, have been of unquestionable benefit in improving the breed of cattle in that part of the country. Similarly, shows at which the best specimens of cattle from the localities most favoured in this respect, are exhibited to thousands of ryots, cannot but be more or less beneficial.

The exhibitions that have been already held at Gooty, Erode and Bellary, have attracted large numbers of ryots, and a fair number of exhibits, and of visitors from the neighbouring districts, and the Salem Exhibition has certainly not fallen short of the others mentioned. Indeed it is probably the best yet held.

The proceedings opened with the usual address from the Municipality to which was also added an address from the Mussulmans of Salem. Neither address, it is worthy of remark, contained any reference whatever to the unfortunate differences which once existed between the Mussulmans and the Hindus of Salem, or to the dispute connected with the mosque which led to the riots of 1882. The address of the Municipality contained the usual words of welcome, and referred to the water-supply of the town for which aid from provincial funds was asked; to the tax on head-loads of fuel collected without, and brought into, the town, which was said to press heavily on the poor; and to the proposed extension of the Madras Railway to Salem, a distance of 4 miles. His Excellency in replying to these addresses assured those present that of all the subjects which came before him as Governor, there were none which caused him greater pleasure to investigate, than those connected with agriculture, on the prosperity of which the present and the future of this Presidency so largely depend. Referring to the water-supply he feared that it was most unsatisfactory, but asked the memorialists to remember how hard it was to decide whether the general funds of the tax-payer should or should not be devoted to the wants of a particular locality. He pointed out the great improvement which has been effected in the forests around Salem as a set off against the imposition of the tax on head-loads of fuel, which of itself did not fall on the poor who collected, but on the dwellers in the town who used, the wood. His Excellency was much disappointed to have to tell his hearers that there was no prospect of the Madras Railway being extended to Salem, as an investigation had disclosed the fact that such an extension would not even pay its working expenses. He invited the Municipality to show, if they could, how a railway could be brought into Salem at a moderate expense, and sympathised very much with a town of 60,000 inhabitants which was avoided by a railway, which passed it at a distance of only four miles.

Of the different sections of the show, those devoted to live stock and implements were the most interesting and most satisfactory. The show of cattle was very fine, the Alambadi bulls being especially remarkable. This breed which takes its name from Alambadi, a town in Coimbatore, is a variety of the Mysore breed, and is probably, next to that of Nellore, the best in the Presidency. The Kangyam bulls also are remarkable for enormous heads, long hanging dewlaps and broad shoulders, the withers being surmounted by a hump. Towards their quarters they fall off, but on the whole, are very imposing and handsome beasts, and greatly valued for the stud. They run from 150 to 300 rupees a pair, and individual animals will, of course, fetch much higher prices. The show of sheep was disappointing although a very good mutton sheep is grown in the neighbouring district of Coimbatore. The show of buffaloes too was poor, probably owing to the fact that this useful milker and drawer of the plough is held in small repute. Among the cattle were bulls sacred to some Hindu god, who roam at pleasure and feed where they will. Most of these had the insignia of the deity to which they were dedicated branded on their velvet flanks. There were antelope, spotted deer, barking deer, and nilgai or blue-bull,—a curious beast which, to the uninitiated, looks like a cross between the antelope and the oryx. These last, however, were mere accessories to the more serious exhibits of the section, as indeed were the sacred bulls who helped by their gaudy clothing and painted horns to lend variety to the long stalls. The show of cattle on the whole was distinctly good, and it is worthy of note that just as Pegu mares seldom or never quit Burmah, just as Arab mares rarely forsake the tents of their own tribe, so do cows of the more highly prized breeds of cattle hardly ever leave the immediate locality to which they belong. The fact is that the ryots decline to part with their cows.

There was an interesting show of country-bred ponies, and their foals, got by the Government stallions. It had been a matter of controversy quite lately at what period of the year the produce of sires, maintained by Government for the purpose of improving the indigenous breed of ponies should best be born, and there was evidence at the Exhibition to show that the decision arrived at, to leave this question to the discretion of local officers, was the only wise and practicable solution. In different parts of this country grass is available at different times and the climate varies greatly, and no general rule such as exists in European studs can well be laid down.

There were several promising colts ; one filly in particular, a daughter of Parfait Amour, attracted much attention.

The Government stallions themselves were paraded in a separate shed. With one exception all were

Arabs or Persians. The difference is not so well defined as might be thought and the circumstances under which both classes are imported into India are not so well known as they might be. The Turkish Government objects to the exportation of Arabs from Bagdad and Busra, the only ports upon the Tigris whence horses can be shipped for the Persian Gulf *en route* to Bombay. On the Eastern side of the river under the jurisdiction of the Persians, there is no such difficulty. When nothing but a river intervenes between the highly prized Arab whose pedigree has been jealously kept by the Sheiks of the Bedouin, and the coarse and under-bred but useful Persian of Arabistan, Luristan and the surrounding country, it is quite natural that the dealers should pass off any good-looking Persian as an Arab, when they can. Indeed the country whence they ship them is locally known as Arabistan, and there is no great stretch of the imagination, no violent departure from truth, in describing its horses, as Arabs of a kind. At any rate, the Persian, be he highly considered or not, possesses just the qualities which are likely to supply the deficiencies of the weedy, narrow-chested and cow-hocked pony of the plains of Southern India. Each animal and his capabilities were discussed by His Excellency in company with the Member of the Board in charge of breeding operations, and the Revenue Secretary to Government, and the subordinate officer employed in the department. Pony breeding operations under His Excellency's own immediate supervision are to be continued upon the Nilgiri Hills where a plentiful supply of grass, and a good climate promise a fair hope of success. An officer lately appointed to report on horse shows in the Nizam's Dominions dwells on the fact that no animals above 2 years old are to be found in the country side. If, as is suggested, the Deccan pony is sold as an Arab, there are unfathomable depths of ignorance and imposture; no two animals could be less alike. The Persian and the Arab have many points of resemblance which are more marked according as the Arab is under-bred, and the Persian the reverse. Size again is a valuable criterion, most of the imported "Arabs" being bigger than the steed of the desert. Of course the Arab varies greatly in size, and natural selection, to use the phrase of the day, evolves different types in different countries. Pure-bred Arabs foaled and reared in England, may be seen at Mr. Wilfrid Blunt's at Crabbet Park, which illustrate by their greater height and bigger bulk, the changes that in time produce such descendants as the English Race horse, or the big bony Turcoman, who bears no resemblance to his putative father.

Leaving the live-stock now for Agricultural implements, perhaps the first thing worthy of notice is the light plough specially adapted to the thin soil in which the Indian ryot sows his dry crops. Large numbers of light ploughs have been sold in the Ceded Districts. The native plough, though it merely scratches the ground, is heavy, and the Swedish plough has been found to be admirably adapted for light soils. Of course for heavy black cotton soil, and irrigated land, a heavier plough is absolutely necessary, but the lighter the implement the better for the ryot, who has no ploughing cattle to spare. There were winnowing machines, cotton cleaning machines, and an improved sugar-cane mill which has proved vastly successful in the north of India, one insertion in which expresses from the canes all the juice they contain, whereas by the native method after three insertions, and considerable waste, much juice yet remains. This Beheea sugar-cane mill is rapidly coming into use throughout the Presidency. The native harrow is very much like a large rake, and generally has only one row of teeth. A Persian wheel was shown at work, but this ancient and useful contrivance is not likely to supplant the more economical and almost equally efficacious *picottah*, whereby water is raised from wells in buckets by a beam suspended on a lofty upright moved by the hand of the worker, who walks up and down it, as the bucket goes up or down. On the whole, it must be said that, except in regard to the light plough above referred to, most of the implements of European agriculture are too expensive for, and perhaps on other grounds not altogether well-adapted to, the simple and primitive, but nevertheless effective methods of agriculture pursued from time immemorial by the native ryot.

Of vegetable products there were specimens enough; rice of all sorts and kinds, cholum, raggi, cumbu, grams of different sorts, oil-seeds, cotton, jaggery, sugar, tobacco, indigo, gums, resins, and vegetables. It is possible to write a book on the different kinds of rice, the golden wire, the white, the ivory, the red, the tailed, the pepper, the needle-pepper, the little bead, and many other species. Some kinds of rice, the food *par excellence* of the upper classes, are far more favoured and more expensive than others. The staple of the masses in many of the districts in the South of India is raggi, which is far cheaper than rice, at least as nourishing, and does not predispose towards certain painful and fatal diseases as does the latter grain. Unfortunately when cereals are exhibited in the grain in small quantities, the samples afford a very indifferent means of judging what the crop may be like. To obviate this, it was agreed that in future all cereals should be exhibited in the straw only. Of fibres there were many specimens; the *Sanseviera zeylanica* which grows in quantities in the neighbouring district of Coimbatore, afforded great promise at one time and attracted the attention of capitalists. There were specimens of other excellent fibres such as *Fourcroya gigantea*, *Rea* and *Musa textilis*. For various reasons, however, chiefly the cost of production, regular manufacture of these fibres for the market has not hitherto proved a success.

We saw iron being smelted by the native process, the ore lying on one side of a small furnace constructed of clay, and fed with firewood. On the other side was the iron extracted from the ore. The hills round Salem abound in valuable iron ore, but unless very cheap coal or fuel becomes available, it is likely that these mineral riches will continue to be unavailing in the future, as they have been in the past. The coal from the Singareni fields which can soon be brought by rail directly to Salem, will not, it is feared, be cheap enough to allow of this industry being prosecuted. It is a great pity, for most admirable steel has been turned out in small quantities by the native method, and a lately deceased smith of Salem had the reputation of manufacturing the best spear-heads for pig-sticking, which have yet been made in India.

Among the animal products were excellent butter and cheese made on the Nilgiris by a retired military officer, and brought down to be exhibited by his daughter, who happily secured six prizes.

The native manufacturers exhibited most of the cloths, wood-carving, silver, copper and brass work well known to all travellers in the south of India. There were Palampores on which were portrayed the story of the Ramayana, the capture of Seeta, the death of Ravana, the return of Rama, and the like, and there were purdahs and cloths of red and white silk so thickly embroidered with gold that they would stand up, yet not of such choice workmanship as one sees at Delhi, or Srinagar. There were bricks from the West Coast, admirable bricks too, such as we saw at Calicut last October in the kilns of the Basel Mission, drain-pipes, indigenous paper, basket-work, lacquered work of which we had already seen better specimens in Kurnool, native saddles of staring crimson cloth, glass bangles, and beautiful woven grass mats from Shermadevi in the Tinnevelly District, so fine that a mat six feet long can be folded up into an incredibly small parcel.

In the evening there was a garden party at the Collector's house, at which Government officials, European and Native, from many surrounding districts were present in large numbers.

Next morning, Mr. Sturrock, the Collector of Coimbatore, came to see His Excellency. He has been on special duty to report upon the proposed transfer of the province of Coorg to the Madras Presidency. This change has been frequently suggested, but no actual steps have ever been taken so far to bring it about. The present administrative arrangements are these:—The small and mountainous province of Coorg is immediately under the control of the Government of India, the Resident of Mysore being also Chief Commissioner of Coorg. Separate acts and regulations and rules apply to the Province, and the question now is whether it shall be attached to Madras, and if the decision be in the affirmative, whether it shall be a separate district or a sub-division of the existing district of South Canara. The Coorgs, a race at once hardy and picturesque, are said to object to being deprived of their present autonomy, or rather their immediate subjection to the Government of India. They are said to object more particularly to being made a sub-division of Canara, regarding the peaceful inhabitants of that district with much the same feelings that the Highlander entertains, or did entertain, towards a Lowlander in Scotland. As usual, it is a question of money, the present administration being more expensive than would be that of a regulation district or portion of a district under the Government of Madras. The question is still * *sub-judice*, and this is all there is at present to be said about it.

* It has been decided since to leave present arrangements unchanged.

On the evening of Saturday the 24th, His Excellency gave away the prizes at the Agricultural Exhibition and spoke commending Agricultural shows as a means of improving agriculture, and congratulating those concerned on the results of the Salem Show.

The same night we left by special train for Coonoor where next day in company with Mr. Burrows, Collector of the Nilgiris, we rode over the Eucalyptus plantations of the Government and inspected the charcoal manufactory, as well as Sim's Park, one of the Government Gardens on the Hills under the control of Mr. Lawson, which was in a highly satisfactory condition.

On Monday the 26th, we came into Ootacamund, where a Guard of Honour of the Nilgiri Rifle Volunteers was drawn up at Charing Cross, and where a large number of the inhabitants were gathered together to bid us welcome to the summer capital.

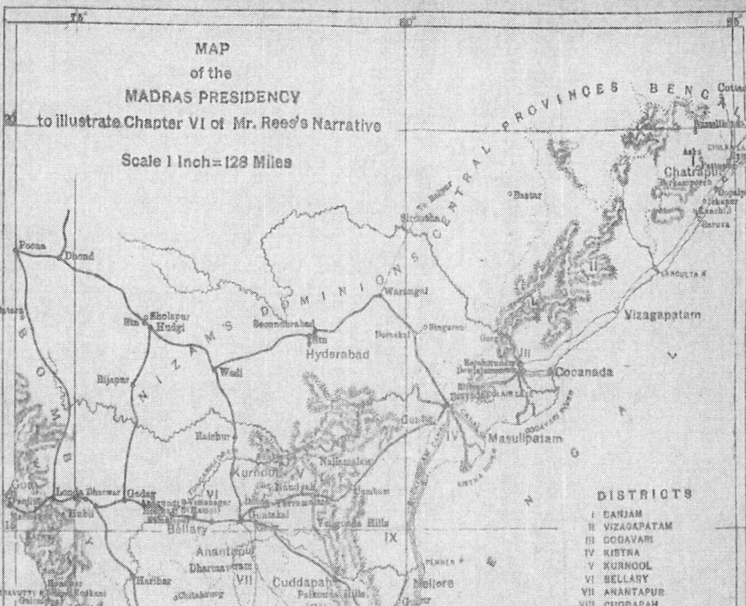
MAP
of the
MADRAS PRESIDENCY
to illustrate Chapter VI of Mr. Rees's Narrative
Scale 1 Inch = 128 Miles
CENTRAL PROVINCES
NIZAMS DOMINIONS
Poona
Dhond
Hyderabad
Warangal
Vizagapatam
Cocanada
Masulipatam
Bellary
Anantapur
Cuddapah
Nellore
MADRAS
Chingleput
Bangalore
Mangalore
Mercara
Mysore
PONDICHERRY
Cuddalore
Calicut
Coimbatore
Trichinopoly
Tanjore
Madura
Cochin
Palamcottah
Trivandrum
Kurnool
Hubli
Gadag
DISTRICTS
I GANJAM
II VIZAGAPATAM
III GODAVARI
IV KISTNA
V KURNOOL
VI BELLARY
VII ANANTAPUR
VIII CUDDAPAH
IX NELLORE
X CHINGLEPUT
XI MADRAS
XII NORTH ARCOT
XIII SOUTH ARCOT
XIV SALEM
XV COIMBATORE
XVI NILGIRI
XVII MALABAR
XVIII S. CANARA
XIX TRICHINOPOLY
XX TANJORE
XXI MADURA
XXII TINNEVELLY
REFERENCE.
Railway line & Station
Chapter VI
District Boundary

1891

CHAPTER VI.*

MYSORE, SERINGAPATAM, BANGALORE, OOSOOR, KOLAR.

Departure from Hills—Our party—Object of tour—Government House, Ootacamund—Scenery *en route*—Toda herdsmen—Korumbers—Overseer's encounter with a tiger—Maharajah of Mysore's Silladars—Brahmin Superintendent of Police—Tippoo Sultan—Fishers' village—Caste in Modern India—At Nanjengode—Native welcome—Hindu temple—Jain Priests—Story of a Hindu King—Reception at Mysore—Chamundi Hill—An Eastern St. George—Visit to palace—Dusserah festival—Mysore forests—State jewels—Tippoo Sultan's sword—Palace library—Bi-sexual divinities—Picture gallery—Visit to Seringapatam—Cauvery bathing ghaut—Daria Dowlat—Hyder—Colonel Baillie—Paintings on walls—Apothecary cicerone—Meer Saduk—Tomb of Hyder and Tippoo—Return to Mysore—Grove of palms—Duke of Wellington—Maharanee's caste girls' school—Lady Dufferin—Departure—Tales of Seringapatam—At Bangalore—Residency—Mandalay mementos—Social functions—National sports—Sky races—Maharajah—Aga Khan—of local water-supply—Race course—Inspection of Remount depôt—At Oossoor—A legend—Hamilton's bones—Stock-farm—Principles of agriculture—Return to Bangalore—Madras Sappers and Miners—Mysore plateau—A story of powder and shot—Departure—Arrival at Kolar road—Hyder's tomb—Social relations among Mussulmans—Inspection of gold mines—Their future—Present prospects—Return to Ootacamund.

One sunny day in July 1888, Lord Connemara, accompanied by his Aide-de-Camp, Lord Marsham, and his Private Secretary, myself, left the hill headquarters of the Madras Government at Ootacamund, on a visit to the Maharaja of Mysore, with which pleasure the Governor meant to combine the business of investigating the water-supply for the Madras troops stationed at Bangalore, and of visiting the Depôt, whence

* This chapter was communicated to the *Asiatic Quarterly Review*, and is now re-published by permission of its Editor.

remounts are supplied to the Cavalry and Artillery of the Madras army.

Government House, Ootacamund, is situated on the slope of the highest hill in Southern India, and our road lay for several miles through evergreen woods of ilex and eugenia, and over grassy downs, covered at this season with a beautiful white balsam peculiar to the Nilgiris. Soon, however, began the descent, happily to the Mysore plateau, and not to the hotter Avernus of the plains. As every thousand feet or so are left behind, the character of the hill-side changes. First we make a short cut through potatoes and barley for a few miles. This is the cultivation of the industrious settler, called, on the hills, the northerner. He and his are fast acquiring the Nilgiris from the indigenous idler, the Toda herdsman, who lives in his wicker and daub oven-shaped house on the emerald turf, and is satisfied with the scanty earnings, which he spends in drink. Next we reach the coffee zone, the plantations looking like red and green chess-boards, and yielding this year a crop, remunerative indeed, though not to the same degree as that of last year.

Here is a rest-house for Europeans alongside a waterfall, by which one of the numerous streams, that we cross and recross when hunting the jackal on the hills, makes two long drops to the larger river it joins below. We ride on, halting a moment to admire a string of dahlias hung across the road by the polite keeper of the turnpike, and some cypresses growing in a road-side garden. Odd it is that the symbol of grace and womanly beauty in the East should be the "hated" and the "funerall" cypress of Horace and of Spenser. However, little time is allowed for literary reflections, when many breakneck miles lie before us, so we pass the rest-house and ride on to the foot of the hills, beyond which the road passes through grassy lawns and uplands, now sparsely, and now thickly wooded. This is a great haunt of the sportsman. Elephants abound, and cartmen will not travel at night. Bison and deer roam about the vast forest that stretches away to the distant Canara, and along the berme of the road are frequent signs of wild pigs, who dig about for roots, and are in consequence highly unpopular in an agricultural country. Not that there is any agriculture here. Fever depopulates the country side, and nothing but the excellent pasturage accounts for the existence of the wretched village of bamboo and daub, at which, after a ride of eighteen miles, we halt for breakfast.

The wild Korumber tribe that lives about these jungles supplies trackers to the manner born, of marvellous sagacity. One of our party, Captain Wyndham-Quin, who stayed behind to shoot, tells us of their skill. How they hurry along like sleuth hounds, deriving inspiration now from a bent twig, and again from a crushed leaf. At one time they will halt to discuss a little foamflake on a bough, at another hold a board of inquiry on a blade of grass, and decide how long it is since a bison has browsed thereby. And in the end it is rarely their fault if you do not see your quarry.

Here we learn that a road overseer lately met a

tiger on the road near the waterfall. He, by his own account, was a stranger to fear, and put the tiger to flight, but his pony, he said, died a week later from fright. Hence to the frontier and for a dozen miles beyond it, our path lies through thick jungle, of which the characteristic features are the waving green feathers of the bamboo, and the giant leaves and monster lilac-like flowers of the teak tree. The little bit of red, dear to a distinguished artist, is not wanting, and two well-mounted lancers of the Maharaja's Silladars canter behind us. Picturesque-looking fellows they are, and a perfect contrast, though not in smartness, to the Brahman Superintendent of Police, son of a late minister of Mysore, who also forms part of the escort.

In front of the bungalow where we pass the night, was the grave of a European killed by a tiger, as we are told by the local official, whose grandfather's sister married Tippoo Sultan.

This village, in the centre of the inland province of Mysore, is inhabited to a great extent by men of the fisher caste, who are occupied in various trades. Let this fact, and the presence of a hard-riding police officer, son of a Brahman prime minister, serve for passing proofs that caste is not inelastic in Modern India, if indeed it ever was, which I wholly disbelieve. In fact its relation to diversity of occupations is generally misunderstood.

Next morning we pass along through fields of Indian corn, beneath an avenue of banyans, till the tower of a temple rising above the cocoanut trees indicates the site of Nanjengode, where we halt through the heat of the day in a spacious house of the Maharaja, on the banks of an affluent of the Cauvery. But first we are smothered in oleanders, champaks, and other holy and heavy scented flowers. The stem of every tree for fifty miles along the avenue is girdled by three bands of paint, a native sign of welcome. There is a famous Hindu temple here, on the site of which some four hundred Jain priests were, it is said, killed two centuries ago, by the Rajah of the day. He had once inclined to the Jain religion, but after succeeding to the throne abandoned it, and finding its priests thwarted his agricultural and other reforms, invited them all to a reception. As each one, after making his bow, walked away down a passage, he was dexterously beheaded and tumbled into a pit dug for the purpose. In this way four hundred malcontents were disposed of as methodically and expeditiously as so many pigs by a pork-packer in Chicago. It is recorded that their removal was so well arranged that the pomp and circumstance of the royal reception were in no way interfered with thereby. A graver historian than I am is the authority for the tale.

In the afternoon we make Mysore, within a few miles of which a whole regiment of the red lancers, another of infantry, six gorgeously caparisoned elephants, a few camels, a state carriage drawn by four white horses, and other paraphernalia of Eastern state await the Governor's arrival. Thence amongst prancing horses, waving lance flags, and drawn swords, we enter the Capital, to the obvious satisfaction of the crowds assembled.

Next morning we rode up the hill sacred to the goddess Kali, of Chamundi, who slew the buffalo monster after whom the province is named. As the Calcutta correspondent of the London *Times* gives of late, I think, the impression that barbarous sacrifices are not uncommon in India, I may say that it is indeed long since the Goddess was propitiated by human blood, and that she is the protecting deity of a state ruled over by so enlightened and benevolent a ruler as the Maharaja of Mysore, whose kind and prince-like hospitality we are enjoying. Like most goddesses she has many aspects, and here she is represented as an Eastern St. George slaying the dragon which devastated the fair province of Mysore. Undoubtedly she has other and more terrible attributes, and in one form or another is the dread divinity that rural India chiefly worships.

The afternoon was devoted to the Palace, which, like a bisected doll's house, presents an open front to one side of a square. Above the deep verandahs of the lower story is a throne corridor, and here the Maharaja at the chief festival of the year sits in state on a throne as gorgeous as the Peacock throne, erewhile of Delhi. All the people can see their Sovereign up above from the open square, but only the rich and great file by him as he sits silent and immovable upon his golden seat. Athletes fight and wrestle below, trumpets blare, elephants scream, cymbals clash, torches flare, and the air is heavy with the scent of ceremonial flowers. The Hindus say that the eyes of mortals blink, because the tears which for their sins they shed have weakened them, but the eyes of the deathless gods blink not at all. Hence an attitude impassive and immovable even to the negation of a blink, is that to be achieved as far as possible on this most interesting and truly oriental occasion. A Raja when he assumes the God should *not* affect to nod.

The forests of Mysore are renowned for teak and sandal and other stout and scented trees. The tall pillars of these halls are all of native wood painted red and yellow, as are the ceilings. Beyond the hall is a courtyard, in the centre of which is a canopied Circus, wherein the little princes will learn to ride, under the eye of their father, a very good horseman himself. A dark and narrow passage, lighted by lamps in the early afternoon, leads to a covered and barred enclosure, where pearls, diamonds, and rubies, silver cords and golden bowls, worth in all perhaps £300,000, are spread out for our inspection on a carpet embroidered with pearls and other precious stones, itself worth £20,000. There are, too, castles of gold and of silver, for the backs of elephants, Howdahs they call them. Let us pass on to the armoury, and wield the sword of Tippoo Sultan, "a very practical weapon," as we are told by the conqueror of King Theebaw, who is present. There is another, and most disagreeable weapon, a dagger with a spring. You drive the blade home, and squeeze the handle, and out spring a few saws and knives, that must catch something vital. Next comes the Library, where we see books scratched by a style upon palmyra leaves, bound with laths, with silver, with steel, and with ivory, all length and no breadth, and arranged like children's bricks in neat towers, with the title of each written on ivory, or graven on metal, as the case may be. In every room are pictures of white-limbed divinities, who seem to have accomplished that bi-sexuality of which the late Lawrence Oliphant told us so much in his latest revelation. To the picture gallery you pass through doors of ivory with carved panels, and within you see other doors of silver with big bosses, a pattern originally adopted, they say, because of the discomfort it occasions to elephants or other living battering-rams. The pictures are most quaint and interesting; the floor is black stone inlaid with brass; and that once precious metal, silver, is freely used in all the appointments of the room, which is low and dark, and has the fascinating air, uncommon in the East, of having been occupied, valued, and cared for, through many a changing year.

All this Eastern magnificence is not incompatible with the use of the latest Western inventions, as we are reminded when a telephonic message is sent to the stables a mile away to say "we may be expected there immediately."

Next morning we visited Seringapatam, crossing the Cauvery river, on the stone-stepped margin of which women were bathing, and washing the brazen household vessels, which flashed in the sunlight. These bathing ghauts are almost always beautiful, and the native women look most graceful, with their yellow silk or blue cotton clothes clinging closely to their figures. Bamboos hang over the water's edge, and vegetation is picturesquely completing the destruction of the Fort, which was begun by the British cannon. We see the corner where the breach was made by which the troops entered, and the place where they divided into two parties: one to push Tippoo further backwards into the Fort, and the other to complete its circuit and to slay its master, as he sought to gain his Palace, and there make a last stand. The Fort is not in itself particularly interesting; but its site on an island, around which flows the sacred Cauvery, is at once strong, striking, and picturesque. A voluble apothecary told us everything. He explained the paintings on the walls of the Deria Dowlat, a beautiful garden house of open halls and verandahs painted most gorgeously, yet most tastefully, in red, yellow, and gold. The boughs of trees penetrate into the upper verandahs, and on the walls are depicted Hyder and Tippoo on the march to defeat Colonel Baillie. Either Prince sits on a state elephant in a golden howdah, smelling a rose—the traditional attitude in which Eastern Kings are painted. Further on they meet Colonel Baillie and proceed to demolish himself and his army. Heads are flying on every side in this Homeric contest, and in the centre Colonel Baillie, splendidly attired in full-dress uniform and seated in a palanquin, bites the thumb of disappointment. Close to him a magazine is exploding, and one native water-carrier, with a skin full of water, essays to quench the flames. The presence of Count de Lally on a prancing steed leads the apothecary, himself a native, to explain that "The French always joined with native States—hence their downfall." He also tells us that Tippoo's General, Meer Saduk, was a traitor "same like the Christian Judas." This summer-house is called the sea of wealth, and its lavish decorations, which cover every inch of wall from first to last, from top to bottom, recall the Palaces of Ispahan, and resemble nothing that I know in India. The common tomb of Hyder and Tippoo somewhat resembles the Taj Mahal, at Agra, in design, though not of course in size or beauty. A walk, bordered by a double row of areca palms and cypresses, leads in a straight line to a white Saracenic dome raised upon a platform, which is supported by black marble pillars. The tombs of the conquered have been well cared for by the conquerors, and everything suggests reverential regard for the dead. The doors of the Mausoleum are of rosewood inlaid with ivory; the windows are of fretwork carved in black marble; incense burns within, and silken cloths cover every tombstone. Solemnity and simplicity, here, as elsewhere, characterise the last resting place of Mussulman Princes.

Then we drove back to Mysore past the Grove of Palms, where the Duke of Wellington lost his way, and many of his men, the day before the fall of the Fort.

There are few prettier sights than a Hindu High Caste Girls' School, and next day at the Maharani's School we saw five hundred well dressed, much bejewelled and intelligent girls running from 6 to 16 years of age, who sang English, Sanscrit and Canarese and played on the Vinah, the violin, and all kinds of instruments. They learn, amongst other things chemistry and physiology, hygiene and needle work, and are much devoted to their Maharani of Mysore, and that warm and true friend of Indian women, Lady Dufferin, who from the walls encourages their studies. Not only are they well educated, but many of them are extremely pretty, and not a few leave their babies daily to come and improve their minds. Herein they seem to surpass their Western sisters in the race for knowledge, but then the babies appear at what their Western sisters would consider an early date.

Next morning the Red Lancers took us to the station and we travelled in the train, over an undulating tableland, past gardens of plantain trees, of sugarcane and areca palms, the eighty-five miles which divide Mysore from Bangalore. The Lancers were a great feature of our journey through Mysore, and Colonel Hay has made them as smart almost as British Cavalry. We entered Seringapatam by the Railway bridge with much greater ease than did Lord Harris and the Duke of Wellington; but the traveller cannot help thinking what a pity it is that a bridge somewhat in keeping with the historical associations, romantic surroundings, and beautiful scenery, has not been built. However, economy before all things, and this metre gauge line was constructed for the very moderate sum of £650,000. We see the bathers in the river as we had the day before, but I have since read in a pamphlet published by the apothecary cicerone that the women of this place are "long-tongued, indifferent to their husbands and frequently to all males." I have learnt too, that when citizen Tippoo appealed to the Republican Governor of the Isle of France for aid against the hated English, he offered his allies "every thing that was necessary for making war, with the sole exceptions of wine and brandy." One other tale of Seringapatam before we leave it. Hyder Ali affected to maintain the ancient Hindu dynasty while himself actually ruling in Mysore; and on the death of the puppet Rajah of the day found it necessary to select from half a dozen children of the royal house one to place upon the empty throne. To discover which had the right stuff in him, he offered the little ones a lot of toys amongst which was a dagger, and the child who chose the dagger was the one he chose for King.

At Bangalore we were received by Sir Harry Prendergast, the Resident, and saw in his charming house some interesting mementos of Mandalay, one of which, a silk curtain embroidered with Chinese dragons, was extremely beautiful and came from King Theebaw's palace. In Burma as in China silk is your only wear, and you have it of all shades and colours, from ordinary orange, red, and blue to such tender and indefinite tints as "pink summer snow."

Social functions and national sports must have their turns, and after more escorts, guards of honour, salutes and the like, we all went to the Bangalore Races, where we met His Highness the Maharaja. We saw too His Highness Sultan Mahomed Shah, grandson and successor of Aga Khan, at once prince and high priest, and, in his day, the greatest patron of the turf in India. It is impossible to convey to the untutored Western mind the real position held by this pretty boy, the founder of whose family, by the way, was the Chief of the Assassins, the Old Man of the Mountains, the ruins of whose eyrie you may yet see in the mountains of the Elburz by the Caspian Sea. The only possible parallel that I can suggest would be that of a horse-racing Cardinal, and this I will not seriously maintain. Had Mr. Launde been a follower of the prophet, his priestly office would never have interfered with his love of horse-racing.

Next day began the most serious business of the tour, and we rode, accompanied by engineering experts, about the country, seeing the sites of various projects for the supply of good drinking water to the troops. The town of Bangalore is situated at a height of 3,113 feet above the level of the sea, and being built itself on a higher level than all its surroundings, no schemes are feasible except such as provide for taking advantage of trifling local depressions, storing the surplus rainfall in convenient localities, and pumping the water to such height as may enable it by gravitation to be brought to the perhaps distant cantonment. Many schemes have been talked of; one has been carried out with only partial success. It is very pleasant to ride over the cool and bracing Mysore plateau, and enquire into engineering projects, but a description of them is far from interesting to the general reader, and there are some who go so far as to hold with the Engineer in charge of the works that regulate the existing supply, that too much fuss is made about the matter. He says that men who are thrown off their horses, and killed *on the spot* at Bangalore, are the only ones that are allowed by the Doctors not to have died from drinking bad water.

Next day is spent in similar inspections and in going again to the races. The course is a beautiful sight on a fine day. Across the crowds of natives clad in garments of all colours, and over the Steeple-chase course, some of the jumps of which are natural hedges of Lantana, you see the famous rock fortress of Savandroog and other high and isolated rocks characteristic of the country, and admirably suited for the fastnesses of armed plunderers in the not long past days of rapine and of bloodshed.

Two more days thus passed in riding about the plateau all day, till the soldiers declared we had water on the brain, and in going to dinners and balls all night, and witnessing one morning a parade of all the troops in the garrison. It was pleasant, in the midst of all our alarms about the army, to see regiments of British Cavalry and Infantry respectively 400 and 900 strong on parade.

On Saturday we left for the Remount Depôt just outside the Mysore frontier and in British territory, 30 miles from Bangalore. Here we saw 700 Australian horses, most of them good ones. The place looks quite English, but a few days ago a gentleman driving a team there saw a cobra on the road, and told his groom to kill it. The groom struck it, and the animal was making off, when the driver moved on, hoping to crush it under the wheel. The enraged snake thereon climbed up the wheel and into the carriage where a lady was sitting. A most curious and exceptional occurrence and a most obtrusive snake. Ordinarily you may pass your life in India without seeing one. Here in the most English looking part of the continent, the most poisonous of snakes positively invades a lady's carriage.

Next day we ride to Oosoor, a polyglot village, where we are received in a gigantic bower of mango branches, inspect silos and stock farms, and preach sanitation. The house we stay in, is in one of Tippoo Sultan's Forts. An English prisoner was ordered to build it, but when the Sultan found it was commanded by a neighbouring hill, he had the builder's head hacked off by the village cobbler with his cobbling knife. So at least the legend runs, and it is generally credited, for some bones, believed to be those of the unfortunate Hamilton, were lately found. Most forts in Southern India, however, are said to have been built by Hyder, or Tippu, and nearly all pretend to the distinction of capture by the Duke of Wellington.

On the rocky hill side was carved a gigantic figure of Sugriva, a lion among monkeys, the magnanimous ape who assisted Rama to recover his ravished spouse.

The stock farm* here is only one of many, unhappily not very successful, endeavours to improve the agricultural stock of the country. It seemed to require a great many improvements itself. Indeed it was considered that a beginning should be made by abolishing it. I remember on board a stage in California,

* Since abolished.

asking a driver why it was that Dakota, I think, was not made a State but remained a Territory; and he said, "Most of the people who live there will require killing before they can be turned into American citizens." Too many of our stock-breeding and agricultural experiments are found in like manner to be of such a character that their total abolition is the first step towards their improvement. We too often forget that the Indian cultivator well understands the cardinal principles of successful agriculture.

Next day we returned to Bangalore and spent a most improving afternoon in visiting the lines of that distinguished corps, the Madras Sappers and Miners, who have been in almost every fight in which the British Army has been engaged, for nearly a century. They are great, however, not only in the art of war, but in the arts of peace. They make all their own equipments and are experts as carpenters, coopers, painters, smiths, armourers, gunsmiths, bricklayers, tile-makers, stone-cutters, masons, telegraphists, photographers, printers, and surveyors. No man is admitted into this corps unless he knows some trade, and no man enlists who, for caste or other reasons, is above putting his hands to anything. No less than 500 children too are educated in these lines, and we saw funny groups of little boys seated on the ground and tracing the figures of the alphabet in the sand. The leader of the tiny class called out the name of the letter, on which all the others took it up in a sing-song chorus and repeated it until its shape and name were well impressed in their little memories. We hear and write a vast amount about technical education, but here apparently we saw the actual living thing.

It goes without saying that the day like every other day concluded with a dinner party and a ball.

It must be remembered all this while, that on the Bangalore plateau the thermometer in July only varies from 72° to 82° in the shade, and that the European can stand a great deal more here than he can on the plains. The Mysore plateau is to the low country all around it what one of its own *droogs* or hill forts is to itself; and the holder of this healthful and beautiful country has always dominated the hot plains with their less strong and less warlike inhabitants. The troopers of His Highness the Maharaja who followed the Governor about on escort duty belonged to the class which furnished Hyder and Tippoo with their fighting men. It is more than probable that they are not in love with these piping times of peace, and say to themselves with the Sikh Chieftain in Sir Lepel Griffin's poem :

> " Cursed be the boasted progress that hunts our sons to school,
> " That breaks the sword, and snaps the spear and bids our courage cool."

The peasantry still regard powder and shot with unconcern, the result however not of use but of natural apathy. Some time ago a battery practising near Bangalore is said to have dropped a shot close to a village, and enquiries were at once instituted as to whether by accident anything of the sort had happened before, and whether the people objected to such dangerous practice in their immediate vicinity. The villagers who were examined said, "O yes! those gentlemen of the artillery are always aiming at us, but as no one gets hurt we have no objection and don't think any change necessary." Historians tell us too that when the south of India was one big battlefield, the peasants would go on cultivating around the combatants, only pausing to ask which side had won. That *was* an interesting question, for it meant a change of masters.

On the morning of our last day at Bangalore we travelled 44 miles by train and 11 miles by road to the Mysore Gold mines. The Railway Station is Kolar Road, and hard by at Kolar is the tomb of the father of Hyder Ali. Here I would remark that, as I understand what is on record on the subject, Hyder Ali was by no means a man of low birth or inferior position, though his family was subjected to the vicissitudes of poverty during his youth and adolescence. It is so usual for historians to assert that men who have risen to the top of the ladder began below its lowest rung that I think it worth while to correct what I believe to be an erroneous impression. However, no one can understand these questions who is not accustomed to Mussulmans and their ways. For instance I was once travelling in Kurdistan with a Mussulman servant, and we lived in every respect on terms of equality; but one day, when I was staying with a village khan, he and I were sitting on the ground taking tea and smoking the hubble-bubble, and he said, "Don't you see your servant standing listening?" "Yes" said I, "I have no objection." "No," rejoined he, "but he can't listen comfortably if he is standing. Can't we make room for him on the carpet?" And so immediately he sat down and joined us at tea. There was no feeling on either side that any one was out of place. Again, I knew a Mussulman official in India of considerable position, who had to be made very much of when he came to call, and I had a dressing boy who also was a Mussulman. In the day, I would make much of the official, and in the evening, he would entertain my servant at dinner. The equality in some sense which is possessed by all followers of Islam *vis à vis* of one another, makes it most difficult for Englishmen to appreciate their social relations. I only assert that Hyder Ali was not from an Eastern point of view, and as a Mussulman, a man of low birth, and of humble position.

To return to the Gold Mines. The first we visited was that of Nundidroog where we saw big lumps of gold mixed with quicksilver put into a crucible, tried in the furnace and converted into ingots, worth £600 a piece, before our very eyes. From this mine—so the officials told us—they had for six months been sending home on an average about £1,500 worth of gold per month.

Then we drove on to the Mysore mine, where 60 heads of Californian stamps were at work crushing the auriferous and diaphanous quartz into thin powder, which passes through tiny perforations at the base of the stamps, on to a copper plate smeared over with quicksilver, in its passage over which the gold is arrested. Below this plate is a bed of quicksilver, and, below that, a slide covered with flannel, which will catch a little gold; and after passing through all these stages the residue is caught in a trough and churned up with quicksilver. The residue in this, the largest mine we visited, is said to produce the respectable sum of £5,000 a year. But nothing had so much effect on me as the ingots of light yellow gold, immensely heavy, and worth £600 a piece, which we saw at Nundidroog Mine, first sparkling in a crucible and next hardened into bars. We heard a great deal about the fuel question, and it seems that it is cheaper to use patent fuel here than coal. Wood, however, yet holds the field against either, though 2½ tons of wood will only go as far as one of coal. There are 2,000 men working in the Mysore mine, and great care is taken to provide amusement for the European miners. A Recreation Room serves for billiards and for church, an extremely undenominational establishment, devoted to the use of any sect that likes to apply for it—the sort of place, I should think, of which a rational Robert Elsmere would approve. We were told that the Mysore Mine sends home on an average about £7,000 a month, and that a local superstition exists here, similar to one I heard in Persia. The native workmen say that a demon guards the gold, and they attribute every accident that happens with the machinery, with the dynamite, or anything else, to the malevolence of this guardian of the subterraneous treasure. They frequently sacrifice cocks at the bottom of the shafts, and hang around their necks necklaces made of dynamite caps. In like manner at Nishapur they say that the Genius who guards the turquoise underground leads on the hapless miner from day to day, and month to month, until at last he finds the precious blue stone, and then the Genius abstracts its colour. Hence it is that buying turquoises is a hazardous affair, and that arrangements have to be made to pay for a stone, when the lapse of a term agreed upon has proved that its colour is fast. We also visited the Ooregaum Mines, and came away with our pockets stuffed with its highly auriferous quartz.

These gold mines are of great value in opening out an otherwise somewhat unremunerative tract of the Mysore plateau. A very competent authority recently reported that the gold fields afforded all around ample evidence of earnest work and rapid progress, of a determination to succeed. The Government of His Highness the Maharaja in an order recently republished in the *Mining Journal*, as were the proceedings from which I quote above, has resolved to extend for a period of 20 years on existing terms all leases under which mining operations have made substantial progress, and are being vigorously prosecuted. It * will be interesting to revisit Kolar after the lapse of a year or two, and see what effects the

* Since the above was written a great advance has been made. Of mines, other than Mysore, it might then have been said that they were experiments. But several mines are now paying dividends, and prospects generally are very good.

energy of the miners and the liberal behaviour of the government have produced.

We had escaped from the evil genius that guards the gold, from the intricate machinery, the noisy stamps, the yawning shaft, and the saluting dynamite, but the day was long and hot, and a garrulous fellow traveller proved to me a greater trial than all these.

> "Hunc neque dira venena nec hosticus auferet ensis;
> Nec laterum dolor, aut tussis, nec tarda podagra;
> Garrulus hunc quando consumet cunque."

> "Sun, fever, dynamite, and sword you brave
> But bores will hunt you to an early grave."

Lest my readers say as much of me, let me hasten to descend the ghaut to the plains below, and after a railway journey of 238 miles, ascend another ghaut to the Nílgiris, there to spend a month before making another tour.

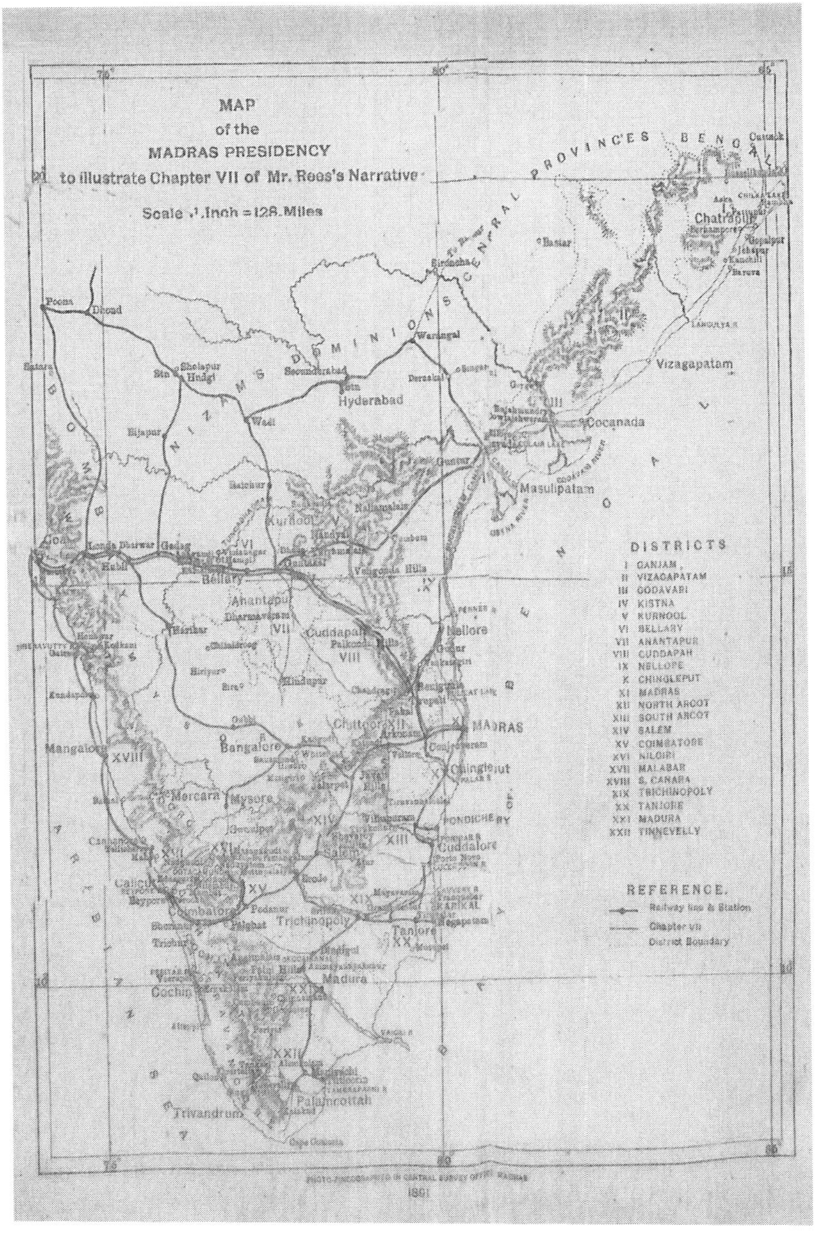
MAP
of the
MADRAS PRESIDENCY
to illustrate Chapter VII of Mr. Rees's Narrative
Scale 1 Inch = 128 Miles
CENTRAL PROVINCES
NIZAMS DOMINIONS
Hyderabad
Vizagapatam
Cocanada
Masulipatam
Kurnool
Bellary
Anantapur
Cuddapah
Nellore
MADRAS
Chingleput
Bangalore
Mangalore
Mercara
Mysore
Cuddalore
Coimbatore
Calicut
Trichinopoly
Tanjore
Madura
Cochin
Palamcottah
Trivandrum
DISTRICTS
I GANJAM
II VIZAGAPATAM
III GODAVARI
IV KISTNA
V KURNOOL
VI BELLARY
VII ANANTAPUR
VIII CUDDAPAH
IX NELLORE
X CHINGLEPUT
XI MADRAS
XII NORTH ARCOT
XIII SOUTH ARCOT
XIV SALEM
XV COIMBATORE
XVI NILGIRI
XVII MALABAR
XVIII S. CANARA
XIX TRICHINOPOLY
XX TANJORE
XXI MADURA
XXII TINNEVELLY
REFERENCE.
Railway line & Station
Chapter VII
District Boundary

CHAPTER VII.

MALABAR, SOUTH CANARA, GOA, BELLARY, CUDDAPAH, NORTH ARCOT AND NELLORE.

Departure from Ootacamund—Passage down ghaut—Railway extension to Calicut—Our party—Corruption in Malabar district—Condition of Laccadives—Rat plagues—Turtle catching—Malabar Tenants' Bill—Waste lands—Sir Charles Turner—Departure from Calicut—*Margaret Northcote*—Sacrifice Rock—Welcome at Tellicherry—To Mahé—A Brahmin gargoyle—"Presentes armes"—Meaning of Mahé—Its inhabitants—Its constitution—Its Administrateur—Addresses at Tellicherry—Christianity in Malabar—Seikh Zeinud-Deen—Departure—At Cannanore—Addresses—Railway extensions—Ramayanam entertainment—Church service—Local Native Chief—Cheruman Perumal—Convict Kunjen Menon's health—*Vanity Fair* on Natives as Judges—Employment of Natives in public service—At Mangalore—Landing—Welcome address—Representative institutions—Basel Mission industries—Government schools—Toddy Drawer's deputation—Tiyyans—Levée—Curious features—St. Aloysius' College—Jesuits—Carmelites—Syrian Christians—Their early settlement—Mar Dionysius—Mar Athanasius—Early Christian church—Xavier—Convent of girls' school—Buckrams—Founders of Jesuit College—Concordat—Exhibition of district products—Silver question—Babel of tongues—An anecdote—At Kundapore—Nambudri Brahmin—Mr. and Mrs. Shujaet Ali—Peculiar fishing—Local dwarf—At Honawar—To Gairsoppa—Falls—Visitor's remarks—Lover's raptures—Panther surprised—Ruins of Jain city—Queen of Gairsoppa—Jain temples—Government and Religion—At Karwar—Coasts of Canara—Arrival at Goa—Reception at Government House—Portuguese power in India—Vasco da Gama—State dinner—Constitution of Government—Native Viceroy of Goa—Old Goa—Its Cathedrals—St. Francis Xavier's tomb—Cape Palace—*En route* to Dharwar—Scenery along railway—At Dharwar—Colonel Lindsay—At Bellary—Stormy weather—Munro Chuttrum—At Cuddapah—Local Civil Dispensary—Disputes regarding burial-grounds—At Renigunta—Addresses—At Chandragiri Palace—Mahant of Tripetty—Ascent of hill—Temple—Sacred hills—Governor's visit to Mahant—Departure—Arrival at Nellore—Dr. Macleane—Levée—Rajas of Venkatagiri and Kalahastry—Latter's establishment—Irrigation works—Civil dispensary—Indian castes—Local Lying-in Hospital—Jubilee memorial—At Venkatagiri—Procession from Railway station—Raja—Arrival at Madras—Results of tour.

On the 9th of October 1888 our stay on the Hills for this year, which had already been broken by a tour in

Mysore and parts of the Salem district, ended in a second descent to Malabar. The passage down the ghaut by night was the only novel experience of this part of the journey, and for those who have never seen a bamboo forest by moonlight, it would be well worth making for the purpose. Before arriving at Calicut by the recent extension of the Madras Railway, we passed over the Ferokh bridge. About this time last year, we had gone up and down over the rice-fields on a temporary embankment and left the train to cross the Beypore river in a boat. On this occasion we * travelled smoothly up to the Calicut station, and were glad to find the Madras Railway possessed of a natural and satisfactory terminus at last.

* His Excellency The Lord Connemara, G.C.I.E.
Mr. Rees.
Major Scott Chisholme, 9th Lancers, Military Secretary.

An avenue of almond trees, flourishing on the way to the Collector's house, is noteworthy, and though there were no signs of woe, and no cause for any, it *might* be said of the officials of the district that they "were afraid and that fears were in the way;" for Mr. Dumergue, who was in temporary charge of the Collectorate, had recently reported one of the native Magistrates of the district for corruption, and he was under trial when we got there. This fact and the recent conviction of a Subordinate Judge for bribery had given rise to a rumour that judicial corruption was rife in the district—an assumption which is probably hardly justifiable, for, doubtless the majority of fair and white-robed native gentlemen, who attended Mr. Dumergue's party in the afternoon, were as free from the suspicion of bribe-eating as need be. There were, among others, at the party some Malabar Rajas wearing very curious, pontifical-looking turbans.

Calicut looked beautiful as usual. There were red-lilies in the tanks, green rice in the fields, fat and prosperous citizens in the streets, and everywhere the date palm—fittest emblem of the prosperity of the country—waved its graceful head, alike above the houses of the town and the fields of the country. One outward visible sign of prosperity is to be found in an abundance of somewhat imperfectly cured fish, from the odour of which we suffered many things at the railway stations.

The Governor inquired at Calicut into the present condition of the Laccadives or Ten Thousand Islands, which form a dependency of the district of Malabar. Life is by no means so dull and monotonous in these remote localities as might be supposed. Quite recently the islanders rose against an unpopular headman, and expelled him with violence. In fact, they take a great deal of administering. They suffer much from a plague of rats, which live in cocoanut trees and subsist upon the tender nuts. The cocoanut trees in the island being everywhere close together, the rats can leap from one to another by running out along the palm leaves; but occasionally the inhabitants combine against the common enemy. Then the trees adjoining those in which the devoted rats have made their dwelling, are each manned by an individual islander, while a crowd below assail the rats with coffee sticks, bats, stumps of trees and other weapons of offence. The hapless creatures being unable to escape on to the neighbouring trees, take headers down to the ground, which, however, they rarely reach alive, for the islanders are experts in killing them on their flight through the air. Owls, rat-snakes, arsenic and many other exterminators have been tried, but all in vain.

Apropos of the Laccadivians, Mr. Winterbotham, Collector of Malabar, told me of the manner in which they catch turtles, which in this latitude are ever fat, and scant of breath. In the crystal clear water of the lagoons the turtle can be followed with ease in its flight. A man with a harpoon stands in the bow of a boat and gives the rowers the direction. Soon the turtle tires and doubles, the boat follows suit, and this continues until the turtle comes to the surface gasping for breath and again disappears. Then the man from the bow dives in after it, seizes it by the eyes, and brings it to the surface. The eye sockets of the fish are large and deep, and the diver can thrust his thumb into one and the forefinger into the other,—a treatment which seems, not unnaturally, to paralyse the turtle, which allows itself to be drawn to the surface, and falls into the boat without a struggle. As its bill is as sharp as a razor, and would take a finger off with the most ordinary snap, this method of fishing requires nerve as well as dexterity. The islanders do not eat the turtle or its eggs, but convert its blubber into oil. They are caught not only in this way, but also when napping on the sands.

However, we are concerned more with the mainland than with these islands.

We heard at Calicut a great deal about the operation of Legislative Acts lately passed, and others now impending, concerning the vexed question of landlord and tenant, and of land tenure. Under a recent Act of the Madras Legislature, evicted tenants can claim the value of their improvements. The great subject of cultivation being the cocoanut tree, it is obvious that much must depend on the value put by an individual judge upon individual trees, and as these begin to bear at the age of 12 years, and as tenancies generally run in the country unrenewed for that term, it is less surprising than it would otherwise be to hear that 90 per cent. of the cases before the Civil Judges are eviction cases. Generally speaking, compensation varies from 8 annas to 8 rupees a tree, but the principles on which it is estimated are vague and leave so much to the discretion of the Judge, as to introduce great uncertainty in the administration of the law. The High Court has taken steps to prescribe a table of rates, and thus and by the creation of case-made law, existing diversities of opinion and practice will, it is hoped, be minimised.

A Bill to control evictions and the monopoly of waste land in Malabar, is now before the Legislative Council, and the opinions of those in England and in India best qualified to judge of the effect of its provision are under the consideration of Government, including that of the late learned Chief Justice of Madras, Sir Charles Turner.

However, it must not be imagined that the number of eviction cases is a proof of the poverty of the people.

Most of these decrees are obtained as evidence of title, and are seldom meant to be executed. Indeed, it requires no intimate knowledge of the Western Coast to come to this conclusion, for plenty is apparent in the face and figure of every man and woman you meet. Few can say here, in the expressive phrase used, not without much eastern hyperbole, the other day by some hill tribes in the northern districts, that "their tongues were dead." They meant atrophied for want of use, though *we* should hardly speak of using our tongues for eating.

So much had been done at Calicut on the occasion of the Governor's visit last year that, instead of prolonging the present halt, we started next morning in the *Margaret Northcote*, a Government yacht of 60 tons, used chiefly for the pearl fishery at Tuticorin. This little steamer is named after a daughter of the late Lord Iddesleigh. She is broad of beam, and light of draught, and rolls as no other ship ever did. A day's coasting voyage in her calls for courage on the part of a bad sailor, hardly inferior to that of Hippalos, the Greek pilot, the first who crossed directly from Arabia to these pepper-yielding shores. However, she brought us safely 40 miles, to Tellicherry, passing on the way Mahé, where a tall flag-post flying the Tricolor, proclaims the existence of the sole remaining possession of France on the west coast of India. I ignore six acres in Calicut as unworthy of notice.

The coast-line becomes bolder as you travel north. Here and there large rocks are found at varying distances from the shore. One we passed stood 50 feet out of the water at a distance of a mile or two from the shore. It is called "The Sacrifice Rock," but claimed no sacrifice from ourselves. The pirates of Angria had slain a ship's crew there. Hence the name. It is now known as producing edible birds' nests, which, so far as I know, are not found in the Indian seas elsewhere. No one here makes birds' nest soup however, and the swallows live so far regardless of the all-absorbing Chinaman, who, by the way, as early as the 13th century had, there is reason to believe, established factories on the Malabar Coast.

Arrived at the pier, the usual welcome was accorded to the Governor, and a most unusual poem was read, which had been composed in his honour, and consisted of a medley of Sanscrit and English, a fearful and hitherto unknown development of Macaronic verse.

Hard by Tellicherry is the little French Settlement of Mahé, consisting of five square miles and governed by an Administrateur Principal, who is subordinate to the Governor of the French Settlements in India, whose seat is at Pondicherry. We breakfasted with him at Mahé, and the drive there was very beautiful. It passed through walled gardens, entered by a succession of stiles from a green lane, deep, narrow and crowned by a high hedge. In every garden the pepper-vine twines around the standards of the taller trees and in one corner is situated a neat thatched house, by the door of which blooms the crimson hibiscus, sacred to the god of blood, in another, an uncultivated little shrubbery festooned with creepers, the shrine of the serpent, whose worship largely prevails in Malabar. On the way I saw a Brahmin with shaven head, and goggle eyes, squatting on his hams upon a garden wall, and looking down into the road. In his mouth, from which water dripped, was a banyan shoot, with which he was cleaning his teeth, and he looked for all the world like a gargoyle on the roof of an old English church.

Arrived at Mahé, a pretty village on the banks of a river, we were received by the French officials, one of whom, the Maire, was a native gentleman wearing two French medals on his coat, and a tricolor girdle around his waist. A guard of native police, armed with chassepots, at the word "presentez armes" given by a native constable, saluted the representative of the neighbouring Power. After the usual polite speeches, which in this case partook of an international character, we breakfasted in a hall beautifully decorated with the cycas.

The word Mahé is said to mean "fishing place," and indeed the odours of the sea were aggressively and odiously fishy, both here and at Tellicherry, during our stay. At certain periods of the year, dead fish poison the water, and pollute the shore. At all seasons fish are freely used for manure. So plentiful is the food-supply of the ocean.

The inhabitants of Mahé, like those of the surrounding British territory, are composed in part of Moplahs, mixed descendants of Arabs and Hindus, in part of Hindus pure and simple. The Moplahs there, as with us, are troublesome fellows, and, lately, when the Administrateur of Mahé arrested one of them, some half-a-dozen of his co-religionists insisted on his release, and threatened the town whereon the Administrateur sent in to the interior of the French dominions for two constables and a Brigadier! No one who knows Malabar and its Moplahs will think the force too great for the occasion.

This little settlement possesses all the institutions of a republic—manhood suffrage, vote by ballot, municipal and local councils, representation at the *Conseil General* which sits at Pondicherry, and in the Chambers at home by a Deputy and a Senator, who, in practice, however, are always residents in France. The Administrateur is appointed from home. He represents the central, and the Maire the local, government. They do not always agree, and a difference of opinion ended, a few days after our visit to Mahé, in the disappearance of the Administrateur who entertained us.

Later on, the Chamber of Commerce of Tellicherry presented an address, praying for railway extensions, and a busy day ended with a levée, a distribution of prizes, and visits to various institutions. The civil hospital here being in the bazaar street, women of the upper classes cannot even pass it without being polluted so as to need ceremonial ablutions before entering their homes. They have no objection, however, to being treated by the officer in charge of the hospital, an intelligent Brahmin, by name, Rama Row.

The Madras Government has, since our visit to this coast last year, endeavoured to remove some of the existing restrictions on the possession and use of fire-arms and weapons of offence, which have been imposed in consequence of their abuse by Moplah fanatics, but unfortunately past experience shows that it is always possible that some outbreak may occur, and here as elsewhere we see none so zealous and so bigotted as recent converts. It is believed that Islam was introduced by Arab traders to the Malabar Coast about 800 A.D., ever since which time the followers of the Prophet have increased and multiplied. The cruel treatment they underwent at the hands of the Portuguese had the effect of strengthening them in their faith, and the Mussulman historian, Sheik Zein-ud-Deen, has some warrant for calling a portion of his work "An account of the arrival of the Franks in Malabar and of their villainous proceedings in that country." This odious and senseless persecution perhaps lighted the torch of fanaticism that burns to this day, but there can be no doubt that agrarian disputes with infidel Hindu landlords are at least equally potent factors in the case.

After a stay of two days we left for Cannanore. The drive of 14 miles was very beautiful. At frequent intervals we reached rivers the bridging of which costs a great deal of money. On the one side of the road is the coast with groves of cocoanuts down to the water's edge; on the other, green fields of rice with a blue background of lofty hills—outlying spurs of the Nílgiris, from which we had descended.

Cannanore is just now suffering from local depression, resulting from the recent removal of the greater part of a regiment of British Infantry to the more congenial climate of Wellington. A long address was received, chiefly from the house-owners, who gave many excellent reasons for thinking that a whole regiment of British Infantry, with its house-occupying officers, should continue to be stationed in their midst.

This town is perhaps the only one in Southern India which contains more Muhammadans than Hindus. The Muhammadans, however, converts from Hinduism, follow the system of succession to sisters' sons, which obtains among the Hindus on this coast. They are Sunnis, but so far as I can make out, they know little of, and take little interest in, the subjects which divide the people of Islam into two great camps.

The country is far opener here than at Tellicherry, and now and again you come to downs, and open uplands. The cantonment is pleasantly situated on a laterite terrace ending at the sea in low precipitous cliffs.

There were the usual addresses, levées and visits to institutions. The Town Council desired, above all things, railway extensions. They wanted a line to connect Mysore with the coast, that the coffee of Coorg might be exported from Tellicherry. They desired an extension of the Madras Railway to Cannanore. These requests were repeated at other places along the coast, but it did not appear, from a conversation Lord Connemara had with the members of the deputations, that they had sufficiently considered the all-important question, whether the lines they asked for would prove remunerative, and it has to be remembered that no further hope of 5 per cent. guarantees from Government can be entertained, and that the exigencies of Imperial finance, and the falling value of the rupee, make it most unlikely that the State will be in a position to supply any merely local wants in the future.

In the evening the native regiment gave a representation of the Rámáyana, the parts being taken by the sepoys. All the actors were gorgeously clad in tinsel and wore prodigious head-dresses, which made them of godlike stature and similar in all respects to the conventional deity of Hindu art. Like Hanuman, the magnanimous ape, the lovely and virtuous Sítá too, was represented by a sepoy, and looked somewhat tall and masculine for the part. The story, however, never fails to please, and is apparently ever present in the mind of the Hindu. Quite recently a holy man came and settled on the Nílgiris of all other places. He struck his tent, and flew his flag on the side of the main street of Ootacamund, and when ordered to remove it, declined. The authorities thereon took it down and told him to move; but through bitter rain and cold he stuck to his ground with the avowed intention of staying there until the authorities should be brought to bury him. He proposed to remain nine months under ground, and to rise again alive and well at the expiration of that period. He said his burial would prove a certain cure for all trouble, sickness and poverty, wherever found around the site of his self-sacrifice. But what introduced the holy man was this. I went to visit him accompanied by a lady, and when we parted he desired me to tell her that she resembled Sítá in every respect. He had every reason to admire her, and I suppose imagination invested the sepoy of the regiment with the charms which should belong to the favourite heroine of the greatest epic of the East, which happily do belong to many an English lady.

On Sunday there was nothing to be done, but to go to church. We drove in a break drawn by a pair of commissariat mules. Behind came a brougham drawn by two trotting bullocks, next the transit of the country,—a sort of diminutive gypsy caravan drawn by ponies, which go well enough at a gallop, but are innocent of any other pace. On the parade ground we met the hounds enjoying, like ourselves, the day of rest. They were of all breeds, from grey hounds to fox terriers, and of all sizes.

The Native Chief who lives at Cannanore is a representative of the Arab Sea Kings, and his title, like that of the Zamorin further south, actually means king of the sea. He is a Mussulman and his family embraced Islam as early as the beginning of the 12th century. It is believed that the last Emperor, Cheruman Perumal, who ruled over all the Malabar Coast, visited Arabia and became a Mussulman in 827 A.D., and, dying a few years later, divided his territories among his tributary Chiefs, exacting from them the condition that they should found mosques and encourage Islam. It is an interesting fact that at Cannanore the Governor actually received a petition from a Moplah basing his claim to certain lands on a copper-plate grant from Cheruman Perumal, who made them over to petitioner's ancestors when he was starting on his pilgrimage. Petitioner pleaded that he was too poor to institute a regular civil suit for the recovery of these lands, his claim to which would seem pretty well barred by limitation.

On Sunday evening we started again in our 60-ton steamer and travelled all night in the direction of Mangalore, which we reached early next morning. Before leaving Cannanore, inquiries had to be made about the condition of the mind and body of the Native Judge of the district, who, having been found guilty of corruption by the courts, was then an inmate of the jail at that station. Just then the mail came in, and in *Vanity Fair* we found the moral deduced from this case that natives should not be made judges. Meanwhile another school wants to put natives into all the most important offices in the country. On the whole, the Public Service Commission has steered a middle course in troubled waters, with more success than might have been expected.

As the ship entered the narrow backwater, on the banks of which Mangalore is built, it passed through a line of boats and native craft, manned not by stalwart and dusky sailors, but by thousands of fair and intelligent school children, who cheered the Governor as he passed down "the long sea lane."

We landed at a lofty temporary shed, under which the trees grew, and through which the birds kept flying to and fro, as a native gentleman read an address asking for various improvements to the port and the town, consideration of which requests was duly promised. This gentleman much commended the efforts of himself and his brother Town Councillors to improve the condition of the town. Then, after a drive along a deep lane, the sides of which were clothed with lichens, we got to the house of the Collector, where a petition awaited the Governor objecting to Town Councillors and their deeds, and praying that the municipal franchise might be taken away, as the petitioners thought things were much better managed by an autocratic Government and its own appointed servants. Here you have a pretty fair representation of both sides of a question which is becoming of great importance. Generally speaking, the educated few are all for representation, and as surely, so are the masses of the people, when they understand what it means, indifferent and probably more or less averse to its introduction.

On the 16th of October, there were Basel Mission industries, and Government high schools to be visited, but the most interesting event was the receipt of a petition from upwards of 5,000 tappers of the palm-tree, the fermented juice of which is the alcoholic drink of the district. Their license fees had lately been raised, and other restrictions placed upon their trade, partly in the interests of the excise revenue, but also in some measure to prevent such indiscriminate sale as might lay Government open to the imputation of encouraging, rather than regulating, the use of intoxicating drinks. These five thousand persons collected together, around the deep verandah of the Collector's house, without a sound. They heard their address read by their spokesman without a word, and when the Governor replied from the verandah, through an interpreter, to the effect that their petition should be considered, though he did not think it could be granted, and explained to them that the extra fees would fall chiefly upon the consumer, and the shop-keeper, rather than on themselves, they dispersed without a murmur. Not that they are a class of people to be driven by any means. I merely mention this as a tribute to their good behaviour and docility on an occasion when much feeling might have been demonstratively manifested. Of course, the matter will be heard of again. At present they are all on strike and the fishermen of the coast complain bitterly that they have been robbed of their toddy, which is to them, their beer.

The toddy-drawers are called Tiyyans and are said to have originally come from Ceylon. They are stalwart, good-looking fellows, and their women are exceptionally fair and comely even on this coast, which is generally fortunate in this respect.

The levée presented some curious features. It is sufficiently startling to one who knows the rigid law of Islam to find Mahomedans, in some cases innocent of the Arabic character, or even the Hindustani tongue, following the law peculiar to this coast of descent through sisters' sons, and, in most respects, in their lives and habits resembling the Hindus, whose religion they have deserted, yet sufficiently fanatical and turbulent to make the presence of European troops essential to the protection of their Hindu landlords. It is startling to see Hindus of high position and caste drinking iced whiskeys and sodas with Europeans, but perhaps the climax is reached when you see a thoroughbred Brahmin march past the Governor to the name of Alfonso de Albuquerque, or Luis de Braganza. Yet among the Catholic Christians of this coast, it is quite usual to find families of pure Hindu descent priding themselves on their Hindu caste, who have taken the names of the Portuguese grandees, who once ruled Western India, when they were received into the Roman Catholic Church. In fact one's ideas of caste, religion, and social relations in general get very much enlarged upon this classic coast, where Jews, Arabs, Greeks, Romans, Portuguese, Dutch and English have, in turn, landed, lived and gathered pepper, and where all have left in a greater or less degree some traces of a more or less permanent occupation.

In front of Mr. Wynne's house, where we stayed, upon a commanding hill, the College of St. Aloysius, an enormous building, dominates the surrounding country. From the great hall, where 400 boys were assembled, the view is one of the finest conceivable. On one side is the Arabian Sea, on another the range of the Western Ghauts rises to a height of six thousand feet, and all the rest is an undulating tableland clothed with groves of cocoanut. Here and there peeps out red laterite soil, and rarely the red-tiled roofs, or the neutral thatch of frequent homesteads. Immediately below the college is a little temple and a tank.

The Jesuits have lately taken over this district from the Carmelites, which order had laboured here since 1600, when the Holy See first began to take measures to absorb the discontented Syrian Christians of the coast. The Carmelites are a proselytizing, and the Jesuits a proselytizing and educational order: hence the transfer.

The mention of the Syrian Christians makes it necessary to say a word or two about them. As early as 350 A.D., about as many Syrians are said to have landed in Malabar, and in the 9th and 10th centuries more came from Bagdad, Nineveh and Jerusalem. The Portuguese, under Vasco da Gama, tried to bring them into the fold of Rome, and to extirpate the Nestorian heresy, which naturally took firm root in a community, whose priests were recruited from Persia and Turkish Arabia. The Dutch put an end to this persecution, and supported the Syrian Christians, who in 1653 sent for a Bishop to the Patriarch, sitting in the seat of Simon Cephas, which is at Antioch. He, on his arrival, was put to death by the Portuguese. From that date to the beginning of the present century the Church "by schisms rent asunder" was administered partly by Native Bishops, and partly by Bishops from Syria; and to this day there are two Bishops amongst them, one, Mar, or Saint, Dionysius, who heads the orthodox, or Antioch party, and another, Mar Athanasius, of the party which is for home rule, and native Bishops. They number some three hundred thousand in all, and hold most tenaciously to differences of doctrine, such as divided the early

Christian Church, and such as nowadays excite a merely academical interest. They are, however, in spite of these internal schisms, a peaceful and well-ordered people, on good terms with the Government, be it British or Native, on the coast, and they retain, in their internal economy, many interesting forms and ceremonies relating to the time when they were governed by a king, who was recognized as such by the native Rajas of the coast. In them, as Bishop Heber says, we probably see preserved many of the rites, customs and ceremonies of the early Christian Church.

To return to the Jesuits, whose success has been, or would be in the case of less earnest workers, phenomenal. As Lord Connemara told them, it is no matter for surprise that the efforts of the Society of Jesus should be so strenuous on the coast where Xavier laboured, and so near the spot where, after his labours, he reposes.

We went to the Carmelite Convent girls' school, where the Roman Catholic Bishop and the Reverend Mothers provided a little entertainment, at once graceful, instructive, and amusing, including music, sacred and secular, calisthenics and singing. "Very delicate and beautiful buckrams," specimens of the embroidery of the girls, were exhibited, the Sacred Heart, the Agnus Dei and the Pelican, emblem of divine love, which gives its blood for its offspring. At all these convent schools, one never fails to be struck with the complete indifference on the part of the Reverend Mothers to any praise or appreciation of their *individual* labours. It is only by asking that you can find out which one, of many present, has brought about the admirable results, for which alone she seems to care.

The girl who read the little address was the granddaughter of one of the founders of the Jesuit College. Amongst other founders and benefactors, whose names are carved in marble in its hall, are the Infanta of Spain, the late Empress of Austria, the Comtesse de Chambord, and Lords Bute and Ripon, whose names are seldom absent from such records from Fort Augustus to Fort St. George.

With reference to the Jesuits and their work a passing reference is required to the Concordat between the Holy See and the Crown of Portugal, whereby their spiritual jurisdictions have recently been defined. The subject is one of the first interest on this coast.

In or about 1600, Pope Clement VIII granted the *Jus Patronalis* or Padroado, that is, the right of protection of Catholic Churches in the Indies, with certain corresponding obligations, to the King of Portugal. The Portuguese King, however, owing to the subsequent decay of the Portuguese power in India, and the supremacy of the Dutch, was unable to exercise this right; and the Pope proceeded to protect his spiritual subjects by appointing Vicars Apostolic, who were exempt from the jurisdiction of the Archbishop of Goa, the Portuguese Primate of the Indies. In 1837, Gregory XVI, by his bull *Multa Præclare*, divided the country into Vicariates Apostolic, and forbade the interference of Portugal. The Archbishop of Goa proved recalcitrant, but the Catholics in general obeyed the Holy Father. As lately as 1861, Pius the Ninth, by a Concordat with Portugal, legalized the then *status quo*, by giving to Goa that of which it was actually in possession, and granting to its Archbishop extraordinary jurisdiction over churches and congregations actually governed by Goanese priests, though remote from Goa, and interspersed among other Catholic congregations immediately under the Holy See. This brings us down to recent times, but we have now another Concordat, which the Papal Delegate, Monsignor Aiuti, is engaged in carrying into effect, whereby this extraordinary jurisdiction of Goa is being expressly defined and limited, and the whole country divided into territorial charges under Goa, or under the Holy See, as present circumstances and past history may require. The delimitation of these dioceses has necessitated transfers here and there of Papal flocks to Goanese Shepherds, and in some cases of Goanese churches to the Holy See. Such transfers, when from Rome to Goa, are unpopular chiefly because the Goanese priests are natives of the country, while those of the Propaganda are French, Italian or English, but no doubt all will be satisfactorily settled by Monsignor Aiuti before he gives up his charge. The British Government are not directly concerned with these changes, but cannot, of course, but be interested in matters of spiritual importance to hundreds of thousands of the Queen's subjects in India.

On the afternoon of the 17th we saw an exhibition of the products of this district. The description of Marco Polo will answer equally well at the present day. He says: "There is in this kingdom a great quantity of pepper, and ginger, and cinnamon, and of nuts of India. They also manufacture very delicate and beautiful buckrams. They also bring hither cloths of silk and gold, also gold and silver, cloves, and spikenard and other fine spices for which there is a demand here." Most of these things we saw on tables, and I cannot think of any others calling for special notice, except knives for cockfighting, a sport to which the people are passionately devoted. There was no silver, however. "Silver," we read in the Bible, "was nothing accounted of in the days of King Solomon," and it seems likely to happen again so. Let us hope that history may repeat itself in another respect, and that we may be able to say soon, in consequence of a prolific yield by the Mysore gold mines, that the reason for silver being of no account is that everything is of gold.

There is a perfect Babel of tongues at Mangalore. Tulu, Hindustani, Canarese, Malayalam, Telugu and good many others may be heard as you walk through the streets. The houses are low and two-storied, and all furnished with screens to keep out the monsoon rains, which here are unusually heavy, and fall for three months almost incessantly. There are no horses to be seen in the streets. It was with difficulty that we could get mounted. I had occasion to send a telegram to the Collector before starting, in answer to one of his, stating that a sufficiently good horse for the Governor could not be got in the district. I said to him: "Good animal not expected, some kind horseflesh essential." This provoked the curiosity of one of my native assistants, who expressed his astonishment, saying that he understood that Europeans preferred beef and mutton.

We left this beautiful and interesting place on October 18th, to go on in the *Margaret Northcote* to Kundapore, the most northern station of the Madras Presidency. Owing to its remote situation, this place had never before been visited by a Governor, unless by one of Hyder's or Tippu's lieutenants from Bednore prior to the partition treaty of 1799. The village is quite small, and beautifully situated in an estuary of three rivers descending from the not far distant hills, which hold up the plateau of Mysore. In such a small place, a traveller would not expect, even when he accompanied the Governor of the Presidency, to see any very noteworthy reception; but nothing could have been more graceful than the little demonstration here. From the landing place to the Assistant Collector's house was formed a lane with living walls. The first line was occupied by pretty and intelligent little girls, each holding in her hand a little paper box containing flowers. As the Governor walked down they flung the petals of flowers over him and shouted, in turn, "*Governor Bahadur Ko Jey*," or "victory to the Governor," and the same rendered into English *Hip, hip, hurrah!* When the supply of pretty little girls was exhausted, a line of men holding leaves of the sago palm succeeded. The shape of this leaf is such that its spathe suits for an upright, and its horizontal branches for the rail of a fence, and all that was not green leaf, was smiling face and holiday attire.

The main street, at all times an avenue of cocoanuts, was turned into a bower, and, for a mile, long strings of mango leaves were hung across and along it.

The people had come in thousands from the surrounding villages to see the Governor, and appeared determined to make much also of the members of his staff. Major Chisholme and I halted, when out walking in the evening, to admire a bower built across the road. The friendly owner—a Moonsiff or subordinate native Judge of the district—came out and invited us to take tea, and before long tea was produced, and some cakes and sweet-meats made on the spur of the moment by the ladies of his family. Our host was a Saraswat Brahmin,—a member of a caste the hereditary occupation of which is the acquisition of knowledge. Remembering an official account of the Nambudri Brahmins, who dwell lower down the coast, one might hesitate to shake hands with such a personage. Hear an account of the Nambudri: "His person is holy; his directions are commands; his movements are processions; his meal is nectar; he is the holiest of human beings; he is the representative of God on earth." Our host, whose learning was greater, if his holiness was less, had no scruples. He seized our right hands in both of his and protested that we must come in. Indeed, the people here are singularly friendly and charming; and the appearance of the whole place is positively idyllic. Even the labours of the scavenger appear picturesque. I saw one sweeping up the mango leaves that had fallen from the trees and a pretty little girl with a short stick assisting him. She kept on stabbing the leaves until, like Aaron's rod, her stick bloomed all over with them; and this was no pastime, but a means of collecting fuel for the family fire.

Our host here, Mr. Shujat Ali Khan, is one of the first of the new order of Native Statutory Civilians. He dresses and lives like a European, and Mrs. Shujat Ali, whose name is Fatimah Begum, is the daughter of the late Sir Salar Jung's Private Secretary; she is an accomplished lady, who plays the piano and sings English and Persian songs, has abjured the purdah, and lives in all respects like a European, as does her husband, except of course that he abstains from the use of alcoholic drinks.

On the afternoon of the morrow we made a long journey in the midday sun, while the thermometer was 90° in our tents, to visit a pond in which a kind of sport is practised, peculiar, it is believed, to this district. A number of fishermen in dug-outs form a semicircle around one end of the pond. They hold a long net from boat to boat from one side of the water to the other. As soon as the semicircle is formed, they commence to beat the boats and shout, and very soon the fishes, being disturbed by the noise, commence to jump and leap into the boats. The net is held, not for the purpose of catching the fish, but as a hedge which they cannot get past. Nevertheless, many of them clear it. Those who strike the net fall into the boat, whereon one of the two fishermen in each dug-out beats them with a stick violently until they die. Some of these fishes weighed 17 and 20 lb., and I saw a man, struggling with one, fall out of the boat. In all 208 were caught in about 20 minutes.

It is said that Hyder Ali was very fond of this, called by the natives the flower fish, and from its appearance I should judge a kind of mullet, and that he kept a post of runners between Kundapore and Bednore, 40 miles away above the ghauts, that his table might always be supplied with it. The sport, though curious was not pleasant to look at. Angling for some reason or other is a peculiarly gentle art, but to beat so many fishes to death appeared cruel.

This fish-killing and a dwarf, perfectly formed, aged 25 years, are the sights of Kundapore. The dwarf was half the height of a sago palm leaf, against which he was leaning when first we saw him. His manners were suave and dignified. He joined the party after dinner, and when asked if he did any work, replied, with unconscious humour, that he did not, but looked after the other members of his family, who did.

Next day we again set sail for Honawar, the site of which is marked by an obelisk erected in memory of a General who died there. We took it for the monument of the English merchants who were killed by natives, who thus revenged the death of a sacred bull, slain by an English bull dog. This monument, however, is lower down the coast.

Landing at Honawar we were within an ace of capsizing in a huge breaker in crossing the bar of the river at low water. Landing and embarking here cause much tribulation, and be it known that October, though elsewhere a good month, is considered by those who live on this coast to be as trying as any in the year. The water is like oil, and, except on the bar of course, as still as the atmosphere. The sun reflected from 7 till 12 o'clock off its unruffled surface, strikes back in your face as from a mirror, and has a peculiarly sickening effect, which is heightened by an ever-present odour of corruption more easily acknowledged, than described.

We were now in the Bombay Presidency, to which the lovely district of North Canara was handed over in 1860, and the Collector, Mr. Blathwayt, had kindly made arrangements for our passage to the Gairsoppa Falls. We went on the same night 18 miles in boats up the moonlit river, grounded on a sand bank, and were pulled off, only to find the rowers had landed to drink success to our future progress, to which this indulgence by no means conduced.

Arrived at Gairsoppa we slept in the travellers' bungalow, awoke to the crowing of the jungle cock, and went on 20 miles by road to Kodkani. Here is another bungalow, whence, you look down into a boiling chaos of waters, formed by the descent of the Sheravati river into a chasm cloven in the mountains, for its exit to the sea.

The road from Gairsoppa to Kodkani is one long bower of evergreen trees and at midday you scarcely see the sun. With the exception of our own party we met nothing on the way, but a huge monkey, and a large snake. We told Mr. Woodrow, the Forest Officer, of this, and he said it was lucky it was not a hamadryad, for he had been chased by one in the jungles, which abound with tigers, bears, bison, and game of all kinds, large and small.

Most of the few visitors to Gairsoppa have compared its famous falls with those of Niagara, but where there are no points of resemblance, there can be no basis for a comparison. At Niagara you have a stupendous volume of water falling by a comparatively small drop, into a large river below, on either bank of which abound hotels, houses, tents, horses, carriages and divers paraphernalia of tourdom and its accessories. At Gairsoppa, you have a comparatively small volume of water falling by a sheer drop of over 800 feet into a rushing torrent below, while above and around are green forests, and unbroken solitude, the undisputed home of beasts of prey. Others, I see in a visitors' book dating from 1843, when Europeans first came here, make the Yosemite waterfalls the standard of comparison. But where again can any basis for comparison be found, between a cleft in the snowcapped Sierra Nevada, a mile deep and five miles long, from the cliffs of which, as if from heaven, one cataract after another comes falling down, and a single, deep and, from its situation, bottomless-seeming rift, in a tropical forest, into which a mountain torrent pours its tumultuous waters, and whence they issue in a placid river to the adjacent sea.

The precipice over which the waters leap is shaped like a sickle, two torrents pouring over the curved blade, and two over the straight handle. A small triangular rock at one end of the curve stands well out from the edge of the precipice like a gurgoyle from a roof. Lying on this with your chin projecting you can see the two nearer torrents of the sickle leap off into space. One goes straight down, four hundred feet, another but a short distance, when it falls into a rift in the rocks, along which it runs and roars some distance, till it shoots out again, and joins the other torrent in mid-air. As your eyes get accustomed to the cloud of spray below, you can gradually discern, another 400 feet below it, the dark sullen pool into which the two torrents plunge, and in which their waters reunite.

The two other falls glide down the straight face of the rock. The water now dissolves into spray, now strikes the rock, and forms again into a cascade. The falls of the sickle and those of the handle are alike beautiful, but the latter are comparatively commonplace and entirely lack the awe-inspiring effects of the leap of the Raja, and the Roarer, into the seemingly bottomless pit.

At night, blazing straw and burning brands were thrown down into the abyss from the gurgoyle rock. Nothing I have ever seen at all resembles the effect produced. The moon, which silvered the water above the edge of the precipice, seemed only to increase, by contrast, the darkness of the chasm below. As you lie on the rock, with your head protruding over the edge, men stand on the brink and throw over bundles of straw loosely tied together. These, like fire-balloons, descend slowly by reason of their lightness, and, sensitive to the rush of air produced by the falling cataract, avoid awhile its downward flight, and consequent extinction by its waters. You see them clearly down to the point where the two first falls, the Raja and the Roarer, meet in mid-air, dimly through the cloud of spray that marks the junction, and once again you get a clear but distant view as they descend further down into the pool at the bottom of the chasm. The heavier burning brands, falling into the water, are more speedily extinguished. The scene is weird, impressive, and exciting, and one, which once witnessed, will never be forgotten.

The visitors' book contains a very interesting account of the manner in which the height of the falls was measured by two adventurous Englishmen, and an American gentleman remarks therein that "Niagara can knock spots off Gairsoppa in point of sublimity, and that this effete old country should arrange for the passage of more water over the falls by the divertation of a few other rivers." One writer says: "Ask the atheist to stand on the brink of this awful precipice and deny the existence of a God," on which another remarks: "But why not throw him over at once." Few, however, confine themselves to prose, and most of the entries read like lovers' raptures. I myself added the following lines to the collection:—

"Love's raptures, it has often been confessed,
Most briefly spoken, are expressed the best;
And how can rushing river's falling flood
Inspire with poetry dull flesh and blood
That not e'en living beauty's potent charm
To love's true language would suffice to warm?
Then leave the muses to the few they love,
Nor add thy tribute to what's writ above.
Or if—since man at once is vain and weak—
Thy vanity or weakness needs *must* speak,
At least be brief. So others you may teach,
Unlike myself, to practice what they preach."

In riding from Gairsoppa to Malemanni, we surprised a panther on the road. The animal, however, made off immediately. The Collector tells us he not unfrequently meets them when marching.

At Gairsoppa we visited the ruins of the Jain City. The Queen of Gairsoppa, called by the Portuguese the *Reinha da Pimento* or Pepper Queen, was a great power in the 17th century. Her subjects were chiefly Jains, by whom the nearest village to the falls is, at present, almost entirely inhabited. Among the ruins of the city are two ordinary Jain temples. The chief native official of the place, one of the new school of educated Mahratta Brahmins, took the Governor and myself to see these temples. I expressed some surprise at finding their worship continued when the site of the city was obviously wholly deserted, whereon he explained: "No one sleeps here; no one lives here. I myself got these gods washed and worshipped for the occasion." This led to more conversation on religion. Our guide said he did not firmly believe in the transmigration of souls. "Having received an English education," he observed, "my mind is in a perturbed state. My father, too, being alive can perform certain oblations and ceremonies. There is no need of more from me. Religion must suit, otherwise we must relax, and above all a Government officer has no time for religion." Let us hope, that this excuse may avail them, in their evil hour.

The idol by the way was most certainly Buddha himself, and not one of the just men made perfect, who these inheritors of Buddhist traditions should worship.

There was nothing remarkable in the city. Through the rank and luxuriant vegetation, which covered everything, you could plainly make out the streets and even the houses. Cities and capitals quickly rise and disappear in India—mushroom cities all unknown to time.

The next day it took us from 10 o'clock in the morning till 5 o'clock in the evening, in the blazing sun, to get down the Gairsoppa river and off to the ship. The thermometer was 96° in the shade and all clothing appeared superfluous. I waited to resume mine until we had crossed the bar, remembering that we were nearly required to swim on the last occasion. The breakers at low water are very aggressive, and this bar has an evil reputation, and has claimed many victims, including one European.

Next morning we arrived at Karwar, and from the house where Mr. and Mrs. Blathwayt most hospitably received us, there is a glorious view. The harbour from which nearly all trade has been diverted by the recent railway extension to Marmagoa, is probably one of the best in India. There is anchorage for the biggest ships that ply up and down the coast close up to the wharf. It is land-locked except on one side, and that is protected in some degree by islands.

The hills of North Canara here come down to the water's edge, right up to which, with no intervening beach, the forest presses. I have never seen more beautiful scenery. Here and there, on the hillside, over the waters of the harbour, a thatched roof indicates the existence of a dwelling house. Otherwise all is forest. The general appearance of the coast much resembles that of the Japanese islands, and the harbour is extremely like the little haven of Tsusima, between

Japan and Corea, which is one of the most beautiful imaginable.

The coast of North and South Canara differs greatly from that of Malabar and Travancore, where the Western Ghauts are farther from the sea. In the former districts the scenery is altogether bolder, and mankind is less mixed as to caste and religion, but the same pleasant and independent spirit of equality is manifested all along, and, in the south of India, is peculiar, I think, to the Western Coast.

On the night of the 25th the weather for the first time proved unpropitious; and we left Karwar in such heavy rain as to make navigation difficult, if not dangerous. Steamers that trade along the coast frequently run down native crafts, which, when they do travel at night, seldom display a light. We were ourselves one night within an ace of a collision with a pattimar or Arab ship which passed in most alarming proximity right under our bows. However, we reached Goa in safety next morning sufficiently early to see the sun rise on the low-lying head-lands, between which we passed up to Panjim or New Goa. Twice on the way, at different stages, the representatives of His Most Faithful Majesty the King of Portugal and Algarves, clad in full-dress uniform, came out to meet the Governor, and at the foot of the stairs of the palace, the Governor-General himself awaited his guest. He, the most illustrious Councillor Don Cesar Augustus de Carvalho, to give him his full style, is an officer of the Portuguese Navy, and the appointment he holds is the highest colonial office in the gift of the Crown of Portugal.

The Portuguese possessions in India, though now small, are not so small as is often supposed, and we had been travelling all night off Portuguese territory, which stretches for about 70 miles along the coast, and extends from 30 to 40 miles inland. The total area of Goa is not much less than 1,100 square miles, and the population is upwards of 400,000. Of the people, all with the exception of an infinitesimal fraction, are practically natives, though they are, for the most part, Roman Catholics and have adopted names illustrious in the history of Portugal. The Chief Secretary to Government, who came out to meet His Excellency, was a Portuguese gentleman appropriately named Albuquerque; and the first telegram I received was from Vasco da Gama, not a descendant of the illustrious navigator and conqueror, but a station on the new extension which connects Marmagoa with the Southern Mahratta railway system.

At the State dinner given by the Governor-General in the evening, the officials of Portuguese India were present; and one was reminded, by seeing several officials wearing Chinese and Siamese decorations, that of the Portuguese Empire in the East, remains Macao, as well as Diu and Damaon. Most of the high officials wore Portuguese decorations.

Goa is directly represented in the Cortes, and the expenses of colonial representatives are paid by the Home Government. The government of the colonies is republican in form, and the franchise extends to all but the most poor and irresponsible citizens. This policy has been pursued by the Portuguese ever since the time of Albuquerque, who conciliated the natives in every possible way, while he subdued their warlike neighbours, who oppressed them.

He carried, however, his principles of conciliation too far, and to the intermarriage of natives with the Portuguese, as much as to the combination in their policy of Sword and Cross, the fall of the Portuguese Empire in India has been due. The chief reason for its break-up was, of course, the decline of the commerce of the Portuguese, when trade followed the flag of the Dutch. As an instance of the practical manner in which principles of race equality are here interpreted, I may mention that in 1835 a native of Goa was raised to the office of Viceroy. It is an instructive comment on the soundness of the principles that led to the appointment, that this officer, after holding office for seventeen days, was compelled to fly the country. I may also mention that officers corresponding to District Judges and Judges of the High Court in British India are invariably Europeans.

Here, as in the neighbouring British districts, excise is one of the chief sources of revenue. Here, as there, the Native Christians keep their caste, and, to a far greater extent than there, have adopted European clothing and habits. To this day there are very few Moslems at the erewhile headquarters of the Inquisition, where the suppression of religious orders in 1835 completed the ruin of their arch-enemies, the Jesuits, whose beneficent efforts have now found an outlet in the British districts along the coast and elsewhere.

On the morning of the 27th, we went up the river

six miles to Old Goa, a city of churches where nothing else remains. There is literally no population in the place beyond the native priests who continue to minister to the religious needs of perhaps half-a-dozen villagers at a time, in churches that could accommodate thousands of worshippers. The Se Primaçial of Goa is a cathedral of immense dimensions, and grass grows upon its steps. Its great bell that once rang at the *auto de fe* now rings out a salute to distinguished visitors, which sounds like a funeral knell. It is hard to retain a sense of the proportions of the West, when sojourning in the East, but the Se Primaçial must be at least as large as Sainte Gudule.

The Convent of the Theatins served for an admirable halting place, where, amid the portraits of some seventy Viceroys and Governors, who looked down from the walls, we breakfasted with the present possessor of the rod of St. Francis, the occupier of the seat of the politic Almeida, the adventurous da Gama, and Albuquerque, "in whose presence the sea trembled." The windows in this charming house were of thin polished oyster-shells, and the furniture consisted of an admirable combination of western ornament and eastern simplicity. On the walls were oil-paintings, on the floors were cool mats, trees thrust their green boughs through the oyster-shell windows, and there was nothing else but tables, chairs and breakfast.

Hard by is situated the church of Bom Jesus, where is the tomb of St. Francis Xavier, a great sepulchre several stories high. The first stage is of jasper, another of bronze, and above all is the silver coffin containing the body of the Saint, which often has been, but now rarely is,* exhibited to the eyes of the faithful. One arm was cut off and sent to Rome by order of the Pope of the day, and since then, the body has withered and shown signs of decay. There is an effigy of St. Francis on the altar before his coffin, and in the right hand thereof is the staff which he used in his life. Another, which he also used, is kept by the Governor of the day, who on arrival takes one from the altar to which on his departure he returns it, the one which was held by the effigy during his term of office, being given to his successor.

We passed the great convent, the last of the nuns of which has died, and the stake at which, it seems, in the 180 years during which the Inquisition flourished at Goa, some 57 victims were actually burnt alive, the others, who were condemned, having been first strangled, and the vast majority having been either acquitted or sentenced to minor punishments.

On the way back, within sight of the crumbling ruins of the once "golden" Goa, an officer of the Governor's staff drew a map of Africa in my pocket-book, and dwelt on the great hopes and intentions of Portugal in that new outlet for the energies of Europe. The Portuguese cherish the glorious memories of their past in India, and yet hope that their days of colonial enterprise are not gone for ever.

After dining at the Cape Palace, which is delightfully situated on the edge of a promontory overlooking

* The exposition of the body has taken place this year (1890), with the usual ceremonies, amidst a vast concourse of visitors.

the bay, we reached the ship, slept in the harbour, and started next day by train for Dharwar, the Governor-General coming to see Lord Connemara start, and his Private Secretary and Aide-de-Camp coming on to the frontier, 50 miles away, where, on the crest of the Western Ghauts, amid the most delightful scenery, the Southern Mahratta Railway comes to meet the Portuguese extension. For the first forty miles the line passes through rice-fields and cocoanut groves, and for the next sixteen it climbs at a ruling gradient of 1 in 40 up the Western Ghauts to a height of 1,800 feet, through green woods and forest glades. At one point a waterfall is bridged at the base of the cascade, and the rushing water falls close to the carriages, into which in rainy weather its spray penetrates, and then passes below them. The scenery is very beautiful, and not unlike that of the Boreghât between Bombay and Poona, and some parts of the hill line from Colombo to Kandy. Tunnels are frequent and the construction of the line was very costly, averaging as much as £50,000 a-mile on the ghaut.

There is said to be a likelihood that it will pay, though in the case of a railway hardly a year old nothing can with certainty be said. Shares are already at a premium, as they are on the connected Southern Mahratta system. The Portuguese would probably never sell if the Southern Mahratta Company were willing, in this case, as in that of the Mysore and Bangalore railway, to buy. Otherwise, it would seem desirable for both lines to be under the same direction. The non-completion of the contemplated improvements to the Marmagoa harbour is at present an obstacle to the prosperity of this portion of the great Southern Mahratta system, and to enable the ghaut portion of the line to keep up with the portion on the flat, it will probably have in the end to be provided with a double line of rails.

The Portuguese Company—its capital was all subscribed in England—has made a special arrangement with the British Indian Steam Navigation Company, whereby grain and cotton are shipped directly to Bombay, but if anticipations are realized and the harbour works completed, of which there is no immediate prospect, Marmagoa should be a formidable rival, so far as Deccan produce goes, to the capital of Western India.

Just beyond the frontier, in the middle of green forest and crowning a precipitous ravine, is situated the rugged castellated rock, from which Castle Rock station, three miles further on, takes its name. After passing Castle Rock, we joined the Southern Mahratta system, which, octopus-like, is sending out branches all over the south of India, to such an extent as to excite the alarm of its less enterprising and more ancient rivals. It is indeed a sign of the times that different railway companies in India are beginning to be jealous, each of the intrusion of the other into what it considers to be the legitimate sphere of its own influence. The railway passes through undulating park-like uplands, sparsely wooded with teak and bamboo and cultivated for the most part with unirrigated rice, to Dharwar, where we spent the next day with Colonel Lindsay, the Agent and Chief Engineer of the Mahratta Railway system, with whom the Governor was able to discuss many questions concerning the recently sanctioned famine extensions, and other railway matters of vital interest to the Madras Presidency.

On the platform at Dharwar were present a guard of honour of Railway Volunteers, and Colonel Peyton, commanding the station, who has shot upwards of 300 tigers. The thermometer was 84° at midday in the tent,—a grateful change after the trying heat of Goa. There is nothing very striking in the town except a fort which affords another of the ever-present evidences in and about the Madras Presidency of the great possessions and enterprise of Hyder Ali. The country around Dharwar consists of cool, green uplands. The climate and scenery are alike delightful, and few stations in India are more favoured in these respects.

Had Dharwar been within the Madras Presidency, we would gladly have prolonged our stay at so exceptionally pleasant a halting place. We had, however, to leave it regretfully after a halt of one day, and travelled in the night, passing Londa, whence a branch of the Southern Mahratta Railway is being made to Bangalore, through the outlying portions of the Nizam's dominions, to the Toongabudra river, over the rocks, trees and water in the bed of which we passed, on one of Colonel Lindsay's bridges, to Bellary. Before coming to the river, you get a good view of the hills and ruins of Vijianagur or Humpi, which were visited last year, and are described in the second chapter.

Here Mr. Goodrich took charge of the party and

next morning we visited the fort, which, of course, was built by Hyder Ali, by whom the builders of which were, of course, put to death immediately afterwards. This story may be true of some, but can hardly be true of all forts in the south of India. What is true of nearly all is that Hyder took them or built them.

On the morning of the 1st November, we left Bellary in a storm and on the way received telegrams to say that parts of the line had been washed away in front of us. Prices, however, were reported to be falling at every station we passed, and if this rain only extends to the Northern Circars it may be hoped that the local * scarcity there, which at present causes some anxiety, may pass off.

At Gooty we learnt that the repairs to the Munro Chuttrum, which the Governor had ordered on his visit last year, were in progress.

At Cuddapah the usual inspections were made and enquiries instituted into the operations of the Agricultural Loans Act, the effect of the house tax leviable under the Local Government Acts passed by desire of Lord Ripon's Government, and into the progress of female medical aid and education. It seemed that the ryots here were not in need of agricultural loans, that they resented the house tax, which, in consequence, has not been imposed, and that the one midwife in the station is meeting with most encouraging success among high and low caste women alike. The Civil

* It ended however in the Ganjam famine described in the next chapter.

Surgeon, a native gentleman, Dr. Ayyasawmi Pillai, bore witness to the readiness of all classes to adopt European treatment. We saw a crowd of women waiting to be treated by him at the dispensary. They were suffering for the most part from fever and from pains or, as they more picturesquely put it, "flames" in their stomachs.

There has been a longstanding dispute here between the local authorities and the Mahomedans, who object to their burying-grounds within the limits of the town being closed. The matter has been happily settled, but discussing it with a Hindu gentleman, I said, "What a pity it is that the Mahomedans do not burn their dead like the Hindus, though after all it is only a fraction of them that burn." He said "Yes, and again not all of that fraction, for if his child is under three years of age, even a Brahmin will bury it." I did not know this, and asked the reason, expecting to hear something based on religious grounds. Whereon he explained that "it is because children of that age are more easily reduced to mud." In this town, where the Mahomedans are poor and many, you may witness the, as I believe, unusual sight of a Mahomedan serving a Hindu as a washerman.

Next day a cyclone raged over a great part of the Presidency, but we nevertheless got safely from Cuddapah, through the jungle that intervenes between that station and Tripetty, to the vicinity of that sacred hill. At the Renigunta station, the Governor received one address from the municipality commending their efforts in their own way, and another from an organized association condemning them root and branch. These addresses were answered together, and in the existence of an organized body of critics was found a proof of the fact that the place was ripe for local self-government, and an incentive and assistance to the municipal authorities, in its conduct. This was not the deduction intended by the opposition.

Another address was received from a body of red-hot social and religious reformers, who wished to abolish religious processions among other things, which would have a serious effect, I imagine, on the Hinduism of the people. They also wished to abolish dancing girls, who, they said, originally resembled the vestal virgins,—a statement which, I think, would take a good deal of proving. The anti-municipal party assured His Excellency that they could render the town "as good a paradise" as the municipality could "in any definite period."

We then drove along the foot of the sacred hills to the fortress and palace of Chandragiri, where we were to camp. In this old and interesting three-storied castle was made the original grant, by the representative of the Vijianagar dynasty of the day in 1639, of the land upon which Fort St. George was built. The Government carefully preserve the palace as a halting place for European travellers. It is most picturesquely situated in the fort and at the back of it is a high rocky hill, on which a fakeer has taken up his abode in a cave, where he beats a drum at all hours of the night.

The castle is built of rough hewn blocks of granite,

which fit, one into the other, with wonderful accuracy. Above the basement, is a second story of lofty rooms and corridors, above this, another of a like nature, and three tall towers spring from the roof. From the back of the building to the precipitous rock behind, on which the fort is situated, is a walled pond full of red and white water-lilies, and around it is a well-kept garden. When the High Priest came to pay his call, galloping up in flannels, he would, on dismounting, perform a simple but effectual toilette on one of the stone steps of the pond, and in a few minutes would re-appear without a spot or stain of travel. Around are green fields and trees, and the walls of the lower line of fortifications. The village of Chandragiri is situated at some distance, and at the palace is most perfect solitude and repose, but for the devotee with the drum.

On the way to Chandragiri, the Mahant or High Priest of Tripetty rode amidst a crowd of natives on a sixteen-hand-high horse with his white garments and turban streaming in the wind behind him.* "His Holiness" has a very good seat on horse-back and altogether is the most amiable and genial of ascetics.

Next morning, in his company, we ascended the sacred hill to Upper Tripetty, which lies in a basin surrounded by low hills, at a height of about 1,600 feet. The temple is of an ordinary character. Monkeys hop about in the streets, and around the houses, just as if they were human beings. The sanctity of

* Unfortunately this Mahant subsequently got into trouble, and he has ceased to hold his high office.

this place is altogether unapproached, I believe, by that of any other in India, with the sole exceptions of Rameshwaram and Benares. For a distance of 12 or 14 miles, you travel over rough paving stones, all of which are roughened that the feet may not slip, and two-thirds of which are engraved with drawings, or inscriptions, or with the names of weary pilgrims. On the way down, I passed some hundreds, all calling in chorus the name of Govinda. Among them was a Brahmin woman with a bar of silver through her cheeks; she had worn this for a year as a vow and was going to have it taken out. As we rode to the foot of the hill, the Mahant and one of his attendants occasionally raced along in front. Both were good if somewhat reckless, riders. The Mahant does not speak English, and is a gentleman of the old school. None the less he has had a telephone wire laid from Lower to Upper Tripetty, which he says saves a good deal of time and trouble. He allowed me to drink milk out of one of his own lotas, and he certainly does the honours of the hill extremely well.

The low hills of Tripetty are well wooded from their base to within a few hundred feet of their summits, when an outcrop of craggy red quartzite, ending at intervals in scarped precipices, crowns the range. The climate has the most evil reputation for fever, and few pilgrims stay even one night on the hill.

Before leaving Chandragiri, where we spent several happy days, the Governor went to return the visit of the High Priest, which ceremony presented no exceptional features except the presentation to each member of the party of little ivory gods seated on lotus leaves and sucking their big toes.

Next day we passed through the Kalahasti zemindary into the district of Nellore by the newly-opened Cuddapah-Nellore State Railway. This line was constructed for the purpose of bringing the rice of Nellore into the surrounding districts and is one of the metre-gauge famine lines.

At Nellore Mr. Macleane, the Collector, took charge of the party, and the day of arrival was signalised by a levée, at which the Rajas of Venkatagiri and Kalahasti, among others, were present. The latter maintains an establishment of 1,400 servants, 6 elephants and 70 horses, some of which, when we saw them paraded, wore bracelets above their knees and necklaces of gold mohurs about their necks.

In the highest posts in this district, Natives and Europeans are about equally employed. The District Collector is, of course, a European Civil Servant; the Judge, however, Mr. Ramachandrier, is a Brahman and a Statutory Civilian, and it is another sign of the times that, at a party at his house in the evening, his married daughter mixed with the other guests like a European lady. The Sub-Collector is a Mussulman, Mr. Mahomed Raza Khan, another Statutory Civilian; the Assistant Collector, again, is a European Civil Servant.

Next morning the Governor visited the site of some desired improvements in irrigation and heard the petitioners explain their own case, and afterwards we went to the civil dispensary, where we saw, among other patients, a boy with a broken leg. The village potter had dressed the wound with a compound of blood and mud, and had fixed a bamboo splint so tightly with string that gangrene was likely to result. The potters, it is said, are the great amateur surgeons in this district, and occupy the position generally held in all parts of the world, I believe, by the barbers. Here I would insert a passing proof of the inaccurate conception of India and its castes which they have, who imagine that objections exist on the part of native women to treatment by persons of a caste inferior or different to their own. The barbers in India, as elsewhere, are generally the amateur surgeons, and midwives, who attend on all castes alike, are almost invariably women of the barber caste, which is one of the lowest and most despised in the country.

At the tank, which is 12 miles around, we learnt that teal and water-fowl of different sorts and kinds are caught by the legs by divers. The fowler, if one may call him so, dives under the water, seizes the teal by its legs, pulls it underneath and swims ashore with it. This is even more remarkable than the fishing at Kundapore.

Everything in Nellore seemed prosperous, and here again we learnt that the ryots utterly decline to borrow money from Government under the Agricultural Loan Improvements Act, preferring to borrow, and being able to borrow, as they allege at a positively cheaper rate, from the much-abused native money-lender.

The lying-in hospital here is doing most excellent

work under the general supervision of Dr. Price, who takes great interest in the female educational movement. He and the matron in charge, Mrs. Rogers, alike agree in what has recently been urged by myself and by other writers in various periodicals, to the effect that there is no caste objection on the part of Hindu women to employing the services of European, Eurasian or low-caste native women as midwives and doctors. In this hospital are four wards—one for Brahmins, one for Sudras and one for low-caste people, and 5 pupil nurses are also being educated, who, when qualified as midwives, will go out to work in the district. There is also a lady belonging to an American Mission working in this district. But her operations are connected with proselytizing, and are consequently to be carefully distinguished from those of the municipal lying-in hospital and of the Countess of Dufferin's Fund.

The Governor laid the foundation stone of a new building for the lying-in hospital, which is being erected as a memorial of the Jubilee.

We arrived at Venkatagiri on the 13th, and, after driving to the outskirts of the town, were met by elephants bearing castle-like howdahs on their backs, which marched in slow procession through the crowded streets, the tops of the howdahs being on a level with the tops of the houses, which were thronged with people wearing white and coloured cloths. Horsemen carrying banners led the procession and after them a troop of cavalry clad in blue-and-white Hussar uniform. Next came dancing-girls with jasmine in their hair, and tinsel on their cloths, then a crowd of macebearers, halberdiers, and torch-carriers, and led horses glittering with cloth of gold. To these succeeded some gold and silver palanquins, a drum camel and a band of musicians which played "under the twinkling starlight" while cymbals clashed, cholera horns screamed, and trumpets blared,—trumpets of enormous length, size and volume, such as those which levelled the walls of Jericho. The main street was lined with a row of spearmen, who held long lances which reached as high as the howdahs. Across the flat and populous roofs, between frequent tamarind trees, the Great Treasure Rock of Venkatagiri looked down from the mountains upon a scene of barbaric pomp and splendour, such as is but rarely seen even in the east, which for once seemed to merit its favorite epithet of "gorgeous."

The Raja, who sat in front with the Governor, on the leading elephant wore in his aigrette an emerald as big as a hen's egg and his brothers wore cross-belts and swords encrusted all over with precious stones. The elephants entered entirely into the spirit of the thing, and walked along with the slow, and, to the oriental mind, graceful, gait, to which, in their literature, they compare a woman's walk.

The Raja not only possesses big jewels but is very rich. His father, a few years back, voluntarily made over all his possessions to him and took to the life of a religious recluse. His eldest son, our host, thus succeeded in his boyhood to an estate the net income of which is not less than £40,000 a-year. His character and manners are alike simple and straightforward.

The condition of the tenants on his estate is good, but neither here nor elsewhere did we hear that it was better than that of those holding directly under Government.

On the morning of the 15th November we reached Madras after travelling by sea 324, by rail 864, by road 111, by river 36, in all, 1,335 miles, and visiting six Madras districts, a foreign territory, and two districts of the Bombay Presidency *en route* from South Canara to Bellary. The Governor had received and answered from first to last 29 addresses.

We met with no accidents, though we passed through a cyclone and had a narrow escape from a collision, and another from boat-wreck at sea, while of a party of three one, Major Chisholme, caught malarious fever, and had to return to Madras. We saw much beautiful country and many interesting peoples and persons, and much on every side, that illustrated the unsafety of holding social, economical or political experiences gained in one part, of equal application in another part, of so large a Presidency, including so many different races and comprising so many tracts of country, which bear one to another hardly any points of resemblance. There was abundant evidence that the people generally in the districts we passed through were prosperous and contented. Their addresses reflected a most reasonable conception of, and attitude towards, the Government, and if they asked for more than could be given, their wants were almost always such as the State would only too gladly grant, were it possessed of a sufficiently long purse.

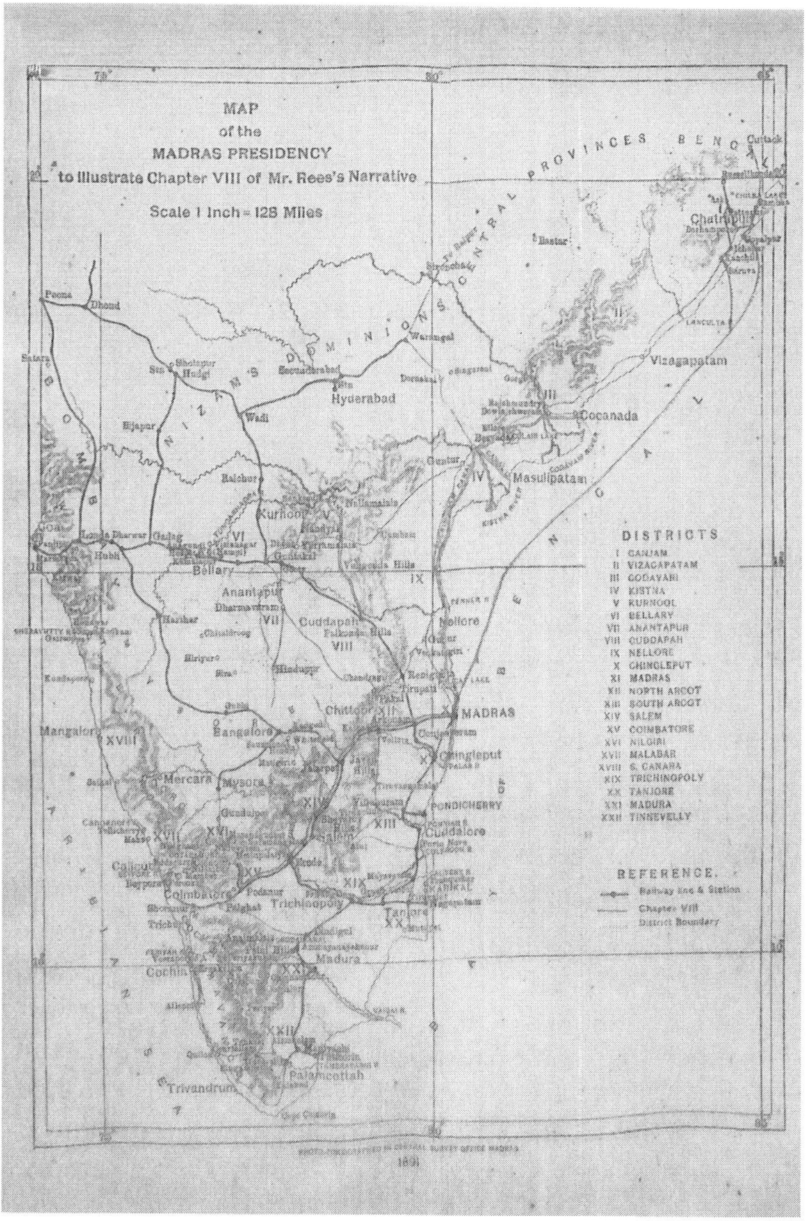
MAP
of the
MADRAS PRESIDENCY
to illustrate Chapter VIII of Mr. Rees's Narrative
Scale 1 Inch = 128 Miles
DISTRICTS
I GANJAM
II VIZAGAPATAM
III GODAVARI
IV KISTNA
V KURNOOL
VI BELLARY
VII ANANTAPUR
VIII CUDDAPAH
IX NELLORE
X CHINGLEPUT
XI MADRAS
XII NORTH ARCOT
XIII SOUTH ARCOT
XIV SALEM
XV COIMBATORE
XVI NILGIRI
XVII MALABAR
XVIII S. CANARA
XIX TRICHINOPOLY
XX TANJORE
XXI MADURA
XXII TINNEVELLY
REFERENCE.
Railway line & Station
Chapter VIII
District Boundary
CENTRAL PROVINCES
NIZAMS DOMINIONS
Hyderabad
Vizagapatam
Cocanada
Masulipatam
Kurnool
Bellary
Anantapur
Cuddapah
Nellore
MADRAS
Chingleput
PONDICHERRY
Cuddalore
Bangalore
Mysore
Mercara
Mangalore
Calicut
Coimbatore
Salem
Trichinopoly
Tanjore
Madura
Cochin
Palamcottah
Trivandrum
Poona
Dhond
Warangal
Chittoor
Hindupur
Chatrapur
1891

CHAPTER VIII.

GANJAM.

BY MR. CLAUDE VINCENT.

Bad news from Ganjam district—Famines of 1877 and 1866—Inaccessibility of district—Means of communication—Causes of present distress—Mr. Garstin's visit—His report—Professional agency works—Civil agency works—Gratuitous relief—Outbreak of cholera—Serious condition of affairs—Governor's departure from Ootacamund—Our party—A mishap—Antonio "killed"—Arrival in Madras—Departure by sea—Calm voyage—At Gopalpur—Dangerous surf—Landing—Luggage-boat capsized—Usual reception—Bishop Tissot—Port of Gopalpur—Condemned pier—Examination of inhabitants—Results thereof—Cholera cases—Drive to Rambha—Mr. Minchin—Anecdote—At Berhampore—Supply of seed-grain—Purchase from Godavery—Visit to jail—Uriyas—Their caste observances—At Aska—Mr. Minchin's Sugar factory—Great heat—At Russellkondah—Maliahs or Hill Tracts—Idyllic jail—Khonds—Their customs—Religion—Meriah sacrifice—Its origin—At Ichapur—Health of party—Queen's sympathy—At Kanshili—Zemindar of Parlakimedi — Addresses — Embarkation — Scene at Baruva — Results of Governor's visit—Real preventive of famine—East Coast Railway—Sanction for its survey—Stormy voyage—Arrival at Madras—Return to Ootacamund—Governor's official minute.

THE Governor's stay on the hills during the hot season of 1889 was rudely interrupted by bad news from the Ganjam district. This district lies at the extreme north of the Madras Presidency, on the borders of Orissa, and, like that province, has been subject to periodical periods of drought resulting in famine. During the great Madras famine of 1877, Ganjam did not suffer much; but in 1866 there was serious scarcity in the district, and it is estimated that 10,000 people then died of starvation.

The district is extremely difficult of access, there being no railway and the only means of communication being by road from the north and south and by means of the coasting steamers. Communication from the west is cut off by a high range of hills and an impassable jungly country. The communication by sea is sufficiently good in fine weather, but becomes difficult during several months of the year on account of the high surf that prevails. For instance, during the famine of 1866, Government bought large stocks of grain, which were sent in steamers to Gopálpur, the principal port of the district. Owing, however, to the heavy surf caused by the monsoon, the ships containing the grain had to lie for several days off the port without being able to land a single bag, while starving people on the beach were clamouring for food and praying to God for fine weather.

The present distress has arisen in consequence of the partial failure of the south-west monsoon of 1888, which was due in the months of June and July, aggravated by the almost complete failure of the north-east monsoon also, which was due in the month of October. The usual results had followed. Crops had failed, prices had risen, merchants had refused to open their grain-stores, grain-riots resulted, semi-panic had developed, and, at the end of October, the District Officers had reported that a severe famine would have to be met. Under these circumstances, Mr. Garstin, C.S.I., then a Member of the Board of Revenue, had, in November, been deputed to visit the district on behalf of Government, and his report, which was received in

December, was more reassuring. He said that the stocks of grain were then ample, that, though prices were high and crops bad, there was no sign of any actual serious distress. Ordinary relief measures were, in his opinion, all that were required for the time.

The distress in the district developed, however, steadily until, in April, there were about 18,000 people employed on Professional Agency works in the Public Works Department on which at least 75 per cent. of a full day's task is exacted from all labourers. About 3,000 people were employed, in addition, on Civil Agency works which provide employment for those who do not come up to the professional standard. About 1,000 persons were also admitted to gratuitous relief, which implies the provision either of a daily money dole or of cooked food in the case of those who are unfit to do any work whatsoever owing to age, sickness or other infirmity. About this time too the Collector's reports became more gloomy. The condition of things, he said, was not improving and was aggravated by a severe outbreak of cholera, which is the usual accompaniment of famine. Deaths from this cause alone amounted to over 1,400 a week. The state of affairs was sufficiently serious to render a visit from the highest authority eminently desirable. The presence of the Governor inspires confidence in the local officers and shows them that their efforts under exceptional circumstances meet with his sympathy and support.

The Governor left Ootacamund on the morning

of the 29th May 1889, a large party of officials and visitors assembling to wish him godspeed. Our party was a small one, consisting only of the Chief Secretary to Government * and the Private Secretary.† A Medical Officer ‡ also joined the party in Madras. All three of us had been through the great Madras famine of 1877-78, and so had had previous experience of the state of affairs that had to be dealt with. The usual monotony of the hot and dusty journey down the ghât was marked on this occasion by what might have been a most serious accident. The phaeton in which His Excellency travelled turned a corner too sharply and rolled over without a moment's warning. The Governor, who was inside, escaped with a severe shaking, but his servant, who was on the box, was thrown 40 feet down the khud. The Governor struggled out of the carriage and went to the side of the road to see what had become of his servant. "Are you hurt, Antonio," he called out, "Killed, your Excellency," cried a feeble voice from the middle of a clump of bamboos. The answer was reassuring and by means of ropes the "dead" Antonio was dragged back to the road, having escaped with a severely-strained arm, which, however, necessitated his being left in Madras.

We arrived in Madras on the morning of the 30th, the few ladies and gentlemen who from force or inclination were braving the hot weather there meeting us at the station. In the evening we embarked on board

---

* Mr. J. F. Price. † Mr. Claude Vincent.

‡ Surgeon-Major McNally, Deputy Sanitary Commissioner.

the S.S. *Nowshera* for Gopálpur. Our voyage was calm and marked by no incident. We carried with us the genial Archdeacon who, formerly in the Royal Navy, was evidently glad to find himself back on his old element.

We reached Gopálpur on the afternoon of the 1st of June. A flagstaff and a few white houses distinguish an otherwise monotonous coast-line, but to ensure vessels making no mistake as to the locality its name is painted in letters 3 feet high on a large sign-board which runs along the roof of the Steamer Company's office, as if the port were a sort of marine Clapham junction instead of being the *ultima Thule* of the Madras presidency and of India. The landing through the much-dreaded surf had now to be faced. The horses that we brought with us and our luggage left the ship in advance, and all landed safely with the exception of one cargo-boat which was overturned in the surf and several very necessary articles of apparel found their last resting place at the bottom of the sea. We ourselves landed in a large surf boat, and the question arose whether we might not have to swim for it. "Can you swim, Mr. Archdeacon," asked the Governor; "no" was the ominous reply, but though thus in the hands of Providence, we felt that, under the circumstances, we were probably fairly secure. And under the charge of the head boatman, who boasted that this was the fourth Governor he had successfully guided through their dangers, we got through the breakers in safety. The Governor was met on the beach with the usual reception and a guard of honour from the neighbouring military station at Berhampore. Bishop Tissot of the Catholic diocese of Vizianagrum, a venerable prelate 80 years of age, lent colour to the scene in his purple robes.

Gopálpur is a port with a fair amount of trade and, at the instance of the local merchants, Government has just completed, at a cost of 3 lakhs of rupees, a handsome iron screw-pile pier which extends nearly 1,000 feet out into the sea. It has been found, however, that the length of the pier is insufficient, as it does not extend beyond the outer line of the surf and boats with cargo to land, find it impossible to lie alongside. It has been proposed to lengthen it, but this, owing to the shelving character of the foreshore, would be a very costly operation, and the latest idea on the subject is to dismantle it and sell the materials.

The Medical Officer of the party held an inspection of the inhabitants of Gopálpur with a view to ascertaining the physical condition of the poorest amongst the population. His examination furnished results which recalled the experience of the famine of 1877. A considerable number of sadly emaciated specimens of humanity were discovered, which pointed to the severity of the distress in the district. As usual in such cases, the children seemed to be the first to have suffered and were in the worst state. Active relief operations appear to be necessary, and above all a system of village relief which would reach starving coolies such as those we discovered at Gopálpur.

On the line of canal between Gopálpur and Chatrapur, the head-quarters of the district, over 5,000 coolies were seen at work. These, however, were in better case, being regularly employed; and though they made some complaints as to the wages they were receiving, they seemed on the whole to be very fairly treated. Three cases of cholera had just occurred amongst them, two of which terminated fatally within a few hours. The third patient was removed from the hospital by some of his fellow workmen, who carried him off, though in a dying state, to his own village.

On the 4th of June we drove 15 miles to Rambha and spent the day in a house belonging to Mr. Minchin of Aska (of whom more hereafter) situated on the edge of the Chilka lake. This lake is a sheet of water 60 miles long and about 10 broad. Tree-covered hills stretch down to the water's edge, and in the cold weather there are myriads of wild-fowl on the lake affording splendid opportunities for the sportsman. The house in which we spent the day is a very fine one and was built by a Civil Servant of the old school, who lived in the days when the pagoda tree still blossomed in India, and could be shaken with some benefit. No record of the cost of building it is extant, as all the papers relating to this subject were lost in a boat which was sunk on a voyage to an island in the middle of the lake.

We were visited at Rambha by two neighbouring Zamindars. One of these, a lad of 18, is still a Minor and under the guardianship of the Court of Wards. He appeared before us in a gorgeous embroidered yellow kincob coat and pink trousers and his bright and open countenance and air of more than usual intelligence impressed us favourably.

On our way back to Chatrapur we were met by bodies of cultivators whose attenuated frames testified to their distress, and who complained of their poverty and their lack of seed-grain in the patient plaintive way typical of the Hindu ryot. The road passed through thousands of acres of cultivable land on which not a blade was visible.

A sharp shower fell in the night, and the next morning, as we drove into Berhampore, bullocks attached to the little wooden ploughs were scraping the surface of the soil into furrows, preparatory to the sowing of the new crop.

The question of seed-grain was one of the most pressing of those that had to be decided. The season for sowing was at hand, but those best qualified to judge asserted that at least one quarter of the cultivators had used their reserve of seed-grain for food, and that no stock of it existed in the district. One ton of grain suffices to sow 30 acres, and it was estimated that 30,000 acres would require to be supplied. Again, the cultivators who had been reduced to the consumption of their seed-grain would evidently be too poor to be able to pay for a fresh supply even if it were procurable, so that importation by Government and distribution with a subsequent recovery of the value seemed to be the only measures possible to adopt, much as State importation is to be deprecated as tending to interfere with private trade, and to alarm the sensitive mind of the native dealer. Orissa was telegraphed to, but replied that not a ton of seed-grain was procurable there, as stocks had been exhausted owing to the drain to Ganjam already experienced. The native merchants of Berhampore were sounded, but did not seem eager to undertake the job, and eventually the purchase of the 1,000 tons was entrusted to the officials of the Godávari district, where, thanks to the magnificent irrigation, a reserve of grain may always be relied upon.

At the Berhampore jail we saw several poor cultivators incarcerated for participation in the grain-riots of October last. Their fields were lying fallow for want of their labour, and they clamoured piteously to the Governor for clemency. It is a curious fact about these riots that many of the rioters got hold of the idea that Government approved of their proceedings. Several poor women were also there, sentenced for stealing, as they pathetically expressed it, "a little earth." It seems hard that the bountiful mother of all mankind should thus, through man's agency, be made to play the part of an avenging deity. But "salt-earth" was what the poor women meant, and salt being a Government monopoly, the removal from the surface of the ground of even a handful of salt-earth is a serious offence. His Excellency has caused measures to be taken for the release of most of the rioters and orders have been given that in the salt cases none but serious ones are to be noticed.

Next morning we drove 25 miles to Aska through what, in a good season, is a mass of rice and sugar-cane cultivation. The correct derivation of the name "Ganjam" is Ganj-i-am, meaning "the granary of the world." It was sad to see a country with so noble a name in such a barren condition. The south-west monsoon is now due and if that brings good rain, though distress will continue till November, when the crops are harvested, the famine will then be over. If it fails wholly or in part, there will be a repetition of the miseries of 1866. No measures of relief can be sufficiently widespread to prevent loss of life in such a crisis. In 1877 the Government of India had to declare that "the task of saving life irrespective of the cost is one which it is beyond their power to undertake," and though relief may be provided for the able-bodied by a well-organized system of public works, the infirm, the weak, the sickly, and, above all, the women and children are bound to go to the wall. In Ganjam the usual difficulties of similar situations are aggravated by the peculiar notions of the inhabitants of the country. Ganjam, being only accessible by sea, is many years behind the southern districts of Madras in its civilisation, and the Uriyas, who inhabit the northern portion of the district, are more than usually rigid in their caste observances. Some of them will not, under the stress of famine, accept a grain of food cooked by strangers, even by Brahmins, so that gratuitous relief in its best form cannot be distributed. The majority of Uriya women will also, under no circumstances, keep away from their houses, which prevents the concentration of labourers on large relief works. The district authorities have, however, got affairs well in hand, a sufficient number of estimates are ready for execution and gratuitous relief on a large scale, either in the shape of cooked food or money doles, will be organized forthwith.

At Aska we stayed in the house of Mr. Minchin, the reputation of whose hospitality and enterprise is widespread. Unfortunately he was absent, but his representative and manager, Mr. Kollmann, a most energetic and charming Hungarian gentleman, did the honours in a princely style. Mr. Minchin has established here a large sugar-factory which employs 1,200 hands, and the yearly outturn of which is about 30,000 cwts. The method employed is the so-called "diffusion process." The cane is cut up into small strips, thoroughly saturated in water, pressed, and the liquid then evaporated. Everything throughout the factory is altogether on a model scale, but business is not so active as it should be. The area in the neighbourhood under sugar-cane cultivation is decreasing owing to bad seasons, and the competition of beet sugar is driving cane sugar out of the market. The factory also undertakes the manufacture of spirits, such as toddy, rum and rice spirits, for the supply of the retail vendors of the district, the annual outturn being about 80,000 gallons of proof spirit. Mr. Minchin has a monopoly of the supply under contract with Government, but complains of the large amount of illicit distillation, and petitions were presented to the Governor by some people who said they were hereditary distillers, and that their means of livelihood had been destroyed by the monopoly system. This system of "abkári" or excise aims at securing what may be concisely termed the maximum of revenue with the minimum of consumption.

The heat at Aska was intense, 106° in the verandahs, but the Governor kindly dispensed with the ceremonial which usually rules in Government House whether established "in court or camp or grove," and business was transacted throughout the day in costume which very much resembled that of Adam before the fall.

From Aska we went to Russellkonda, a town at the foot of the Maliahs or hill tracts of the Ganjam district. It is very picturesque, being surrounded by hills on which grows the graceful bamboo jungle. The usual assemblage of people met us at the entrance to the town, and the whole population, several thousands in number, turned out behind the carriage and followed it to our temporary residence, forming a running procession several hundred yards long. The jail at Russellkonda is the most civilised imaginable. In other places jails are always surrounded by high walls to prevent the escape of the prisoners, but either these walls are an unnecessary precaution or else the idea of escape has not penetrated the minds of the Russellkonda prisoners, for the jail there has a wall only about 3 feet high, such as surrounds an ordinary dwelling-house. A prisoner could easily jump over it, and yet the record of escapes or attempts at escape is *nil.* When we were passing in the morning all the prisoners crowded to the wall to see us go by, and in the evening when the Governor inspected the jail all the townspeople peeped over to see what was going on. In short, quite an idyllic jail, and possibly the poor people are happier in it than elsewhere.

The administrator of the Maliahs, Mr. Horne, met

us in Russellkonda and we heard much from him regarding the curious customs of the inhabitants of the hills who are called Khonds. Their chief amusements are dancing and getting drunk, which they combine. They will do no work and will pay no taxes. Previous to our occupation of the hills, and indeed for many years subsequent to it, human sacrifices were common among them. Their custom was to buy grown-up men and women or children from the villages in the plains and keep them until they had occasion to think that their tutelar deity, the earth goddess, required propitiation. Then the victim, who would meanwhile be treated as a favoured mortal, was garlanded, intoxicated, and finally beaten to death with clubs; or with the heavy brass armlets worn by the inhabitants; or cut to death with knives; or, more horrible still, burnt with brands until he was incapable of struggling, under the belief that the next fall of rain would be proportionate to the number of tears he shed. A general orgie with all sorts of sensual excesses celebrated the occasion. When dead, he was hacked to pieces and portions of his flesh were carried off in triumph to the different villages and buried in the earth in honour of the goddess.

The reported origin of this barbarous custom is curious. The Khonds believe in one Supreme Being, Boora Pennu, whom they sometimes call the God of Light, sometimes the Sun-God. In the beginning he created for himself a consort, Tari Pennu, who became the source of all evil and the earth-goddess. Afterwards he created the earth; and walking upon it one day with Tari Pennu, he was so enraged with her, because she refused to scratch the back of his neck, that he resolved to create out of the earth a new being, man, who should render to him the most devoted homage. He also resolved to create out of the earth all that was necessary for man's existence. Filled with jealousy, Tari Pennu attempted to prevent the fulfilment of these purposes, but only succeeded in altering the order of creation. Taking a handful of earth, Boora Pennu threw it behind him to create man, but it was caught by Tari and cast on one side, whence arose trees, herbs and all kinds of vegetable life. In like manner she intercepted, caught and flung aside three other handsful of earth, which became respectively the fish of the sea, the beasts of the earth, and the birds of the air. Then, seeing what his rebellious consort had done, Boora Pennu put his hand on her head, to prevent any further interference with his will, placed a fifth handful of earth on the ground, and from it was the human race created. The goddess then placed her hands over the earth and said "let those beings you have made exist; you shall create no more;" whereupon the god caused an exudation of sweat to proceed from his body, collected it in his hand, and threw it around, saying "to all that I have created," whence originated love and sex and the continuance of species. At first the human race was sinless, went about unclothed, and enjoyed free communion with Boora. They lived without labour and in perfect harmony. But all this was changed by Tari, who "sowed the seeds of sin into mankind as into a ploughed field." Then came the loss of innocence, which was followed by disease and death. The earth became a jungle, flowers became poisonous, and animals became savage. The god and goddess fiercely contended for superiority over the new creation; and the supposed result of this conflict is the source of a division in the religious belief of the mountaineers. One sect—those who follow Boora Pennu—believe that he was victorious, in proof of which they allege the pains of childbirth which have been imposed upon the sex of Tari. The other sect—those who worship the goddess—believe that she was unconquered, and that, although she is the source of all evils, she can confer every form of earthly benefit, indirectly, by not obstructing the good which flows from Boora, and, directly, by her own act. They also believe that she appeared on the earth in a feminine form, called by them Umbally Bylee, and that while under this form she introduced order and the art of agriculture, as well as all other blessings into the world. As Umbally Bylee, she was one day slicing vegetables, and accidentally cutting her finger, the blood drops fell on the soft barren mud, which instantly became dry and firm earth. "Behold the good change," exclaimed the goddess, "cut up my body to complete it." But regarding her as one of themselves, the people declined to do her bidding, and in order that it might be carried out they resolved instead to purchase victims from other peoples. This is the origin of what is variously termed the Meriah, Tokki or Keddi sacrifice. At first its efficacy was confined to those who personally practised the rite, but afterwards Tari ordered that all mankind should be included in the benefits it was to confer. Hence the sect of Tari believed that the responsibility for the well-being of the whole world rests upon them. The practice of a rite so horrible on such purely benevolent principles is one of its most singular features.

The followers of Boora Pennu, though condemning the human sacrifices practised by the followers of Tari, yet were themselves guilty of the practice of female infanticide. To justify this they urged the authority of their god, who was evidently a philosopher even if also a misogynist. He is supposed to have said: "Behold! from the making of one feminine being what have I and the whole world suffered. You are at liberty to bring up only as many women as you can manage."

The number of human sacrifices used to be very large. On the occasion of the new-moon feast of 1841 there were as many as 240 victims, and between 1837 and 1854 one English officer alone saved 1,506 intended victims, of whom 717 were males and 789 females. The practice has since been put down by the Government and the Khonds acquiesce readily in the measures adopted as they find that the earth is not less fruitful without being so propitiated and they are saved the expense of purchasing their victims which used to vary from 60 to 200 rupees apiece. The Khond dialect has no alphabet and is therefore unwritten, so it is very little known, and communication with the inhabitants is not easy.

A large irrigation reservoir was in progress at Russellkonda which is to cover an area of 4½ square miles.

It was curious to observe the immense brass armlets worn by most of the women, which extend in a series of rings from the wrist to the elbow, are welded on, and often weigh as much as 7 lb. on each arm.

Numerous memorials were here presented to Lord Connemara, one of which began with the somewhat original invocation of *gloria in excelsis.* It went on to speak of the "regal visit of his Divine Lordship to this part of the country away from the metropolis especially in this most tiresome torrid season." With this latter expression we all more or less agreed, for the heat was tremendous (107° in the shade). The expression used recalled the address presented to the Bishop of Madras in Tinnevelly one June, in which some Native Christians thanked His Lordship for deigning to visit them "in this hell of a hot weather."

Russellkonda showed a larger proportion of emaciated people than any place we had hitherto visited. A muster of the population showed many of them to be not only suffering from famine but also largely from small-pox and the inspection was very trying to our senses of sight and smell.

The jailor here, an old artilleryman, has shot over 100 bears, with which the neighbourhood abounds.

By this time we were all more or less knocked up with the heat and exposure, the Governor getting a rather bad attack of malarial fever and the Collector suffering slightly from sunstroke, so we spent two days more in Mr. Minchin's luxurious house at Aska, recruiting, arranging statistics, and discussing with the local officers the measures of relief to be adopted. The people we found were beginning to sell their jewels, which is always a bad sign, and some gold necklaces and metal bracelets, both of wonderfully original and graceful design, were purchased by us.

From Aska we went to Pattupur, the centre of the most severe distress. Mr. Carr, who is in charge here, has just started a relief-kitchen where 100 poor little starvelings of children are fed twice a day. But he is met by a curious difficulty. Little tin plates were made on which the food, consisting of rice and curry, is served. Brahmins are employed to cook the meals, otherwise they would not be eaten, but so strong are caste prejudices that the cooks will not wash the plates off which the children have eaten, and the children will not again eat off the plates if they are washed by persons of inferior caste. The remedy is either to give each child a plate of its own, which it can keep and wash, or else to provide the ordinary leaf plates of the country, which are thrown away after every meal.

Another instance of the strength of caste feeling was that of some emaciated Brahmin children who were looking hungrily on while the food was being distributed; they were asked to sit down and partake, but they shook their heads and said "no, we are Brahmins and cannot eat in public."

A deputation from the brother of a neighbouring Zamindar brought a dead spotted deer and sambur as presents. We had seen him on the road in the morning holding in his hands, as we passed, a large vase of burning camphor, which is the offering they make to their gods.

A number of Khonds from the neighbouring hills were also on view. Their arrows are most formidable-looking weapons, but we were assured they seldom manage to hit anything at a distance beyond 20 yards.

About 8 o'clock in the evening a noisy blowing of trumpets announced the arrival, to pay his respects to the Governor, of the Peddakimidi Zamindar, one of the large landed proprietors of the neighbourhood. He is a most truculent individual and gives the local officers a great deal of trouble. He had been warned to come in the afternoon and his late appearance was a piece of swagger, so he was not received. This is the gentleman who, not long since, when received by a high official, ostentatiously washed his hands and feet immediately after the interview in order to purify himself. However, he is a religious devotee, which may account for his bad manners. He is said to have performed the rite of the million rose-leaves which consists in scattering one million roses petal by petal on to the shrine of his favourite god. The number of roses is probably somewhat exaggerated but he went on scattering petals for three days and so became a very holy man.

Coming into Ichapur the next morning after a 30-mile drive we were met by a Police Inspector on a white pony who gallantly showed the way through the town. His devotion to duty was great, but he was evidently no equestrian. The pace alarmed him, and we saw his attendant run up behind, and catch and keep hold of the pony's tail to prevent its going too fast! Thus quaintly led we arrived at our halting place, once a mess-house, in the days when we were fighting with the Mahrattas for the possession of the district, but now a travellers' bungalow.

Our elephants, of which we had three or four travelling with us, brought in our camp in good time. These animals are kept for use by the District Officers when travelling in the hills.

The meaning of Ichapur is "city of delight," but we scarcely found it to be such. The Governor had a return of fever, the Doctor was also ill and the heat was great.

However, we were all cheered in the evening by the receipt of a telegram from the Secretary of State to the following effect:—"Balmoral, 13th June. The Queen-Empress of India appreciates your endeavours to alleviate the distress in Ganjam and desires that no efforts may be spared. Her Majesty deeply sympathises with the sufferings of her people in that district." The Governor at once ordered the translation of this into Telugu and Uriya, which are the two vernaculars of the district, and copies to be sent to every village.

At Kanshili, the next morning, we were met with the usual deputation and address and by the Zamindar of Parlakimidi, resplendent in blue velvet and gold and adorned with a most elaborate pearl necklace. He is the best of the Zamindars we have met, having had a good English education under a competent tutor.

The address thanked the Governor for coming among the people "at a time when a dreadful pestilence and a painful famine struggle for supremacy, the former confining a great majority of the people to their houses, and the latter driving them out in search of food. We hope that Your Excellency's auspicious tour would soon expel these contending tyrants from us"!

Another address said: "It is not necessary for me to borrow Gargantua's mouth to express my gratitude" &c.!

Next morning we drove 8 miles to the port of Baruva, where the British India Company's steamer *Booldana* had been ordered to meet us. We had sent all our luggage on in advance expecting to go straight on board, and it was an unpleasant surprise when we arrived at the seashore to find no steamer there. Various were the conjectures, but after an hour's waiting she hove in sight having overshot the port, if a piece of bare sand with a flag-staff on it can be so called. Thousands of natives from the neighbouring villages lined the beach to see the Governor embark. The surf was high, but after waiting ten minutes for a lull, amid frantic shouts and yells, we passed through it with nothing more than a splashing. As the boat started all the people on the beach put up their hands in the attitude of prayer, invoking the protection of the goddess of the waters. By 11 A.M. we were steaming south to Madras, and though rather battered, worn, and dilapidated, both as to ourselves and our belongings, by our fortnight's touring, we congratulated ourselves that, in spite of the heat and the cholera, we had no casualty to record.

The Governor's visit was no doubt peculiarly well timed, and the relief measures he ordered will be the means of saving many poor people from the most lingering and dreadful of all deaths. The result of elaborate examinations made by the Medical Officer who accompanied us was that 5 per cent. of the population are in a state of dangerous emaciation, and the best estimate of the District Officers was that, even if the monsoon is good, 12,000 people will have to be employed on Professional Agency works, 8,000 on Civil Agency works, while not less than 30,000 will have either to receive money doles or be fed in relief-kitchens until the new crop is harvested in November or December. If the monsoon fails 100,000 people will probably have to be relieved, and the resources of private trade in an inaccessible district like Ganjam will be severely taxed to cope with the crisis. The district is not only one of the most populous but also one of the most fertile in the Madras Presidency, but it is deficient in irrigation works, and the rice cultivation on which the large majority of the people rely for food is therefore mainly dependent on the quantity and seasonableness of the periodic rains. In most other districts similarly circumstanced the various kinds of millets, which require no irrigation and far less rain than the rice crop, are largely grown, but the explanation of the preference for rice cultivation in Ganjam is that if it is successful the outturn is double in quantity and treble in value of the corresponding millet crop.

The real preventive of famine in Ganjam, as elsewhere, lies in the improvement of communications. A glance at a railway map of India will show a great blank in this corner of the Eastern coast of the peninsula and a * railway project is now before Government for the construction of a line from Bezvada, in the Kistna delta, where two lines now terminate "in the air," so to speak, through the rich Godávari and Vizagapatam districts, to pass through Ganjam and on to Orissa, there to join a line that is to be run to the sacred shrine of Juggernath at Pooree from the Bengal system of railways. There can be little doubt that such a line would be remunerative, and no doubt that it would be the salvation of the Ganjam district from future scarcities and would speedily place it abreast of the most flourishing portions of the Madras Presidency. It was satisfactory to learn by a telegram from the Viceroy before we left the district that the necessary funds for the survey of this line would be sanctioned.

We had a stormy voyage back to Madras, which we reached on the morning of the 19th June, and after halting there for a day we arrived at Ootacamund on the afternoon of the 21st.

---

* For an account of the ceremony of cutting the first sod of this railway see Chapter XIII.

CHAPTER IX.

TANJORE AND SOUTH ARCOT.

BY MR. CLAUDE VINCENT.

Departure from Ootacamund—Our party—Arrival at Trichinopoly—Mrs. Shujat Ali—Municipal address—At Negapatam—Meaning of Negapatam—Visit to South Indian Railway workshops—Municipal address—Karikal—Its early history—Story of Yanam—Mottos—At Karikal—At Tranquebar—Mr. Ratnaswamy Nadar—Major Helmich's tomb—Barthelom Ziegenbaig—Evening service—Representations of Last Supper—Visit to Nagur—Return to Negapatam—Arrival at Kumbhakonam—Meaning of name—Cauvery waters—Government college—Higher education—Reception at Railway station—Native entertainment—Busy day—Town *en fête*—Hail, hero of Ganjam—Visits to institutions—"Young India's" manners—Mr. Seshaya Sastryar—Ceremony of weighing against gold—Interesting picture—Sports at Kumbhakonam college——Exhibition of local manufactures—Caste girls' school—Incident—More addresses—Gambling in district—A story—Tank illuminations—Departure—At Cuddalore—Its early history—Fort St. David—Rama Raja—East India Company—Fall of Madras—Dupleix—Collector's house—Clive's attempt at suicide—French in Pondicherry—Victories of peace—Addresses—Visit to Fort St. David—Arrival at Guindy Park.

ON September 5th, 1889, the Governor left Ootacamund, making a short tour through the Tanjore and South Arcot districts on his way to Madras. The departure from Metapolliam was by the evening instead of by the usual midday train so that Ootacamund was not left till 4 P.M. A large gathering of officials and others assembled on the slopes of the Government House gardens to wish His Excellency good-bye.

The descent of the ghât in the light of the setting sun was lovely in the extreme. It was the first day of brilliant fine weather we had had after two or three

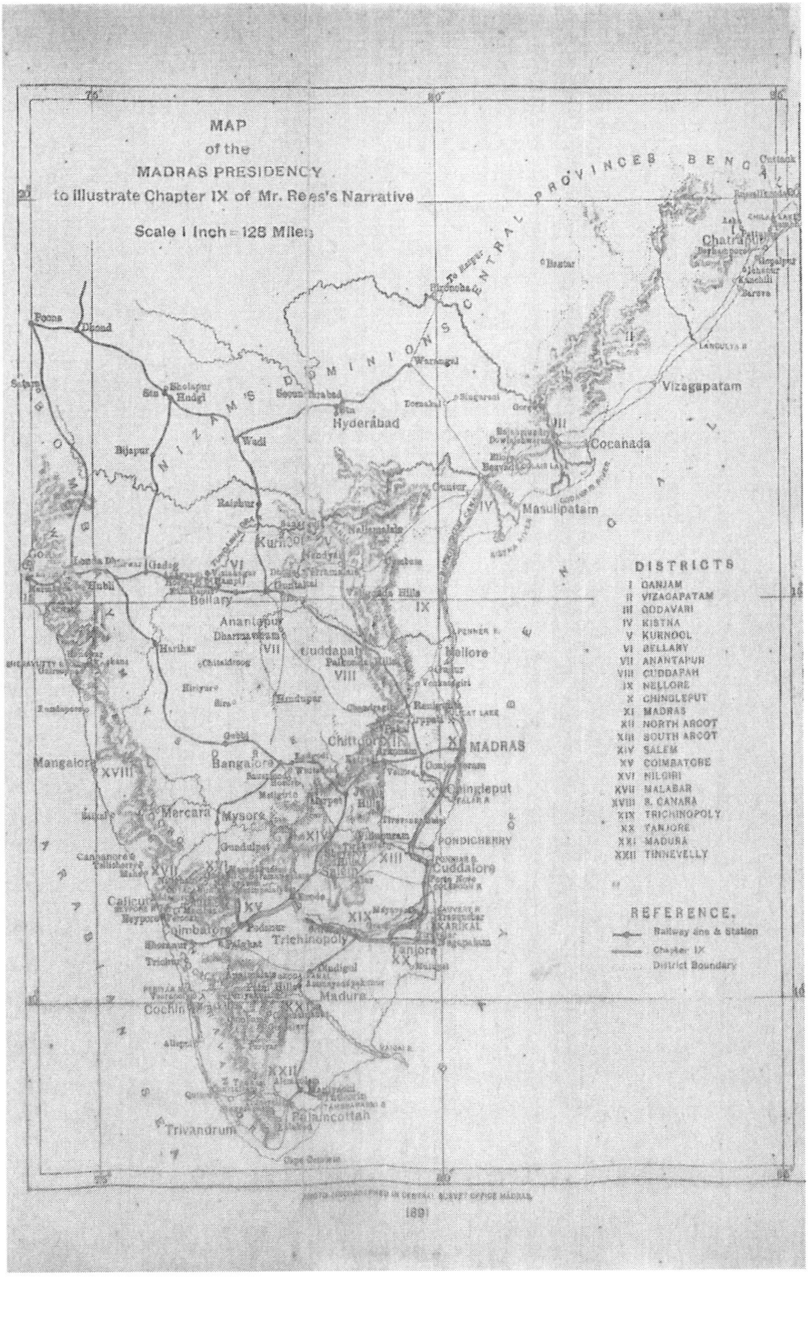
MAP
of the
MADRAS PRESIDENCY
to illustrate Chapter IX of Mr. Rees's Narrative
Scale 1 Inch = 128 Miles
DISTRICTS
I GANJAM
II VIZAGAPATAM
III GODAVARI
IV KISTNA
V KURNOOL
VI BELLARY
VII ANANTAPUR
VIII CUDDAPAH
IX NELLORE
X CHINGLEPUT
XI MADRAS
XII NORTH ARCOT
XIII SOUTH ARCOT
XIV SALEM
XV COIMBATORE
XVI NILGIRI
XVII MALABAR
XVIII S. CANARA
XIX TRICHINOPOLY
XX TANJORE
XXI MADURA
XXII TINNEVELLY
REFERENCE.
Railway line & Station
Chapter IX
District Boundary
CENTRAL PROVINCES
NIZAMS DOMINIONS
Hyderâbad
Vizagapatam
Cocanada
Masulipatam
Kurnool
Bellary
Anantapur
Nellore
Chittoor
MADRAS
Chingleput
Bangalore
Mangalore
Mercara
Mysore
PONDICHERRY
Cuddalore
Calicut
Salem
Trichinopoly
Tanjore
KARIKAL
Madura
Cochin
Trivandrum
Palamcottah
1891

months of monsoon, and as we drove down, the hills in the distance stood out in sharp purple relief, while below them the plains appeared covered with a deep blue haze. The bright green foliage of the jungle, above which towered steep masses of rugged rock, formed a fitting foreground.

We* dined at Metapolliam and were brought to Erode in the middle of the night, sleeping there till the early morning, when we changed into a special train of the South Indian Railway, the engine of which was gaily decorated with flowers and foliage. By 10 o'clock we were at Trichinopoly, where the Governor was met by the residents, and at breakfast we had the rare privilege of meeting a Mahomedan lady who took part in the meal, and joined in the conversation in the most charming manner possible. She was the wife of a Mr. Shujat Ali, one of the so-called "Statutory Civil Servants," who is Head Assistant Collector and Magistrate of the district. It was not the first time His Excellency had had the pleasure of meeting Mr. and Mrs. Shujat Ali as he was their guest at Honawar last year (see 7th Tour). For Hindu ladies to mix in European society is becoming a by no means rare occurrence, but the rules of seclusion are much stricter among the Mahomedans, from whom indeed the Hindus probably took their ideas on the subject, and it was an encouraging sign of the times to meet with a lady who had had the necessary inde-

* His Excellency The Lord Connemara, G.C.I.E.
Mr. Claude Vincent, Acting Private Secretary, and Captain Williams, A.D.C.

pendence of character to break through a foolish tradition.

After breakfast the Governor received a municipal address on the platform, a portion of which had been railed off for the occasion and was rendered fragrant and pretty by means of garlands of oleander flowers.

We halted at Tanjore for a few minutes and in the evening arrived at Negapatam, where we were met by a large crowd and a guard of honour of the South Indian Railway Volunteers. The whole population lined the streets as we drove to Mr. Crighton's hospitable mansion, triumphal arches spanned the roadway at frequent intervals, while school children sang Tamil hymns and showered flowers upon us as we passed.

Negapatam, the meaning of which is "snake city," is one of the oldest towns on the east coast of India. It is mentioned by a Chinese traveller of the 7th century. It afterwards formed one of the earliest Portuguese settlements, was taken by the Dutch in 1660, and from the latter by the English in 1781. It is now a flourishing port with a rising trade, and the terminus of the South Indian Railway Company.

The next morning we were conducted by Mr. Crighton over the railway workshops of which he is in charge. It was a gala day and while the outside of the shops was rendered gay with bunting, the severity of the inside and of the many intricate machines there in use was relieved by means of bright garlands. An allegorical picture at the entrance, a production of local talent, showed us the South Indian Railway in the guise of an ostrich proudly marching ahead, while its rival, the Madras Railway, typified by a small bird, was lagging hopelessly in the rear! We saw the sights usual on such occasions, masses of molten metal under the steam hammer, &c., but these so unnerved one of our native attendants that he fairly turned tail and ran as if he had seen the fiend incarnate.

There was a municipal address and levée in the afternoon, and in the evening the Governor inaugurated a new Club for the European residents.

The next morning we drove 20 miles to Tranquebar, the "place of waves," an old Danish settlement which was granted to the Danes in 1620 by the then Raja of Tanjore in consideration of an annual payment. It was taken by the English in 1807, but restored to Denmark in 1814 and remained in her possession till 1845 when it was bought by the East India Company for £120,000.

The road to it lay for some miles through the territory of Karikal, which is a small French settlement, and so within the space of one morning we had been over ground which may be said to epitomise the history of the conquest of the east coast of India, ground which had formed the subject of rivalry, friendly or hostile, between the leading colonising nations of Europe, Portuguese, Dutch, Danes, French and English. Of these, the two latter only now remain, and while the one has spread its arms over the whole country, the other is restricted to a few square miles of territory, which it continues to hold more from a feeling of *amour propre* than from any possibility of usefulness that the retention of them can serve.

Besides Karikal and the large colony of Pondicherry France has two other settlements in the Madras Presidency even smaller than Karikal, Mahé and Yanam. Of the latter an amusing story is related, which is typical. A visitor was going round the place with the "Administrateur." They came to a room which was evidently intended for prisoners but which was empty and the door of which was open. "You are fortunate in having no prisoners," said the visitor. "Oh! indeed, we have," replied the "Administrateur," with his pride somewhat ruffled, "that is," he added, "we have one." "Where is he?" was the question. "Well, you see," was the reply, "it is hardly worth while keeping up an establishment for the sake of one prisoner, so we allow him to live where he likes on condition that he reports himself on the first of every month!"

There was a marked contrast in the condition of the road over which we drove in its English and French portions, the latter being sadly in need of repair, but the town of Karikal was bright and clean enough, and the house of the "Administrateur," with the Tricolor flying over it, situated in a small "place," looked very comfortable and smart, and the whole place reminded one of a French provincial town. It was curious to read over the shops in this out-of-the-way corner the familiar signs of "debit de tabac," "salle des ventes," &c.

Tranquebar, after its purchase from the Danes, was constituted the head-quarters of the Tanjore district, but with the location of the railway terminus at

Negapatam its importance declined, the head-quarters were transferred to Tanjore in 1860, and it is now falling into decay. The town is still surrounded by its old wall which is in a fair state of preservation, and the streets are laid out in the European fashion with the houses side by side and without verandahs, which must make them very hot. The house we stayed in was, however, a very fine one, close to the sea, and beautifully cool. It was the old Government House but now belongs to a Mr. Ratnaswami Nadar, a large "abkári" contractor, and one of the richest and most influential men in this rich and progressive district.

In the evening we visited the citadel which has nothing remarkable to distinguish it. As a curious link with the past we saw in one of the many graveyards the tomb of a Major Helmich of the Danish army, whose son had visited the Governor in the afternoon. This gentleman had been born in Tranquebar and had served 47 years as a Civil Servant of the British Crown in Western Australia where he had risen to be Postmaster-General and Superintendent of Telegraphs. Retired now on a pension he had returned to the scenes of his childhood and what changes he must have observed.

Tranquebar has the reputation of having been the first seat of the Protestant Missions in India, and in one of the churches we visited we were shown a tomb purporting to be that of the first Protestant Missionary. Barthelom Ziegenbaig was the name inscribed thereon, born in 1683 and who died in 1719. The church now belongs to the Leipsic Lutheran Mission.

In the evening we attended divine service in a church which formerly belonged to a Danish Mission, but is now in charge of the Society for the Propagation of the Gospel. The service was intoned by a native clergyman. In the vestry of this church is a representation of the Last Supper, not by Leonardo da Vinci. It is carved out of wood, the figures being in high relief and painted in bright red and blue and green; altogether the most extraordinary representation of the sacred feast it is possible to imagine.

The next morning we drove back to Negapatam, stopping on the way at Nagur, a great Mahomedan centre, where there is a fine mosque which is the object of pious pilgrimage from all parts of India.

In the afternoon the train took us to Kumbhakonam stopping at Tanjore. Kumbhakonam is a very ancient town, the local tradition attributing its foundation to a date immediately subsequent to that of the deluge. Its name signifies the mouth (literally nose) of a water-jar, and is justified by its position on the sacred river Cauvery which irrigates in Tanjore district an area of 800,000 acres of rice-land. Kumbhakonam is the great Brahminical centre of Southern India, and as such has necessarily become the centre also of the modern "High School" education which is in a large measure a Brahmin monopoly. As an educational residence the place has one decided advantage over all other resorts of learning in the world. The waters of the Cauvery at Kumbhakonam are said to be so refreshing that a student after the hardest day's work has only to bathe in them to find the true elixir of life, and to have all his fatigue of mind or body completely washed away.

The Kumbhakonam College under the intelligent management of Mr. Bilderbeck is a most flourishing institution and sends up a number of successful candidates for degrees at the examinations of the Madras University. A number of High Schools are also in a very prosperous condition and serve to furnish either students for the College or candidates for the various examinations that have to be passed to qualify for the public service. The demand for higher education among the Hindus, particularly among the Brahmins, is exceedingly keen, and they show themselves to be the most eager and apt of pupils. It is a misfortune, however, that almost every youth who passes an examination looks upon the Government service as the goal of his ambition. The supply of educated material is largely in excess of any possible demand Government is likely to make upon it, and though this causes a not unhealthy competition and a very high standard of excellence in those who are selected, yet it results in a feeling of dissatisfaction—active or passive, but not seldom the former—in those who do not succeed in getting into the Government service. The learning too is almost exclusively book-learning, the practical application of the arts and sciences not flourishing, partly owing to want of opportunity for instruction and partly to a lack of inclination and aptitude on the part of the young Hindus.

The Governor was met at the station by the usual municipal deputation and address. The latter was, however, unusual in this, that it merely offered a welcome and preferred no requests. After dinner we were present at a native entertainment which terminated unfortunately. A large temporary shed, the inside of which was beautifully decorated, had been put up for his reception, but sparks from a display of fireworks outside set fire to the thatched roof and in five minutes the structure was in ashes. Although there was an immense crowd of people luckily no one was injured.

The next day was a busy one and the Governor had to make no less than five speeches. A reception committee had organised the proceedings, the whole town was "*en fête*," and the principal points of interest had been lavishly decorated. We were reminded of our last tour by the inscription "Hail, hero of Ganjam" on one of the triumphal arches. The Governor's visit there in May and the benefits resulting therefrom have earned him the warm encomiums of all sections of the community.

We began the day by visiting the two principal Native High Schools, in each of which the Governor gave some good advice to the students about their behaviour towards their superiors and inferiors. There have been numerous complaints of late that the demeanour of Young India is sadly lacking in respect, but perhaps the fault lies not a little with the teaching staff, boys in such matters being taught more readily by example than by precept.

In one of the schools the Governor selected a boy aged only 12 and told him to explain the 15th proposition of Book I of Euclid, which he did without a moment's hesitation or a trace of shyness. We doubted whether an average English boy would have been so ready.

We afterwards visited the house of the Native Chairman of the Municipality, Mr. Thumbuswami Mudelliar, and that of Dewan Bahadur Seshaya Shastri, C.S.I., now Dewan Regent of Puducotta, one of the most accomplished and agreeable gentlemen it would be possible to meet. He was formerly Minister to the Maha Raja of Travancore and has in his house an interesting reminiscence of that country in the shape of a picture presented to him by the Maha Raja, showing the latter seated in a scale being weighed against gold. This is a ceremony which each successive Maha Raja of Travancore has to go through, the gold being subsequently distributed to charitable institutions. The painting is in oils by a native artist, and is very well executed. Little pots of growing rice are pictured before the Maha Raja as a sign of plenty. The Dewan's house realises the utmost desires of an orthodox Brahmin in Southern India. Situated in the holy town of Kumbhakonam and so placed on the banks of the sacred Cauvery that a portion of it is built on arches through which the river runs, the happy owner has a private bathing platform, and can thus perform his ablutions and offer his prayers to heaven within the seclusion of his own walls.

In the evening we drove to the Kumbhakonam College where we saw the final heats of some athletic sports in which great proficiency was displayed. A leading student in thanking His Excellency for presiding, quoted Shakespeare in support of physical culture!

We had previously seen an interesting exhibition

of local manufactures, especially the famous Tanjore metal-ware and silk-weaving. A class of a caste girls' school was also brought to the College in charge of a Native Mistress who spoke English fluently, and nothing could be prettier than the sight of these children gaily got up with jewels and bright coloured cloths. They showed great proficiency in drawing and sang an English song in the most charming manner possible. But two of them aged about 12 were shortly to go through their second marriage ceremony and to leave the happy innocence of school-life while scarcely yet more than infants.

Two more addresses were presented at the Town Hall, one of which complained of the increase of gambling. As regards this the Collector, Mr. Gibson, told us a curious story. It seems that, in this district, a mania for lotteries had developed, promoted by shrewd merchants who thus obtained the money wherewith to extend their trading operations. They gave good prizes, but kept the capital in their hands for a long time and so obtained the use of it and the interest on it. The gambling spirit spread to the schools and boys got up lotteries amongst themselves. It was time for the authorities to interfere, but after the Collector had taken steps to suppress the lotteries he received a letter of remonstrance from a schoolmaster who took up the original ground that lotteries encouraged habits of thrift, and compared them in this respect to the Post Office Savings Bank very much to the disadvantage of the latter!

We afterwards drove round a very fine bathing tank, which was beautifully illuminated, and returned to our hospitable quarters almost smothered with the lovely flower garlands that are presented here on State occasions in great profusion. We had had a most interesting and instructive day.

The next morning we proceeded to Cuddalore, "the town at the junction of the rivers," which is the head-quarters of the South Arcot district and a place intimately connected with the history of our conquest of Southern India. For here was Fort St. David which in August 1690 was sold by Ram Raja, king of the Chenchi country, to the "Right Honourable East India Company" for the sum of 40,000 chuckrums and who generously promised "to assist and defend you in the quiett and free possession thereof from ye French and from all other European nations and other." On the fall of Madras in 1746, the British Administration withdrew to Cuddalore, which was soon afterwards twice unsuccessfully besieged by the French under Dupleix. The head-quarters of the Presidency remained here till 1752, when the Government returned to Madras. In 1758, the French occupied the town, and stormed and destroyed the fort, but in 1760, after the battle of Wandiwash, the British regained possession. In 1782 it again fell into the hands of the French and their ally Tippu Sultan, by whom the fortifications were sufficiently renewed to enable it to withstand in the following year a siege and several assaults. During the siege a drawn battle was fought in the roadstead between the French and English fleets. In 1785, Cuddalore was formally restored to the British, and in 1801 it was included in the cession of the Carnatic.

Here too is the house, in which we stayed, wherein Clive in 1749 made his famous attempt at suicide. But the ancient military glory of Cuddalore has departed. Traces of the famous fort still remain but what is left is in ruins and though the place bears the reputation of being a very pleasant "up-country station" and though its residents are remarkable for their sociability, there is nothing else that is noteworthy about it. Its inhabitants have no longer the fear before their eyes of rival European nations spreading war over the land. Pondicherry is only 12 miles distant, but the French now find the pursuits of peace more attractive than the toils of war and cross the frontier rather in the hope of marrying the fairest of our daughters than of making prisoners of the bravest of our men.

And so the addresses from municipalities to the Governor in this place so rich in historical recollections consisted merely of the usual prosaic requests as regards water-supply, drainage and the provision of the necessary funds. "Ask that it may be given you" is the sage motto of these intelligent and enterprising bodies.

In the evening we visited Fort St. David, charmingly situated close to the sea and on the edge of a backwater. We were shown an underground passage lined with brick which used to pass all round the line of defences.

A very hot night in the train brought us in to Guindy Park, Madras, early on the morning of September 13th.

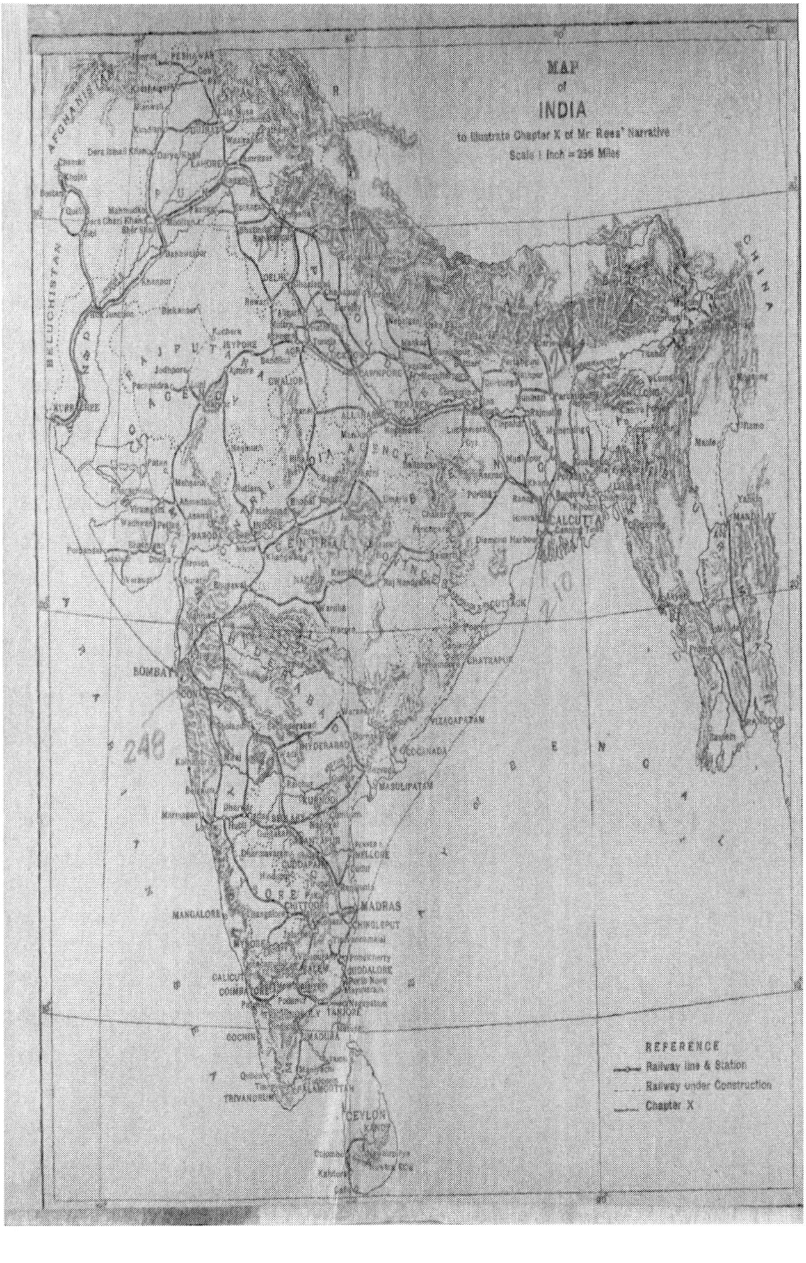
MAP
of
INDIA
to Illustrate Chapter X of Mr. Rees' Narrative
Scale 1 Inch = 236 Miles
REFERENCE
Railway line & Station
Railway under Construction
Chapter X
AFGHANISTAN
BELUCHISTAN
CHINA
PESHAWAR
LAHORE
DELHI
JEYPORE
GWALIOR
CAWNPORE
ALLAHABAD
BENARES
CALCUTTA
INDORE
BARODA
NAGPUR
CUTTACK
CHATRAPUR
BOMBAY
HYDERABAD
VIZAGAPATAM
COCANADA
MASULIPATAM
KURNOOL
BELLARY
NELLORE
CUDDAPAH
MADRAS
CHINGLEPUT
MANGALORE
CALICUT
COIMBATORE
TANJORE
COCHIN
MADURA
TRIVANDRUM
CEYLON
KANDY
MANDALAY
RANGOON

CHAPTER X.

CALCUTTA, DARJEELING, ALLAHABAD, SIMLA, QUETTA, KURRACHEE AND BOMBAY.

Governor embarks for Calcutta—Our party—Arrival at Hoogly—Saugor island—Landing at Calcutta—Conference with Sir Steuart Bayley—East Coast Railway—Journey to Darjeeling—Darjeeling railway—Scenery *en route*—"Shrubbery"—Maha Raja of Cooch Behar—Himalayan snows—Kangchenjinga peak—Observatory hill—Senchal hill—Sikkim frontier expedition—Tibetians—Chinese amban—Connaught Rangers—Tiger Hill—Mount Everest—Bazaars—Bhooteans—Lepchas—Buddhist temples—Best Lama twist—Curious religious ceremony—Kurseong—Arrival in Calcutta—Local opium dues—Allahabad—Visit to fort—Junction of Ganges and Jumna—Mr. Justice Straight—Agra—Fort—Akbar's tomb at Secundra—Taj by moonlight—Saharunpore—Umballa—General Galbraith—Black Mountain expedition—Kalka—*En route* to Simla—Himalayan trees—Liliputian rice-fields—Sonawar—Dagshai—Solon—Arrival at Simla—Viceregal lodge—Goorkhas—Jutogh battery practice—Wiltshire regiment—Prospect hill—Sutlej and Jumna—Fakir—Kerosine oil tins—Busy days—Departure from Simla—Arrival at Lahore—Lieutenant Governor's house—Cathedral—Mayo hall—Shalimar gardens—Fort—Sir James and Lady Lyall—Camel-riding—Mosque—Tomb of Runjeet Singh—Sikh Bible—Fort armoury—Durbar hall—Departure from Lahore—Rohri—Lansdowne bridge—Bukkur—Sukkur—Indus—Sadh Bela—Sindhis—Sind-Pishin line—Chappar rift—Bostan—Kilah Abdulla—Khojak pass—Khwaja Amran Mountains—Beloochistan—Khelat territory—Quetta—General Sir George White—Sir Robert Sandeman—Fort—Market—Parsi merchant—Anecdote—Durbar—Duranis—Popalzais — Barukzais — Presentations—Governor's speech—Sirdar Asad Khan—Benefits of British rule—Baleli—Gulistan—Railway from Kilah Abdulla—Kandahar—Punjaubis—Pathans—Shalibagh—Old Chaman—New Chaman—Murder of Captain Harris—Book on thieves—Headman of Kasee village—Brahui entertainment—Departure from Quetta—Sir James Brown's railway—Chappar rift—Hurnai route—Sibi route—Bolan pass—Babar Kach—Ruk junction—*En route* Kurrachee—Tragic occurrence—Sehwan—Kotri—Manora headland—At Kurrachee—Frere hall—Campanile—Signboards—Saint and his crocodiles—Sind population—Local buildings—Trade—Embarkation—Dwarka—Somnath—Bombay harbour—Reception at Apollo Bunder—Duke of Connaught—Sir Harry Prendergast—Bhore ghaut—Arrival at Madras.

THE Governor arrived in Madras from his ninth tour on September 13th, and, after spending eight days at Guindy Park, embarked for Calcutta on his way to Simla, whither he had been invited by the Viceroy to confer on several important public questions.

We * left Madras at 6 P.M. on September 21st, 1889, in the S.S. *Kapurthala* of the British India Steam Navigation Company, and arrived at the mouth of the Hooghly, after a pleasant and uneventful voyage, on the morning of September 24th.

Taking our pilot on board we went on as far as Saugor, where the tide failed us and we had to anchor. The afternoon was utilised in visiting the lighthouse and telegraph station whence the arrival and departure of ships are notified to Calcutta. An extensive view is obtained from the top of the lighthouse. The island of Saugor consists of a close jungle which swarms with deer and pig, and the whole of the buildings are surrounded by a strong palisading to protect them from the attacks of the tigers with which the place used to be infested. Returning to our steamer we found the surf rising, so we had to wade out to our boat, and one of the party took an involuntary bath in the water of the sacred Ganges.

The next morning we went on to Calcutta, and at 4 P.M. His Excellency landed, being received by Captain Currie, on behalf of the Lieutenant-Governor, by some of the Bengal officials and by a guard of honour

---

* His Excellency The Lord Connemara, G.C.I.E.
Mr. Claude Vincent, Acting Private Secretary.
The Viscount Marsham and Captain Fowle, 21st Hussars, A.D.Cs.

of the 4th Bengal Infantry. We were not due at Simla till October 5th, so the Governor took advantage of the occasion to pay a visit to Darjeeling, and to confer there with Sir Steuart Bayley, the Lieutenant-Governor of Bengal. The proposed East Coast Railway, now likely soon to become an accomplished fact, and the distress in Ganjam and Orissa, which are adjoining districts of the two provinces, formed topics of common interest.

On landing we drove straight to the railway station, and by 8 o'clock the following morning, after a hot night in the train, we were at Silliguri, whence starts the remarkable little railway that runs up to Darjeeling, ascending 7,000 feet in 50 miles.

It is on the 2-feet gauge, and the passenger carriages are simply platforms on which are rows of seats, with a covering overhead to protect one from the sun and rain.

The engines weigh from 10 to 15 tons and are very powerful, dragging up a train of 15 or 16 carriages at a good speed, the ruling gradient being about 1 in 28. The inception and execution of this useful line are due to Mr. Prestage, and it has proved a great financial success, paying nearly 10 per cent. on its capital. The line follows, for the most part, the old cart-road, but various ingenious devices, such as spirals and reversing stations, have had to be resorted to in order to get it over some of the more difficult portions.

It was a lovely day and we had beautiful glimpses as we ascended of the plains below us and of the surrounding hills. Sometimes the line passes through what looks like an artificial avenue of forest-trees; sometimes it traverses dense jungle in which we see growing huge tree-ferns and the broad leaves of the wild plantain and calladium, while colour is given by the purple clusters of the so-called Sikkim rose; sometimes it skirts perilously near the edge of a sheer precipice.

As we neared Darjeeling there was a rift in the usual evening mist, and we had a fine view of the snowy ranges.

Sir Steuart Bayley was at the station to meet Lord Connemara, and accompanied by a guard of mounted volunteers we proceeded to The Shrubbery, the picturesque and charming residence of the Lieutenant-Governor, at the gate of which was drawn up a guard of honour from the European troops stationed at Darjeeling. Several officials and the Maha Raja of Cooch Behar were also present to welcome His Excellency.

The next day we were up early to get a view of the snows, which, if visible at all, are generally so in the early morning before the sun has drawn the clouds up out of the valleys. They are often invisible for days and weeks together, but fortune favored us. The morning sky was cloudless and Kangchenjinga—"the five pinnacles or treasuries of snow"—stood before us in silent majesty and matchless purity. The highest peak is 28,156 feet high and is only distant 45 miles in a direct line from Darjeeling, but it is difficult to realise its enormous elevation, principally, no doubt, because of the height from which it is viewed. With a telescope we were easily able to see the precise formation of the range and to note the places from which avalanches of the recently-fallen snow had thundered down. Observatory Hill, from which a fine panoramic view of the whole of the semicircle of mountains is obtained, is close by and we made the ascent. This hill is locally sacred, and while there we observed several hill people performing a curious ceremony. Long strings of parti-coloured cloth are sewn together and cut into jagged edges, each point representing a prayer, and are then hung up on to trees looking towards Lhasa, "the seat of the Gods," which is the Buddhist Mecca. Oblations of rice and fruits are meanwhile offered.

In the afternoon we descended about 2,000 feet to see the Tukwar Tea Estate, which, under the management of Mr. Curtis, turns out about 300,000 lbs. annually of tea of a very fine quality, fetching a high price in the London market. Everything was very well-ordered and prosperous. On our way back we were pointed out the local Mount Ararat, Tendong by name, where, according to Buddhist tradition, humanity was saved during the flood. Religions vary in their developments, but the underlying traditions are common to nearly all, and the last Mount Ararat we had seen, was pointed out to us by a Persian believer in the faith of Islam near the Caspian Sea.

At dinner that evening we had the pleasure of meeting their Highnesses the Maha Raja and Maha Rani of Cooch Behar.

The next day we ascended Senchal Hill, 1,600 feet above Darjeeling, where there used to be barracks for the convalescents of European regiments. But the mists and the rain made the place unhealthy and the lack of occupation engendered depression of spirits, so that fever and suicide became common, and the place had to be abandoned. Now only the chimneys of the barracks remain to mark their site, and these are weather-beaten and moss-grown, and looked ghostly through the mist in which we saw them. A mountain battery of artillery, under the command of Major Keith, R.A., was collected on the hill, and we were shown some excellent mimic warfare with blank cartridge. The guns are of the Armstrong pattern and have a range of over 3,000 yards. They are so constructed as to take to pieces readily and to pack on to the backs of mules, and the unlimbering and limbering up that we saw done did not occupy more than two minutes. This battery has recently been engaged on the Sikkim frontier expedition, the object of which was to drive the Tibetians out of Sikkim, which is a protected State. The Tibetians had practically occupied the hills, and trade was at a standstill. The object of the expedition was accomplished after one fight, and the Tibetians have retired behind their own border, but it has been found necessary to keep * some troops in Sikkim to prevent incursions, and half a battalion of British Infantry, the Connaught Rangers, besides native troops, are encamped 100 miles from Darjeeling in the wild hills.

---

* They waited there a long while for the advent of the Chinese Amban, or as the soldiers called him the Chinese Umpire. They were as facetious as ever in spite of the cold, and were always saying, "Well we can't find this umpire, now we have come to *seek 'im*." J.D.R.

We heard a characteristic story of this little war. The Tibetians had announced themselves as prepared to exterminate all the troops we were presumptuous enough to send against them, and they built a strong stone wall and awaited our attack. After a sharp action, they had to retire in the utmost confusion. Whereupon remarked a man of Sikkim to a captured Tibetian: "If you cannot stop the British when you are behind such defences as that, what is the use of your expecting to stop them anywhere?"

After luncheon we went up Tiger Hill, from which on fine days Mount Everest, the highest point in the world, is visible. But it was cloudy and we did not see it. It is 854 feet higher than Kangchenjinga, but owing to its distance its height appears less.

The next day was Sunday, and we saw in the church a tablet to the General Lloyd who was the founder of Darjeeling. The pulpit is "in memoriam" to Lady Canning, who is buried at Barrackpore (see Chapter IV).

After service we went through the bazaar accompanied by Mr. Paul, the Deputy Commissioner. It was market-day and the place was crowded with Bhooteans and Lepchas, who are the local inhabitants, and there were also many Tibetians. It was a busy scene. They all had on their best and brightest clothes, the women were gay with coin necklaces and with silver ornaments covered with rough turquoises or other stones, and many of them had on their wrist a curious bracelet cut out of shell, which would seem to bear some sort of affinity to our marriage ring.

The natives of Darjeeling are a pleasant good-humoured set of people, fond of a joke and always with a smile on their faces. They are not handsome but many of them are almost as fair as Europeans and have a high colour. Many of the younger women are however passably good-looking.

We also visited the shop of a Mr. Paul Möwis, who is a great collector of curios, and saw there some fine weapons, some of the Buddhist praying wheels, which, if turned in one direction yield prayers, and if in the other curses, some wooden sundials in the form of walking sticks, and a beautiful collection of local butterflies and moths. Of these some had their wings coloured exactly like dead leaves. There is one swallow-tailed butterfly found only here which is the *rara avis* of collectors. A good female specimen of this is said to be worth £20.

In the afternoon we visited a * Buddhist temple and witnessed the queerest religious ceremony imaginable. The Governor was met by a procession of priests, who presented him with a sacred scarf, and then, preceded by drums and trumpets, we entered the shrine. In the doorway was a huge praying wheel which the local Buddhists engage a man to turn at so much an hour, and thus offer up vicarious

---

* The temples here are very disappointing. On an altar not far from Darjeeling two bottles containing flowers proved, on inspection, to bear labels of Highland whiskey and Plymouth gin. It is a far cry from Sikkim to Columbo, but in the large Buddhist temple near the latter town, one of the altars is disfigured by pictures taken from the wrappings of English cotton goods. Curiously enough, the paper, with more sense of propriety than was possessed by the priests, was inscribed with the words, "Best Lama Twist."
J.D.R.

prayers. Three images of Buddha were behind glass in the shrine, and the priests sat down in two rows in front of these and repeated a prayer, the burden of which was the mysterious Buddhist invocation:

> "*Om mani padme hum.*" Oh Lord of the jewel and the lotus.

There was a musical accompaniment, and the noise caused by the trumpets, the cymbals, the shell horns and other instruments was prodigious.

On Monday morning, at 12 o'clock, we left Darjeeling with the same ceremony that had attended His Excellency's arrival, but instead of going down the ghât in the ordinary train, we went down on a trolly under the charge of Mr. Cary, the General Manager of the Railway Company. This enabled us to start an hour and-a-half later than the other passengers and catch them up at the foot of the hill. It is a novel form of travelling; indeed, as one of the party observed, it is worth while coming up to Darjeeling if only to experience the sensation of going down on a trolly. An engine took us up to the top of the slight incline at the bottom of which Darjeeling lies, and then, casting us off, left us to descend by the force of gravity alone. We started gently, but quickly gathering speed, we went whizzing along round curves and past the edges of precipices at a breakneck pace. It is a form of travelling that looks dangerous and feels dangerous, and the description of which sounds dangerous, but it is undeniably a most fascinating mode of progression, and the trollies are so absolutely under control by means of powerful breaks that there is really very little risk about it. Accidents, however, do happen. Lady Bayley and her daughter were thrown out recently while going down, and a note on the trolly-pass which was handed to us looked ominous as it told us that the Company would not be responsible for any accident or injury to passengers or their property. The speed in descending averages 15 miles an hour, but it is often more. We halted at Kurseong, a lovely spot, for lunch, and finally about 5 P.M., with a final race along a straight piece, we joined the train, which had been waiting for us at the foot.

The next morning we arrived in Calcutta, where the Governor was the guest of Mr. Charles Moore. In the afternoon, in the company of the Commissioner of Police, he visited the opium-smoking dens, a gruesome sight, but less harrowing perhaps than the sight of the drunkenness in the slums of our own great cities. Opium-smoking is a form of vice that is at least silent and hidden away. In the evening we went on by the mail train to Allahabad, where we arrived at 5 o'clock on the afternoon of October 2nd, being received by Mr. Justice Straight, with whom His Excellency stayed. A guard of honour from the East Surrey regiment was on the platform. Here Mr. Rees, who had been to England on leave, rejoined His Excellency, and I handed over charge of my duties to him.

While staying at Allahabad, where Mr. Vincent to our regret left us, we visited the fort. There is indeed but little else to see, except the junction of the Ganges and the Jumna, at once the glory of the city and its *raison d'être.* It was extremely hot here, and the house had to be closed, and the day spent in darkened rooms. Our kind host, Mr. Justice Straight, assured us, however, that the heat was exceptional for this time of the year. I remember being told the same thing, when I was at Allahabad before.

Next day we went by train to Agra, to halt the night and see the Taj Mahal by moonlight. The fort and Akbar's tomb at Secundra were also visited in the course of a busy day. The Taj has been too often described to justify any attempt to describe its beauties in this narrative. The last and by no means the least beautiful description of its moonlit glories appeared so lately as last May in the *Nineteenth Century*, from the pen of Lady Jersey, one of the most observant of recent travellers in India. To those who have not seen it in its moon-silvered aspect, I would say they have by no means tasted of the fulness of its glories.

After travelling all night and all day, we reached Umballa on the evening of the 5th of October, the snows of the lower Himalayas becoming visible about Saharunpore. At Umballa Colonel Cook entertained us on behalf of General Galbraith, the General commanding the station, who recently commanded a brigade in the Black Mountain expedition.

Another night's travelling—this time in a dâk gharry, or posting carriage,—brought us to Kalka, at the foot of the ascent to Simla. Only one of the party succeeded in sleeping, and a continuance of hot days and sleepless nights made the prospect of Simla more than ever agreeable. The road is, however, white, glaring, and dusty, and the scenery not particularly fine. Himalayan trees, extremely like Scotch firs, sparsely dot the hillsides, and as the road winds along its gradual ascent you look down into great valleys, terraced into Lilliputian rice-fields. Sonawar and Dagshai, each perched on its respective hill being left behind, we found breakfast at Solon, and at 2 o'clock arrived at Simla.

The new Viceregal Lodge is built on the top of one of the highest hills, and is approached through a wooden gateway of a Buddhistic appearance which is heightened by the presence of a guard of Mongol-faced Goorkhas. The gate is of wood on a small, what those of Pekin are, of stone on a large, scale. The guards naturally salute in the usual military style, but the Buddhists have among them some curious fashions of salutation, and at Darjeeling, at a Lama Serai the Governor visited, the priests welcomed him by putting out their tongues, and wagging their heads. So do the little toy-chinamen whose heads when pushed continue to wag with hanging tongues for several minutes. Thus what we take for a humorous caricature of the celestial, may be a faithful picture of his priest.

On the morning of the 9th October, the Governor accompanied the Viceroy, the Commander-in-Chief, and the Military Member of Council, General Chesney, to watch the operations of the Jutogh mountain battery, which is stationed on the top of the next hill to that on which the Viceregal Lodge is situated. At a point where two narrow hill-roads meet, the battery passed by in such review order as the path and the hillside permitted. Seven-pounder screw-guns were packed on the mules' backs, and the carriages, and the wheels and ammunition, and all the belongings of the battery. The mules were of an average size and admirably groomed. Behind the battery marched a company of the Wiltshire regiment. After passing the saluting point, where the Viceroy, Governor and Commander-in-Chief were stationed, the battery marched down a precipitous hillside, to a point where the guns were put together in an incredibly short time. Soon afterwards they commenced firing at screens placed at a distance of 850 yards, solid ball and shrapnel. The latter bursting in the air precipitate a shower of bullets, while the base of the shell travels on to the target, which, in this practice, is very generally hit. Meanwhile, the company of the Wiltshire regiment formed a covering party to protect the battery while being worked. Subsequently, two batteries played from another point upon different targets, and most excellent practice was made throughout the day.

The afternoon was left vacant for work, and walks about the hills, through the deodars, rhododendrons, and Himalayan oaks. From "Prospect Hill" an admirable view of the country around Simla can be obtained, taking in the snowy mountains and exhibiting the ridge, on either side of which the waters of the

Sutlej and the Jumna collect and flow down towards the plains. The country had a dried and burnt-up appearance, and there was little colour but for patches of amaranth here and there on the terraces of the hill-sides.

Simla, unlike many of the hill stations in India, contains no native population apart from that which is accessory to the Europeans living there, and dependent upon them, for its occupation and maintenance. At this time of the year, when the most distant hills show but little snow upon their summits, it is hard to realize that for many months the roads in the station are almost closed with snowdrift, and that snow lingers, as I have seen it, on the Mall till April.

At the top of the hill on which the targets were placed, but well out of range, is a little temple where a Fakir dwells surrounded by rhododendrons and kerosine oil tins. The latter, long since a prominent feature of urban India, promise to make themselves felt in the landscape also. At Quetta we found a soldiers' bath and a school-house spire constructed from these ubiquitous and useful articles.

During the days at Simla the Governor was busily occupied in interviewing the Members of Council and other high officers concerning matters affecting the interests direct or indirect of the Madras Presidency.

Early on the morning of Saturday the 12th, after enjoying the charming and genial hospitality of the Viceregal Lodge for five days, we left Simla, and by 1-30 P.M. had reached the foot of the ghâts after a drive of 58 miles, the greater part of which the horses galloped, taking the corners and sharp turns of the winding hill-road in the most marvellous manner. On the way we passed the mail cart, which delivered a bag of letters and offered others belonging to people who were expected to journey down that day—with such perfection are our postal arrangements made in India. After a brief halt we drove 38 more miles, travelling some way alongside the embankment, which is destined to carry the train to Kalka from Delhi and Umballa, which we had good reason to wish had been already completed. There was very little water in the two rivers we passed, and the broad straight cantonment roads of Umballa were covered, to the depth of perhaps an inch, with fine white dust, which penetrates everything and everywhere.

Next morning at 6-30 A.M. we arrived at Lahore, early enough for a morning walk before church. The air was crisp and cool till the sun was high, and the architecture of the houses, European and native, is adapted as much to cold as to heat, both of which indeed the inhabitants of Lahore experience.

The railway station here resembles in appearance one of the forts of the country, and is in fact a fortified position itself, as are most of the stations on the line where it approaches the frontier. We drove from the station to the Lieutenant-Governor's house in a *char-à-banc* drawn by four camels, on each one of which was seated a driver clothed in scarlet and wearing a cloth of gold head-dress.

Sir James Lyall's house, at which we had the great pleasure to stay, has been built around the tomb of a wrestler, who, however, after building it, elected to be buried elsewhere. The area covered by the dome is now the dining-room, and a very admirable dining-room it makes. Arches around it serve as recesses for side-boards and the like, and through slits in the dome the room is provided with that dim light which is so grateful in the tropics to the tired eye.

The cathedral is a large red-brick structure, in which the officiating clergyman is almost isolated from his congregation. In front of it is a very beautiful new building for the High Court, in the Saracenic style, which harmonises admirably with the ancient buildings, history, and atmosphere of Lahore. Of course the Governor visited the Mayo Hall, a very handsome and spacious edifice erected to the memory of his brother, Lord Mayo.

In the afternoon we rode and drove to Shalimar, a walled garden thickly planted with mango trees and divided into compartments by long reservoirs. In the centre is a pillared marble kiosk, from which on one side descends a screen of white marble ornamented with black lines. Down this the water ripples into a pond below, whence it falls into another reservoir, leading to the extremity of the garden. Outside all is glare and dust; within all is green foliage, white marble, cool reservoir, and rippling cascade.

Next morning we visited the fort. The Governor and Lady Lyall drove; Lord Marsham, Captain Fowle and I rode on camels. Each camel carried besides its rider one of the Lieutenant-Governor's red chuprassis. The reins in camel-riding have to be rested on the top of the camel's head and kept between the beast's ears, as every camel is a star-gazer and holds his head up pointing towards the sky. My off rein came away from the bit, but my companion on board the camel said it did not matter; nor did it apparently—which showed how little my steering effected. Wherever the leader goes the other camels follow. Their favourite game is "follow my leader." The streets of Lahore are narrow, the houses are almost invariably three or four or even more stories high; the ground-floor is generally a shop; in the next floor are bow windows projecting from the façade of the house and resting perhaps on peacock buttresses. The fronts of the houses are in general profusely painted and ornamented. As you sit on your camel you are on a level with the occupant, who is very probably looking at you as you go by from the first-floor window. Sikhs and Muhammadans alike are very fair here. Many of the mosques and gateways are ornamented in Persian fashion with blue tiles inscribed with texts from the Koran.

The great mosque is approached by a huge paved courtyard surrounded by a red sandstone wall. The minarets at each corner of the quadrangle and the mosque itself are built of the same material, on which, in the case of the latter, are worked white marble flowers and traceries. The whole is crowned by three white marble domes, on the summit of each of which is a little golden pinnacle. The effect of the red sandstone and the white marble relieved by nothing but green trees within the square is very simple, and I think very impressive. The wings of the jay supplied the only other bit of colour, and the crescent moon just visible in the daylight looked down upon its not unworthy temple. The mosque is, however, generally out of favour, because, among other reasons, it was built by Aurangzeeb out of the estate of his murdered brother Dara.

Close by is the tomb of Runjeet Singh. On it are eleven knobs of marble, each one representing one of the Maha Raja's wives, who committed suttee and burnt themselves with their deceased lord. Two more knobs are in memory of two pigeons from the neighbouring fort, who also immolated themselves in his honour. The knobs which represent the queens are crowned, while plain knobs record the sacrifices of equally devoted, but less legal wives. Here also is a copy of the Sikh Bible, which is illuminated like a mediæval Missal.

Within the fort is a very interesting armoury containing weapons, armour and ammunition taken from the Sikhs. Herein you see little crowsfeet, which, thrown upon the ground, lame the horses of cavalry, ponderous battle-axes, murderous maces, and a flail called "the morning star," a kind of whip, all, handle, lash and terminal knot alike, of iron. There were cuirasses from France, steel shields exhibiting the rays of the sun, mosquitoons or bell-mouthed pistols called "tigers' whelps," and swords, guns and daggers of every kind and description. The armoury is situated in the Durbar Hall, a corner of the fort whence, through ivory latticed windows, you may, as Runjeet

Singh did, view the country around. There is a curious little hall in this quadrangle, the marble roof of which is shaped like an inverted boat. In the interior it is entirely lined with bits of glass like the well-known hall in the palace at Amber. In the armoury we also saw the uniforms of Runjeet's soldiers and the flags his standard bearers carried into action, on some of which are figures of the Hindu god Hanuman, "the pearl of quadrumanous creatures."

On the evening of Monday, the 14th, we left Lahore and travelled 270 miles in the night, crossing the Sutlej at 7 o'clock in the morning at Adamwahan, whence till nightfall we journeyed through a sandy and level plain, covered with the "ferash" tree, which much resembles a stunted casuarina. Tall grasses, acacias and euphorbias relieved the dull monotony of the plain. Wherever water was available it was apparent that the soil, in spite of its forbidding appearance, amply repaid cultivation. Most of the stations along the line were built in the Saracenic style, with flat roofs and domes. This resulted not only from the possession of taste, but from the absence of wood, on the part of the builders. The names of the stations were tastefully worked in blue letters on glazed tiles, Mooltan, which we passed in the night, being famous for this kind of work.

Just at sunset we came to Rohri, on the eastern bank of the Indus, and crossed the river by the new Lansdowne bridge. Sir Richard Temple has just described this as a "mighty work." On the eastern bank, and on the island of Bukkur are constructed two enormous cantilevers, each of which is 310 feet long, and their extremities are connected by a central girder resting on them, 200 feet in length. The whole makes one span of 820 feet, which is understood to be the* longest in the world, other than spans effected by suspension bridges. The weight of the bridge is 3,300 tons, and in a mean temperature of 100° the iron contracts and expands to such an extent that the noses of the cantilevers rise and fall 6 inches from the effects of temperature. This very successful and remarkable engineering work cost Rs. 38,22,000, including the ordinary girder bridge by which the island of Bukkur is connected with the western or Sukkur bank of the river.

The Indus here pierces a low spur of limestone hills, of which the high ground of Rohri and Sukkur, and the island of Bukkur are portions. It is the most beautiful as well as the most practicable spot for bridging the great river. The houses on either bank tower tier above tier from water-level to hill-top. The island is fairly well wooded and possesses a fortress and a shrine, and as you cross on the great iron roadway you see the lights twinkling in the shrine on Sadh Bela further down stream. In twilight, at any rate, the scene is one of considerable beauty, and in the glare of day and in the blinding sunlight it is sufficiently striking. The advance which has been made in communications in this portion of the world is very much brought home to a traveller, who, like

* This was written before the Forth bridge was opened.

myself, not many years ago crossed the Indus here in a ferry boat.

From Sukkur we travelled all night in the train awaking 180 miles further on, amongst the frontier hills at a distance of about 670 miles from Lahore. The first thing that strikes you here is that it is very apparent that the railway you are travelling on was not constructed for commercial purposes. It passes through a succession of bare and rocky hills between which are valleys of all sizes. Here you understand how it is that amongst the Arabs, a valley and a river are accounted one and the same thing, for many of these little valleys have to be bridged from side to side. Sometimes you pass through a tunnel into a little defile, cross it on a bridge, and find another tunnel on the other side, after passing through which you curve around the inside of a second and a larger valley, in the middle of which another watercourse has to be bridged. Occasional tufts of coarse grass, euphorbias, tamarisks, acacias and camel-thorn make up the vegetation; camels, mules, goats, and the ubiquitous pariah dog are the only animals seen.

At the stations, which are pretty frequent—37 in 305 miles—the employés are mostly men from the plains below, but occasionally you see the Beloochee whose handsome Hebraic cast of face, with ample curling jet-black beard, would attract attention anywhere as a model of its own type of beauty. He wears a large twisted turban of more or less white linen, and a loose white robe of the same material.

At Sukkur it was impossible to help contrasting

civilization and uncivilization, to the disadvantage of the former, in respect of costume. The Sindhis, with their close-fitting buttoned tunic, broadcloth trowsers and polished leather boots crowned the hideousness of their attire by the national hat, which is exactly like the black silk hat we wear in London, except that its brim is at the top instead of at the bottom. The usual three-legged station dog was amongst the occupants of every platform. Most Indian stations of any importance possess a dog which has lost one leg in a railway accident and so has established a claim on railway travellers for the rest of its life.

The Sind-Pishin line has taken a great deal of engineering, and now that it has been completed a notice on the back of the Railway Guide informs travellers that the Railway Administration "will not accept responsibility for injury to any passenger or for loss of or injury to any kind of traffic to a greater extent than Rs. 1,000," say, £100, though they are unfortunately by no means one and the same thing.

The railway ascends from the plains through the Chappar rift, a cleft in the limestone range, to the Hurnai pass. Bostan is the junction whence the line takes off for Kilah Abdulla and the Khojak pass in the Khwaja Amran mountains, which are visible from the station. Near the station is a little orchard, from which presumably it takes its name, though Lord Marsham and Captain Fowle at once named it Boston junction, and would hear of no less commonplace derivation. The presence of apple, nectarine, peach and other fruit trees, the crisp coolness of the air, and a corresponding elevation of the spirits,—all evidence the fact that India is left behind, and that we are now in Central Asia. After passing through parts of Sind and Beloochistan, we have travelled across the Pishin district, ceded to the British by Afghanistan in 1879, and again entered Khelat territory at Quetta at 7 o'clock on the evening of the 16th October, after a journey of nearly 800 miles from Lahore.

On the 17th the Governor, accompanied by General Sir George White and Sir Robert Sandeman, visited the fort of Quetta, from the ramparts of which we saw in one direction the Bolan, and in another the Amran mountains and the Khojak pass. Below us lay the bazaars and barracks, and the public and private buildings of Quetta embosomed among apricot, poplar, mulberry and willow trees.

In the morning a visit was paid to the market, where excellent grapes from Cabul, peaches, pomegranates, apples, and many other fruits were exposed for sale, also to a mill, where an enterprising Parsi makes flour with the latest and most approved machinery. This gentleman has also discovered a coal-mine, or rather is opening a hitherto unworked coal-mine not far from Quetta, the existence of which has long been known to the authorities. That morning I asked an intelligent acquaintance I had made for his views on the frontier. He said they were not at all good. On which I said I thought that he had better let me judge of that, whereon he replied that he would sell me his views. I subsequently discovered that he referred to photographs.

At the Durbar held in the evening were present representatives of the Duranis, Popalzais, Barukzais, and others. Most of these gentlemen were of tall stature and possessed fair faces of a Jewish cast, long black hair and curly Ninivesque beards. They wore fur robes and ample turbans; and most of them gave a friendly look at Sir Robert Sandeman as they got up in turns to bow to the Governor. One of them had a red beard dyed with henna Persian fashion. He was a refugee from Cabul and a follower of Shere Ali. Some of them had their beards divided into two long sausage curls, which trailed down their chests in front. All sat down on their knees on the carpet, while we sat on chairs. Sir Robert Sandeman encourages trade in this frontier district by giving the leading merchants a seat in Durbar. Hence the presence of the Hindu and ubiquitous Parsi. The Governor, after each gentleman had been presented to him, made a short speech, saying that he was glad to make their acquaintance and that he came there as a private individual to see their country. As the representative of the Queen in Southern India, he wished, however, to say that he was very glad to find that merchants from this country came as far south as Cape Comorin, to sell horses, fruits, and other articles of merchandise. He said that those who came south to trade, must go back reporting how peaceful and prosperous Southern India was; and he was quite certain that his hearers appreciated such peace, which always resulted from the supremacy of the British, and now characterised these districts so lately given over to riot and rapine.

His Excellency doubtless did not think this the occasion to say that, besides the *bonâ fide* trader, other Afghans and Beloochees come south, whose appearance in a Hindu village causes much the same panic among the people, as the arrival of a handful of Arabs does among the inhabitants of the east coast of Africa. Sirdar Asad Khan replied on behalf of the Sirdars, thanking the Governor for his kindly sentiments. He said that in the last 14 years he and his brother Sirdars had had ample opportunities of appreciating the benefits of British rule.

On Friday morning we went by train to Baleli, where General White, and other officers of the Royal Engineers and Royal Artillery, took us to inspect the fortifications around Quetta. His Excellency and the General rode horses, but most of us were mounted on very good mules, who never made mistakes in the difficult, stony passes and precipitous hillsides. The horses of the cavalry escort carried their nosebags on the near side of the saddle, while on the off side hung nets containing forage, so packed as to exactly resemble "fenders," board ship. All along the road were strings of camels on their way to Kandahar, some laden and some empty, the latter with their noses turned up and their heads in the air, following one another in Indian file. The camel-riders were mostly clad in sheepskins. After passing Boston junction, the plain is covered with low limestone hummocks, resembling more or less pitched tents. Seen from a little distance a group of them has quite the appearance of a camp. To me it seemed very picturesque, but I dare say many would say, as Sir Charles Napier did, when the country was called picturesque in his hearing, that it was undoubtedly the place where God shot the rubbish when he made the world.

After Boston comes Gulistan. In some places in America you can see that the names of the stations along the railway have been taken as they came in a page of the Classical Dictionary, and here it would seem as if the best known works of Persian literature had supplied the railway nomenclature. Gulistan, the rose garden, is an arid plain covered with camel-thorn, but Boston, the flower garden, does boast of one orchard.

At Kilah Abdulla, the last station to which the line is so far open, at a distance of 59 miles from Quetta, the boundaries of Afghanistan and British Pishin march and a survey is now being made here. I asked the surveyor whether the natives did not misunderstand the purpose of his theodolite and his flag. He said they did, and that one idea they have of the theodolite is that it photographs like a camera, and that pictures are taken, as by the camera, upside down. More than this, they think a person using the theodolite can see through the walls of houses, with the appalling result that the ladies of their families are photographed by the infidel standing on their heads. Consequently, the surveyor is highly unpopular, and is apt to be shot at. A frontier surveyor's existence is interesting and unconventional. There was a question just then as to the strength of the guard which should accompany the surveyor, who, however, was prepared to go without any, and having killed two bears in a hand-to-hand fight, was ready to meet any number of Afghans.

From Kilah Abdulla the line ascends about 1,000 feet to a point whence a tunnel is being pierced through the Khwaja Amran range. We halted the night at the eastern extremity of the tunnel, where we were the guests of Colonel Paterson and the officers of the 23rd Pioneers, and in the morning rode up the hill-side passing the first shaft and up to the summit of the Khojak pass, whence Kandahar, at a distance of 60 miles, would be visible, but that it lies between ranges of low hills rising out of a sea of red sand in the plain below. We rode from choice, but for the purpose of construction and for the transport of material from the eastern to the western side of the tunnel, a tramway leads from the first to the second shaft, and from the second shaft a funicular railway ascends to the top of the range, whence a level line runs along the top of the pass to another funicular, down which plant is passed to the western extremity of the tunnel.

We had some conversation with one of the miners, who had come on from the Severn tunnel. Lord Connemara asked him how he got his work done, and he said he had formerly been obliged now and again to use his revolver, but that at present he was getting on very well. Asked whether Punjaubis or Pathans were the best workmen, he summed up their respective merits briefly, simply and effectively, by remarking that "Punchaps are good chaps, but Pattuns are badduns."

In the tent at Shalibagh, on the eastern side of the Khojak, the thermometer registered 48° and when we awoke in the morning it was freezing outside and little icicles were hanging on the railway carriages. The mess-house tent was kept very warm by a huge pan filled with burning charcoal.

From the top of the Khojak we looked down upon Old Chaman and the New Chaman. At the latter place only a few days before our visit a Pathan came to see one of the contractors of the railway works, alleging that he was owed Rs. 30 for some work he had done a year before. The contractor referred him to the local authority, whereon he, knowing nothing of, and caring nothing for, the local authority, went away disappointed, and shortly afterwards met a mule-driver belonging to the works riding one mule and leading another. It entered into his head that he would take this mule in satisfaction of his debt. So he fired his revolver at the muleteer, who fell off, and went off himself on one of the mules. The muleteer gave the alarm in camp, and the frontier police were about to start in pursuit when Captain Harris, commanding the Royal Engineers, called out to Lieutenant Rooke, of the Bombay Lancers, "let us go and see the fun." So these two young officers rode off, and outstripping the mounted police soon came up with the Pathan. Captain Harris pointed a pistol at him, whereon the Pathan fired two barrels of his five-chambered revolver, missing with both. Captain Harris and Lieutenant Rooke then fired at him and both missed. Then he fired again and shot Captain Harris through the heart, who fell off his horse, just exclaiming "I am hit" before he died. Next the robber turned and fired at Lieutenant Rooke. The ball caught Rooke on the shoulder-blade and glanced off into his throat, and he too fell. The Pathan thereon picked up the revolver of Captain Harris, who lay dead on the sand, and made off with the mule. Soon afterwards the police came up and shot him in two places, and he was brought into camp to be tried. He said he had killed two Englishmen in the war, that these two sahibs pointed pistols at him, that he made as good a fight as he could for his life, and would leave the rest in the hands of God. Soon after he died of his wounds. By post at Shalibagh I received the prospectus of a new work on Indian and Burmese thieves. The author divides them into 37 classes, and gives them names worthy of word-stringing Aristoplanes himself. I give a few examples:—"The reckless but remarkably tender-hearted and moral-dagger-thief"; "the pillow-portmanteau bed, bundle and mattress thief"; "the dreadful back-water pirate or thief"; "the giant-like 'puckey' or the wonderful thought-speed-travelling thief"; "the lamplight-dimming and snake-producing-wick thief." All classes, however, do not rejoice in such lengthy names; for instance, there is "the dead-child using thief"; "the marine equestrian thief," an Indian relation, I suppose, of the Horse Marine; "the tiger-growl-imitating thief"; "the dreadful strangling thug"; and "the inconsiderate and fearless thief," in which last class, I imagine, the author would place the bold Pathan.

We saw the tents in the clear light air,—the tents where these occurrences took place. Though seven or eight miles from where we stood, they seemed quite near. Distances are ever most deceptive in the desert. As you walk in the streets of Quetta too, in the straight broad roads between the avenues of plane or poplar trees, you see at either end of the road the hills which, though at a distance on all sides of upwards of ten miles, seem close at hand, and just at the end of the avenue.

Near Quetta, surrounded by a mud wall, is the village of Kasee, the headman of which is very friendly to Europeans. When you go to his house he shakes hands with you,—most of the Afghans here seem to have adopted that form of salutation. In his reception-room are vases containing paper-flowers and some ordinary dinner plates are stuck in niches in the walls. I took tea with him and a circle of his friends. They gave me a chair, and all sat on the carpet drinking tea in such a manner as to make that bubbling sound characteristic of the camel. After some conversation, and the exchange of some stock quotations from the standard Persian authors, a visit to a Brahui encampment, where some wandering musicians played upon a Beloochee fiddle, completed the early morning ride.

Early on Monday morning we left with regret the hospitable house of Sir Robert and Lady Sandeman. It was bitterly cold in the railway carriages and all the way along the Quetta valley and the Pishin tableland. I have attempted to describe the chief features of the route through the Hurnai pass by which we came and by which we returned. It is a treeless, arid, wild and mountainous country, such as stretches, with no exception of any great importance, but the valley of the Tigris and the Euphrates, from the Indus to the Mediterranean. A few facts, however, may with advantage be given concerning the remarkable railway constructed by General Sir James Brown between July 1884 and March 1887.

This line, of 5-feet 6-inch gauge, and laid with 75-lb. steel rails, offered exceptional difficulties to the constructor. In Sind he had to work in a climate where the thermometer often registers 124° in the shade. Higher up, in the mountains and valleys, it frequently registers 18° below zero. At Hurnai he is 3,000 feet above the level of the sea, and he had to take his iron road 6,600 feet above that level before he reached Quetta. In 224 uphill miles, with a high ruling gradient throughout, he had to make 4 miles of bridges, one mile of rocky tunnel, and one mile of lined tunnel, and to contend throughout with landslips and floods. All this too, he had to do in a country with a population of two to the square mile.

At one point, just before the high tableland is reached, the line passes through the Chapper rift. Here the rocky mountains are split through as if in the glacial epoch another

> "Alpheus bold
> On his glacier cold
> With his trident the mountains strook
> And opened a chasm
> In the rocks."

The broken sides fall away from the top, and along the bottom is a waterway, down which in the rains rages a foaming and uncontrollable torrent. The line enters the rift by a little tunnel, comes out in a cutting, enters a second tunnel, and then runs along a terrace, excavated in the soft treacherous soapy earth of the almost vertical hillside. At the end of the rift it runs into another tunnel at a height of 250 feet above the river below, and emerging at this altitude from the heart of the hill, comes out upon a bridge, which conducts the train in mid-air to the opposite side of the chasm. Here the line runs for some distance through a shallow tunnel only a foot or two within the shelving rocky surface of the hill. For ventilation's sake and for convenience in working, this tunnel is pierced, along the outer side of the hill with openings. The natural roof serves to carry over it the drainage of the hillside and the débris of its landslips. Through the openings you look across the valley, on to what seems like another line, but is in fact your own, which, after a circuitous descent, reaches the level of the river you have crossed. This is the most heavy part of the work, but it only gives a fair idea of the enormous difficulties from floods, landslips and the nature of the country, which the engineer has encountered and overcome. The alternative route—55 miles shorter than this—from Sibi, through the Bolan to Quetta has lately been washed away. The Sind-Pishin line is said to pay its working expenses. Passenger traffic seems brisk, but so far it would appear that the competition of caravans is severe, for the camels of the migratory Brahuis can be seen all the way, marching alongside the iron road.

The line through the Bolan pass, like the Darjeeling-Himalayan railway, started with a roadway more or less ready-made, and this of course greatly reduced expenses. Take it all in all, the Sibi-Pishin line seems a work to be proud of. It is doubtful, however, if the contractors would concur in this somewhat complacent survey of the work; for, out of six, one died of cholera, two of fever, and one was murdered.

At Babar Kach we saw the petroleum which is brought up from a place some few miles distant and used as fuel in the Khojak works. The discovery and exploitation of this most valuable mineral oil is entirely due to Sir Robert Sandeman, and it is fervently to be hoped that its use, and also that of the coal which has been discovered in the Quetta valley, may arrest the destruction of the little vegetation there is around the town.

On the night of the 21st, we ran through to Ruk junction, and in the morning were travelling down the Indus valley on our way to Kurrachee. This being a purely unofficial narrative is not the place for opinions or reflections on the frontier or on any political question, nor for remarks upon military and commercial subjects, which a visit to Quetta obviously suggests.

The down train from Lahore was late owing to a tragic occurrence. The clothes of a European woman, who was travelling in the train, caught fire by contact with one of the sparks from the engine. To save the child she had with her, she flung it down, and in her terror jumped out of the carriage. The driver of the train was her husband, and on arrival at the next station he went back on his engine to pick her up. His child was dead and his wife was dreadfully injured. The bedding of one of our own servants caught fire in the same way.

The line to Kurrachee passes for the most part through an alkaloid plain, covered with babul and scrub jungle. At many points, however, tall crops of millet testified to the fact that the soil is not so barren as it looks. At Sehwan the rail passes along a cutting in the hills, which here run up to the Indus bank; and at Kotri they are only half-a-mile from the river. For the greater part of the way the Indus is invisible; but a false Indus was created on our right by the mirage. After the sun had set, the lighthouse and the headland of Manora were visible in the sun's departing glow, which seemed like a halo just over the city. At night-fall we reached the cantonment, where the usual guards, and a large assemblage of officers were present to meet the Governor, who stayed with Mr. Trevor, the Commissioner of Sind, in the house built by Sir Charles Napier during his tenure of that office.

Kurrachee is too well known to need description here. Sir Charles Dilke has "pronounced" it the least Indian, and the pleasantest of Indian cities. It certainly is most un-Indian, and very pleasant, but I hope not very pleasant, because it is un-Indian. The town possesses some of those fine buildings for which the capital of the Presidency is renowned. Its market and Frere Hall are worthy of Bombay itself, and its broad streets allow of that indefinite expansion of traffic, which is expected when the anticipated new line from the north comes straight across the desert to the sea. This railway would attract very little trade on the way, but it is believed that it would bring down great quantities of wheat from Delhi and the Lower Punjaub, owing to the directness of the route. On this account it is alleged to be preferable to the connection through Omerkote, and the south of the Rajputana desert, with the existing Rajputana line at Pachpadra, which was so strongly urged by the Kurrachee people not long ago. The exports of Punjaub wheat from this port have varied to an enormous extent during the last five years.

The most striking feature of the town from a distance is the tower of the church, which they say was built in imitation of the campanile of the Duomo at Florence. Perhaps this association and the fact that the number of windows increases campanile-like in each story, led me to think next day that it seemed top heavy, and inclined to lean to one side as some well-known towers of this description do. It is a conspicuous land mark from a long distance and quite the lighthouse of the plains, as that on Manora point is of the adjacent sea.

Some one has written a History of England from its signboards, and at Kurrachee, as at Port Said or in a Californian camp, you see the most diverse legends written above the shop windows, and such as characterise the meeting of different nationalities in one place for the purposes of trade. Hajee Rahmat Allah, "the pilgrim of the Grace of God," and "Hajee Younas" or holy Jonas have sandwiched between them "Mrs. Marks the Milliner," and similar curious combinations may be seen all down the street.

The sight of the neighbourhood of Kurrachee, is the crocodile saint and his crocodiles. The track to Peer Mugger runs along an open billowless plain, all along which the campanile is visible, till you strike a low spur of hills running down into the sea. This little range is pierced by a pass invisible until you reach it, and at a short distance on the other side, is situated a small pond surrounded by a low mudwall, and situated in the middle of palm trees. A wild tulip tree hangs over the puddle, which is not a dozen yards long or half-a-dozen broad; and close by on a hillock overlooking it is the little tomb place, wherein the saint lives and prays and collects rupees from his visitors. I was looking at the pond and asking where the crocodiles were, when I saw what looked like a log of wood moving on the sand just beneath my eyes and not two yards away. This was one of the reptiles, and by and by a Mussulman, called the "padre," came down and summoned his pets, whereon they all ran into the water, the level of which they raised several inches by their united bulk. One only was refractory, and the "padre" beat him over the head with a stick. I remember a dignitary of the Church in India, now deceased, telling me that he had such influence with the people of the country that when he laid his hands on their backs they burst into tears. This "padre," with more practical persuasion, laid his stick on the back of his recalcitrant pet, who did not burst into tears in spite of the proverbially lachrymose disposition of the crocodile, but opened his jaws and hissed loudly and looked as if he would bite the "padre" but abstained from the actual commission of such sin. Inside the thick and dirty water, the heads of these beasts appeared sticking out like shapeless little rocks. Though their mouths were shut the teeth in their lower jaws protruded, growing seemingly in random fashion without any regard to order or uprightness, just like almonds in a piece of nougat. One of the attendants, when questioned, said that these reptiles, of which there were 80 more or less by his account, were created by the saint by a mere act of volition, a power which fortunately is not possessed by many. What particular connection they had with the holy tomb, or with religion in general he could not say, and I cannot help thinking that, they are a mere speculation, their proximity to the tomb an accident, their sanctity fortuitous, their *raison d'être* an excuse for a collection, the only religious association to which they can rightly lay claim.

The population of Sind is perhaps the most Mussulman in India. The followers of the prophet are nearly 80 per cent. of the whole. The Arabs first settled here. They used to crawl along the coast to the mouth of the Indus before the daring voyage of Hippalos, who committed himself and his fortunes to the monsoon, which he had observed to blow with regularity towards the coast of India at a fixed season, whereby they learnt that the voyage across the open sea was practicable. A traveller from whom I asked the way to the crocodile saint's abode afforded an illustration of the geographical proximity of, and historical connection of this coast with, Arabia. In answering me he said "it is just beyond the mountain (جبل)." Now, nowhere else in India have I heard the Arabic word jabal used for mountain.

Among the finest buildings in Kurrachee are, as very frequently happens elsewhere in India, the Roman Catholic church and the Roman Catholic schools. These, it is said, do an immense amount of good in the country, the education being so much appreciated that the schools are well nigh self-supporting. The extremely handsome and commodious buildings were erected from the funds of the Society of Jesus. The church was open. It is a pity this is not generally the case, but of India, as of England, it will not be immediately that a great divine and poet will say:

"I cannot walk the city's sultry streets,
But the wide porch invites to still retreats,
Where passion's thirst is calmed, and care's unthankful gloom."

We saw enormous quantities of wheat being hoisted into ditchers bound for London, Antwerp, and elsewhere, and learnt that the trade of the port has been steadily increasing though it has fluctuated largely in the last two years. Reports show too that the trade in the Persian gulf is much greater than it was five years ago, when I travelled down from Bagdad along the coast to Kurrachee, which is larger, greener, and altogether more prosperous, than it then was.

As we left, the harbour was full of ships, all dressed in their best in honour of the Governor. The lighthouse and the ever-present Campanile are the most prominent objects, as Sind and Kurrachee fade in the distance, and we steam away to Bombay.

Leaving at 1 o'clock P.M. on the 23rd, we arrived in Bombay harbour at noon on the 25th, after a quiet and pleasant voyage, sailing along the coast of Guzerat and getting a good view in passing of the temples of Dwarka and Somnath. But little of its former glory remains apparently to the latter temple, to sack which Mahmood of Ghazni made a journey somewhat similar to what we have just accomplished, from Afghanistan to the country beyond the Indus.

It is impossible to imagine any greater contrast than is afforded by the scenery of Bombay and its unrivalled harbour, to that which we have left behind in Sind. Here everything speaks of an abundant rainfall, hills rise upon hills from the sea-coast to the top of the ghauts, and every hill is clothed with grass and covered with forest. When all the landscape glowed in the crimson hues of the setting sun it seemed as if the isle of Bombay itself was the place the Laureate had in his mind which charmed the wanderer out in ocean:

> "Where some refulgent sunset of India
> Streams over a rich ambrosial ocean isle,
> And crimson-hued the stately palmwoods
> Whisper in odorous heights of even."

In the harbour at Bombay was Her Majesty's ship *Griffon*, which had just come from the African coast where she lost her first Lieutenant in a brush with a slaver, and liberated 120 slaves. The yards were manned as the Governor went past. Among other ships was a Turkish man-of-war, taking out an Osmanli Order to be presented to the Mikado of Japan.

At the top of the steps of the Apollo Bunder His Royal Highness the Duke of Connaught, accompanied by all the officers of his staff, and the civil officers of Bombay, received Lord Connemara. His Royal Highness drove His Excellency to the station, where another guard of honour was paraded, and the Resident in Baroda, Sir Harry Prendergast, and other high officials were present.

The palmwoods on their odorous heights were just ceasing to be crimson-hued, when we reached Khandala at the top of the lovely Bhore ghaut, and it had not long been dark, when we reached Poona, where we dined. The Parsi contractor, who supplied an excellent dinner, informed us that his people had beaten the Europeans at cricket at Bombay and that the "Zoroastrian horn" was accordingly "exalted." It may be said of the Parsi that he does well everything that he attempts to do. It is believed that there is no place to which our troops penetrated in Afghanistan, at which a Parsi merchant has not also arrived, with tinned provisions, bottled beer, wine and whiskey. At Quetta, the most forward station we have on the frontier, an enterprising Parsi has been granted the title of Khan Bahadur for his services as contractor for railways, founder of mills, provider of stores, discoverer of coal, distiller of spirits, and possessor in short of boundless and indescribable enterprise.

Next morning, after a rough night in the train,

during which only the police officer was able to sleep, we breakfasted at Wadi, in Hyderabad territory where the Nawab Khursheed Jah, whose jaghire this part of the State is, entertained us.

After breakfast we ran through the pleasant uplands of the Hyderabad Dominions, well cultivated with cotton and other crops, and dotted here and there with little walled villages, and the rocky droogs of the Deccan, nature's forts which require little aid from art to make them defensible. In the afternoon we reached the Madras frontier, after crossing the great rivers Krishna and Tungabudhra, both of which were full of water. Then we steamed through crops of millet, cotton and castor-oil, all in a most flourishing condition, until nightfall, when we reached the great rock fortress of Gooty, after passing carefully over a portion of the line damaged by the recent floods. Beyond this the railway passes through low hills and park-like grassy lawns, full of groves of tamarind trees, till at the Pennér river we passed over its new bridge, which had only come into use a few days before a portion of the old one was carried away by floods. We saw the fallen stone pier in the water, and the iron girders, which had rested on it, were discovered some seven miles down the river.

Next morning at ¼ past 6 on the 27th October we arrived in Madras after a journey of 200 miles by road, 4,230 by rail and 1,270 by sea.

CHAPTER XI.

COCONADA, RAJAMUNDRY, ELLORE, BEZWADA, SINGARENI AND HYDERABAD.

Duke of Clarence's departure from Madras—Grain riots in Southern districts—Object of tour—Our party—On board S.S. *Sirsa*—Madras harbour—H.M.S. *Bondicea*—Sir Edward Freemantle—Coast of Masulipatam—Its historic associations—Colonel Forde—Marquis de Conflans—Religious wars—Secular wars—English and Dutch at Masulipatam—Charles II—At Coconada—Harbour—Trade of port—Plan of East Coast Railway—Chamber of Commerce—Steam dredger *Connemara*—Local self-government—Female medical aid—Agricultural Loans Act—By canal to Rajamundry—S.S. *Arthur Cotton*—Scenery *en route*—Godavari Irrigation Works—Dowlaishweram—Incident of journey—S.S. *John Mullins*—Landing—At Rajamundry—Peepshow—Departure for Gorge—Hero worship—Mr. Puckle—General Haig—Marquess of Tweeddale—Scenery *en route*—S.S. *Victoria* — Local tobacco — Shipwreck—Description of Gorge—Sir Charles Trevelyan—Sir Mountstuart Grant Duff—Return to Rajamundry—Rumpa country—Incident of Rumpa rumpus—Mr. Martindale—Lord Guillamore—Human sacrifices to Kali—Hill people—Rajamundry and Rumpa contrasted—Jail—Hospital—Excise system—Ellore—Enthusiastic reception—Primary education — Carpet manufacture—Journey to Bezwada—Pitt and regent diamonds—Story of Sindbad the Sailor—Deccan Mining Company—Tom-tom telephone—Arrival at Bezwada — Anicut—S.S. *Alexandra*—Tadipalle — Bellary-Kistna State Railway—Singareni—Colonel Orr—Extent and cost of dam—Kondapille toys—Muslin—Halcyon's feathers—Railway communication—Mr. Arundel—East Coast Railway—Future of Bezwada—Afternoon reception—Deputation from Nizam—Mr. Harrison—Buddhist cave temple—Mr. Wolfe-Murray—Ascent of hills—Kali temple—Brahmin priest—Tiled houses—Two devotees—Illuminations of town—Excise system—Operations of Agricultural Loans Act—House tax—Local Punchayets—Departure—Nizam's Railway saloons—Kumumett—Nawab Badr-ud-Dowlah—Conditions of British and Native rule—Singareni coal mines—New year's day—Arrival at Hyderabad—Reception at Railway station—Visits from Nizam and minister—Nizam's Palace—Char Minar—Char Mahala—Titles—Title of Nizam—Fireworks—Illuminations—Second names of cities—Nawab Afsar Jung — Fort of Golconda — Bradlaugh's Congress speech—Congress agencies—Nawab Vicar-ul-Oomrah—Falaknumah—Lucknow modellers—Features of tour—Return to Madras.

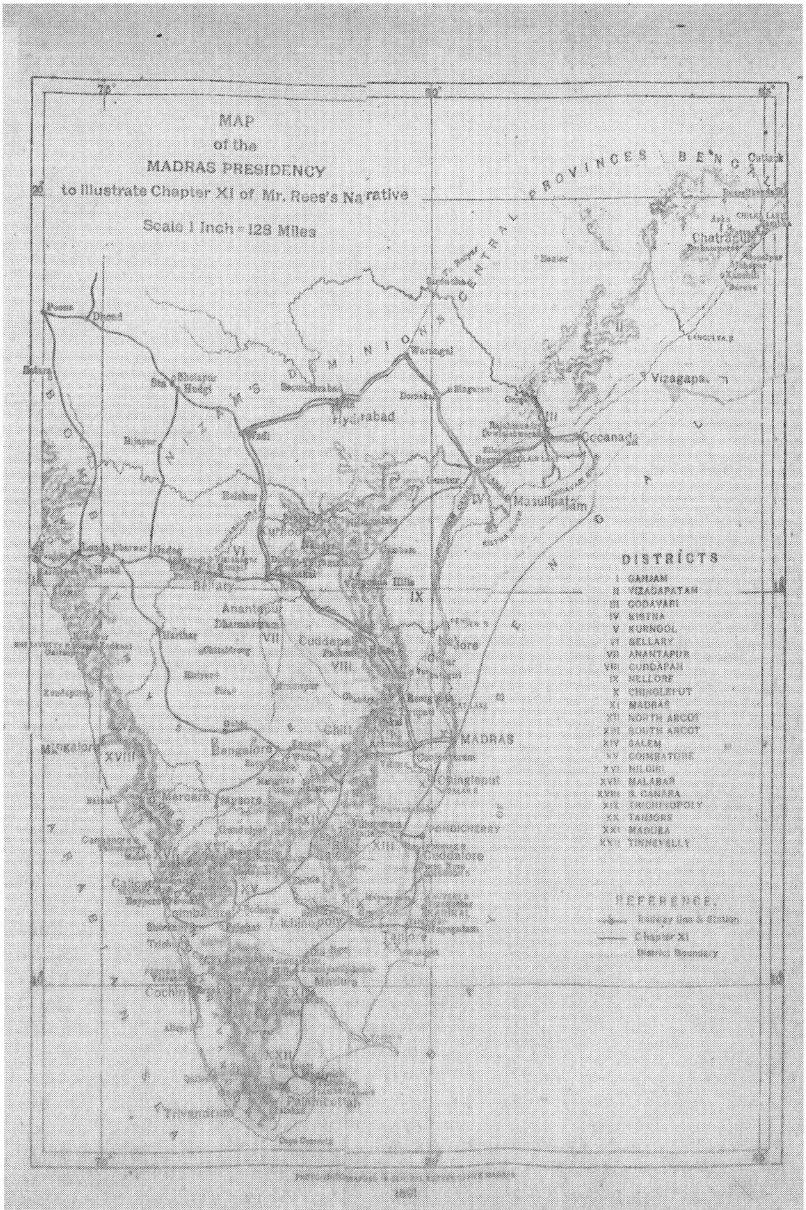

MAP
of the
MADRAS PRESIDENCY
to illustrate Chapter XI of Mr. Rees's Narrative
Scale 1 Inch = 128 Miles
CENTRAL PROVINCES
BENGAL
NIZAM'S DOMINIONS
Poona
Sholapur
Hydrabad
Warangal
Secunderabad
Wadi
Bijapur
Raichur
Kurnool
Bellary
Anantapur
Cuddapah
Nellore
MADRAS
Chingleput
Bangalore
Mysore
Mangalore
Mercara
Calicut
Coimbatore
Trichinopoly
Tanjore
Cudddalore
PONDICHERRY
Madura
Cochin
Palamcottah
Trivandrum
Cape Comorin
Vizagapatam
Cocanada
Masulipatam
Chatrapur
Guntur
DISTRICTS
I GANJAM
II VIZAGAPATAM
III GODAVARI
IV KISTNA
V KURNOOL
VI BELLARY
VII ANANTAPUR
VIII CUDDAPAH
IX NELLORE
X CHINGLEPUT
XI MADRAS
XII NORTH ARCOT
XIII SOUTH ARCOT
XIV SALEM
XV COIMBATORE
XVI NILGIRI
XVII MALABAR
XVIII S. CANARA
XIX TRICHINOPOLY
XX TANJORE
XXI MADURA
XXII TINNEVELLY
REFERENCE.
Railway line & Station
Chapter XI
District Boundary

His Royal Highness Prince Albert Victor left Madras after his second visit to Lord Connemara on the morning of the 16th December for Rangoon; and three days later, the Governor, started for his (eleventh) tour, in the Godávari and Kistna districts. In the interval of three days, to the great relief of the Government, rain had fallen in most of the southern districts, where prices had risen so considerably as to give ground for much anxiety. The trifling grain riots which had occurred in Trichinopoly, Cumbaconam and Tanjore, were of no great moment, being brought about chiefly by the bad characters to be found in all large towns, who welcome any period of distress as an occasion for plunder, and seek their private gain in the public loss and misfortune. It was not only to visit the great irrigation works of the Kistna and the Godávari, but also to inquire what stocks of grain might be on hand to assist other districts where scarcity prevailed, that Lord Connemara proposed to make this tour during the Christmas holidays. His Excellency had not long before, during the famine in Ganjam, called these favoured deltas to the aid of their less fortunate neighbour.

The rain had fallen in torrents all Tuesday and Wednesday, and on Thursday morning the flood-gates were still open when on the 19th December 1889, * we embarked on board the S.S. *Sirsa*, and the waves were running high through the yawning eastern

* H.E. The Lord Connemara, G.C.I.E.
Mr. Rees, Private Secretary.
The Viscount Marsham, A.D.C.

entrance of the ever-unfinished Harbour. The Governor's departure was private, but a salute was none the less fired from the Naval Commander-in-Chief's Flagship *Boadicea*, and the Admiral, Sir Edmund Fremantle, who was just starting for Zanzibar, came off to the *Sirsa* to bid His Excellency good-bye.

After tossing about all day and all night we reached Masulipatam on the morning of the 20th November. Nothing was visible but the long low coast over which in 1864 a storm-wave burst, penetrating seventeen miles inland, and destroying thirty thousand people, and innumerable head of cattle. The traveller does not realize, in these times of peace, that the coast along which he travels was long the scene of desperate conflict between the English and the French for the supremacy of India, and that one of the most gallant fights of this land of battle-fields, was fought here by Colonel Forde, who defeated the Marquis de Conflans at Masulipatam in 1759, rising superior to the most desperate circumstances, and attacking under every possible disadvantage, a far superior force entrenched within a strong and well-provisioned fortress. In ages past, there had been religious wars between Buddhism and the indigenous idolatry of the country. Buddhism conquered, and in its turn was driven out by Brahminism, which rules supreme to this day. Subsequently came secular wars. The Mahomedan Kingdoms of the Deccan overthrew the Hindu rulers of the south, and the Great Mogul triumphed over them in turn, and finally a lieutenant of the Great Mogul came under the influence successively of the French and the

English, and ceded to the latter the districts, wherein we are about to travel, and whence we proceed to the capital of his successor, the Nizam of Hyderabad.

It is curious to reflect that the jealousy and rivalry of the Dutch originally led the English of Masulipatam to found a factory in Madras, and that in 1679 the representative of the East India Company on tour presented a purse to the King of Golconda's lieutenant at Masulipatam, as being "a person rising in the favour of the Court to whom a small summe of ready money given privately would be more acceptable than a greater summe given publickly." The English and the Dutch had been competing at Masulipatam for the commerce of the coast for more than a half century, before spotted deer and water-fowl were sent thence to His Majesty King Charles II of England. The picture of King Charles, surrounded by his subjects, feeding the water-fowl in the Park, has ever been a favourite one with the English people, and it would be odd if those water-fowl had come from Masulipatam. But on to the royal table, or into the royal parks they certainly went.

After a brief halt at this historic site, we travelled on along the coast of the district, which in size is about equal to the principality of Wales, and next morning arrived at Coconada in the Bay of Coringa, ten miles north of the Gautami mouth of the river Godávari. To the north and north-east of the anchorage, low hills come down near the water's edge relieving the coast from the barren and desolate appearance, that it presents near Masulipatam. The harbour was alive with boats bearing on their sails huge red crosses, anchors, moons and such like devices, whereby their owners may recognize them from the distant shore. The Collector, Mr. Power, met us on board, and another voyage of 6 miles in a steam launch landed us between the groynes which form at once an entrance to the town of Coconada, and to the canals which extend thence to the great anicut of the Godávari, since the construction of which the trade of the town has advanced by "leaps and bounds," the value of its exports and imports having risen from £300,000 in 1862 to £740,000 in 1872 and £1,500,000 in 1888. Trade, to which a considerable impetus was given by the American war, which was the cause of extensive shipments of cotton, suffers a little at present from the construction of the Nizam's State Railway to Bezwada, whence much delta produce finds its way to Bombay. It is expected, however, that the extension of the East Coast line to Coconada will more than counteract this effect, and it is hoped that it will also convert the port into an important outlet for the coal mines of Singareni, which we are going to see. The roadway on the sea-wall was covered with natives wearing bright and many-coloured garments, and on arrival at the jetty we found present the usual assemblage of European district officers, zemindars in purple and gold, and municipal councillors in more sober and business-like attire. A feature not quite so invariable on such occasions, was the presence of an astrologer, who was prepared to predict, and prophesy, for a consideration. Immediately the Governor landed, a choir of ten pandits or wise men sang a chorus of Sanscrit benediction, and then followed a more prosaic and practical address, which referred gratefully to the Governor's efforts in obtaining the sanction of the Secretary of State and the Government of India to the construction of the East Coast railway, the survey of which is actually in progress. In reply, the Governor alluded to the fallacy of the opinion that the existence of maritime and canal communication rendered a railway unnecessary. He pointed out that the proposed line would not only develop the internal resources of these districts and rouse into life its dormant industries, but would also increase the sea-borne trade both in regard to exports from, and imports to, the coast.

At present the rich and populous districts of Ganjam, Vizagapatam and Godávari are entirely bereft of railway communication with the outer world, and the proposed line will extend from Bezwada over the Kistna river to Samulcotta, 8 miles from Coconada, and thence through Vizagapatam to Vizianagrum, whence it will proceed to Cuttack,—a distance of some 500 miles from Bezwada. The first portion of this line from Bezwada to Coconada, whither a branch is proposed from Samulcotta, is necessary in order to connect the Bellary-Kistna and Hyderabad State Railways with the rice-producing deltas of this district and of the Kistna, while its continuation to Vizianagrum will, it is believed, prove a remunerative undertaking, on account of the rich and populous nature of the country through which it will pass. Then it is thought highly desirable that the line should be extended to

Ganjam, which so lately suffered from famine. This district is cut off from communication with the other parts of the country, being a mere strip of land between the Eastern Ghâts and the Bay of Bengal, isolated at all times from railways, and during a part of the year from maritime communication, owing to want of harbours and a turbulent sea. For the same reason it is thought equally desirable to connect Ganjam with Cuttack on the north, more especially as the latter place will, it is believed, be finally connected with the Bengal-Nagpur Railway system.

The town of Coconada was, as is usual on such occasions, beautifully decorated and the archways displayed some original mottoes such as "Receive with *grande cher apropos*" and "Welcome with *gaieté à la mode*." In the centre of each of these remarkable inscriptions stood the effigy of an *embonpoint* Telugu lady, who emptied trays of flowers on the Governor's head as the carriage passed underneath the arches.

In the afternoon the Chamber of Commerce presented an address, in which they deprecated the closing of the irrigation canals for annual repairs, which seems, however, unavoidable, these canals being primarily irrigation works, and of secondary, though of great importance, in respect to navigation.

In the afternoon the new steam dredger *Connemara* was launched by the Governor, and christened by Mrs. Simson, wife of the President of the Chamber of Commerce. This little ceremony was very well arranged, and as the champagne bottle burst on the port beam, the Governor touched a string, and the ship slipped gently off its cradle into the water. At dinner we were glad to learn that many contracts for the urgent supply of rice to southern districts, which had been entered into by Madras merchants, had been suddenly cancelled,—a proof of the change which recent rains have made in the prospects and situation in the south.

Among the official matters considered at Coconada were some which possess general interest, for instance, the progress of local self-government. Into the municipal councils of the district the electoral system has been largely introduced, but the municipal administration has not altogether met with the approbation of the Government, as would appear from orders published, which have been communicated to the Press. The provision of female medical aid is receiving the attention of the authorities, and seven certificated midwives are at work in the district, but the prejudice against European methods of treatment seems stronger in the Northern Circars than in the southern districts. The East Indian midwife attached to the Coconada hospital attends on an average to only twenty cases in the year. In Rajamundry, again, which is considered intellectually as an advanced centre, the objection to European attendance and European treatment is particularly strong.

The ryot population of the district, being generally well-to-do, does not borrow under the provisions of the Agricultural Loans Act, and when loans are required the much-abused Sowcar here, as elsewhere, is preferred to the more reasonable, but less lenient and elastic, Government.

Next morning we took a walk through some native villages. The soil near the coast is sandy and covered with the delicate purple flowers of the goat's foot convolvulus (Ipomæa Pescapræ). This sandy soil, however, is by no means barren, and supports besides groves of palmyra trees, orchards of cashew-nut and guava. The pathways to the villages pass between hedges of aloe and prickly-pear.

We first came upon a hamlet inhabited by persons engaged in drawing toddy. Arrangements are being made for regulating the traffic in toddy or fermented palm juice, but the inhabitants of the toddy-drawers' village did not view the future restrictions with favour, and followed us for a long distance repeating their objections, which I endeavoured to translate into English from their euphonious Telugu. Next we come on a village of herdsmen, and one old shepherd, solicitous of the Governor's weal, advised him to be very careful in going over a primitive bridge near the village. After that we came on some washermen beating their cloths on stones. One of these was gathering earth impregnated with alkali, which they use as a substitute for soap, and a fairly efficient substitute it is believed to be.

On Sunday, the Native girls' school and the hospital were visited, and inquiries made as to the progress of female medical education. The church too was inspected, that certain repairs might be considered, before divine service, with which the day ended.

Next morning, the 23rd, we rose early and left by canal for Rajamundry,—a distance of 44 miles more or less. We were towed along in a little convoy of house-boats by the steam launch *Arthur Cotton*, named after the celebrated Engineer, who constructed the great Godavari irrigation works. In the river from the head of the delta there is a continual fall, consequently we had a continual rise, and passed three locks, one a double one, with a rise of 18 feet. The canal banks were green and banyans shaded the road which ran alongside. All around us were fields of stubble, and innumerable strawricks. The character of the country, but for the palmyras, much resembles that of the fens. When you get within a few miles of the great dam which stems the stream at Dowlaishweram, first one canal and then another, takes off in different directions. After the separation of each canal the artificial waterway grows broader and broader, till near Dowlaishweram it becomes as wide as the Thames at Maidenhead, but probably contains a great deal more water. At last it ends in a lock; and when we leave the boats and mount the banks, an expanse of water stretches some 4 miles before the eye. Immediately in front extends the first portion of the great anicut which, with the help of three islands at the head of the delta, holds up the river, and diverts its waters on either side, so as to irrigate upwards of 612,000 acres of fertile rice-bearing lands, and to water with gold a delta of 2,000 square miles. Every river in India is a Pactolus, but this great stream has been made more subservient to the wants of man than perhaps any other of its size in the world. Practically at the present moment it ends at this great anicut above which you see nothing but a vast expanse of water, and below which spread miles of yellow sand.

It is in the nature of such works that they are never finished. In 1852, the dam and some of the distribution works were completed for the exceedingly low figure of £150,000. Labour was then cheap and material abounds on every side. Many times since have these titanic works been considered complete. In 1880, eighteen years later, they were completed at a cost of £868,000 and now in 1890 it is believed they are pretty well completed at a cost of £1,180,000. Whatever they cost, however, so long ago as 1877, the returns directly due to the water distributed amounted to upwards of £2,000,000, and in 1879 it was calculated that goods of the value of upwards of £3,500,000 passed over the canals, while the value of the exports and imports of the district which in 1847, before the construction of the anicut, amounted to £170,000 had risen in 1887 to upwards of £1,500,000. The great dam itself rises some 14 feet above the level of the stream and consists of three long portions and one short one, amounting in the aggregate to 3,982 yards in length. The navigable channels, which distribute the water are 528 miles long, and the total length of distributive channels is not less than 1,600 miles.

Just before we got to the anicut a "dugout," or boat made by hollowing out the trunk of a palmyra, came off from the shore with the post. Among the letters was an elaborate book of advertisements from

Treacher, the Bombay merchant, which I threw overboard into the canal. The small plunge of the disappearing publication, was followed by the larger plunge of a man from the bank, who rescued the book and swam after the boat with it. It is impossible to escape from advertisements.

From Dowlaishweram the S.S. *John Mullins* brought us up to Rajamundry, the Judge's house "*impositum saxis late candentibus,*" becoming visible, long before we reached it, over the broad expanse of water. As you steam away from the anicut, and get from under the lee of the island, to which its first portion extends, you see beyond you more water, and as you get higher up you see beyond that a still greater breadth; and finally across the four islands you catch a view, soon to be obscured by other islets, of an unbroken sheet of water four miles wide.

Arrived at last at the landing place at Rajamundry, we find the bastions of the old fort and the river bank crowded with people, who overflowed into the banyan trees, which were filled with living fruit, clad for the most part in clothes as red as its own berries. The crowds here are much more gaily dressed than they are in the southern districts, and nearly every man has a cloth or a turban of bright red. It was an extremely orderly crowd, as may be inferred from the presence of large numbers of Telugu babies, "brown, fat and fascinating," as Lady Dufferin calls them in her recently-published book. At bed-time a troupe of girls played the game of stick at the back of the house. In this game, a troupe dances around, each girl holding two sticks in her hand, and as they meet and pass each strikes the sticks of the other, and the sound of a continual tapping arises, not in itself unpleasant, but not conducive to sleep. It has often been remarked how sounds suggest past associations, and the tapping of these little bamboos recalled a similar and greater tap-chorus at Seoul, the far distant capital of Corea, where at nightfall the women get up in this way the linen of their husbands, who are extremely well turned out. Those who are not engaged in this species of ironing may go out for a walk at that hour. The sound serves also as a kind of curfew for men who, if found about at this the woman's time for exercise, are very apt to be taken up by the watchman, and bambooed.

Among the various apparatus of *tamasha* in the town was a small peepshow, and coming up behind the exhibitor, I heard him chattering in quick and fluent Telugu, "Walk up, ladies and gentlemen, and see His Excellency the Governor of Madras get into his carriage in front of Government House." On peeping myself, I discovered a gentleman, extremely unlike the Governor, getting into a carriage, unknown to His Excellency, in front of a house not at all resembling Government House. So while our friends were being amused by Barnum in England we were not without our consolations in Rajamundry.

Next morning we rose at 5, and left at 6 o'clock, in the *John Mullins*. It is the custom here, after a decent lapse of time such as may add an element of antiquity or mystery to that of high reputation, for the Engineers in charge of these great irrigation works to be canonized as the representatives it may be of the river-god. Amongst the natives some such process as this continually goes on, and the English community here apparently acknowledge the same principle to the extent, at any rate, of naming the little ships of the flotilla of the Godavari, after the most eminent Engineers, who have controlled and distributed its bountiful and beneficent waters. This makes the ships very interesting to those who, like ourselves, had actually met in the flesh those eponymous heroes, Sir Arthur Cotton and General Mullins. The fact should also stimulate Indian executive officers in their efforts to cope with their ever-increasing duties.

No earnest district officer can be sure that he is not qualifying for a hero. In Tinnevelly the people say of the largest anicut across the Tambraparni begun by Mr. Puckle, that it was a god-like work, built by one who was like the gods. A religious character is ever a great factor in the evolution of gods from men. Sir Arthur Cotton, in reporting to Government the completion of the Godavari anicut, hoped that its accomplishment might lead to an increasing appreciation of a Christian Government, and trusted that it was only the beginning of a series of works worthy of our nation, of our knowledge, of our religion, and of the extraordinary power God has been pleased to place in our hands. To this day Sir Arthur maintains a colporteur who distributes Christian tracts in the country irrigated by the aid of his great dam. One of his assistants, General Haig, recently came out from England to do a hot-weather's duty for a sick missionary in Godavari. The respect and veneration of the natives for men of this stamp is boundless, and if a temple were erected to either of them in the delta, it would not lack worshippers. The Governor of the day, the Marquess of Tweeddale, should also live in the grateful recollection of the people, for his strong aid was needed, and was freely given, to obtain sanction for such gigantic works from the Court of Directors.

We steamed away gaily up the slightly narrowing river as far as a picturesque island-hill crowned by an ancient fane. The scenery here is just such as the traveller would be requested by the guide-book to pause and admire, and we did pause for a longer period than we had intended. At one point below, where the existence of a shoal was known, all preparations had been made for dragging the steam launch off had she grounded, and crowds of coolies stood in the shallow water, their white turbans looking like the tops of mushrooms, of which their heads were the black stalks. Just here a raft of wood about 300 yards long passed us. Woodcutters thus bring timber down the river to Dowlaishweram, living themselves for perhaps a month on their rafts. We also passed now and again alluvial islands such as are repeatedly formed by the deposit of the rolling silt of the descending river. These islands are well enough when they rise out of the river, but loose quicksands below it are the bane of its navigation, as we soon experienced. After steaming eight miles past groves of acacias and rows of sentinel palms, and now and again passing through the half section of a hamlet cut in two by the impetuous floods of the river, we left the *John Mullins* for the *Victoria*, and proceeded slowly and anxiously up stream. The steamer draws 3 feet, and at the bow a man with a leadstick continually calls the soundings. He pokes into the water a long bamboo on which feet and inches are marked. He calls 4 feet, 3½ feet and then 3 feet. The Telugu captain gesticulates wildly and gives multitudinous orders, all of which are repeated in a shrill voice by a boy, who appears delighted with our parlous state. After 3 feet are called we see the yellow sands below us. We hang for one moment on the apex of disaster, and finally clear the sand bank and go on. We then passed another alluvial island, and learnt that the tobacco grown here is not all sent to Burmah to be made into cigars, but that part is manufactured in the district into cheroots, which sell for a shilling a hundred. A specimen cheroot is being examined, when the man with the leadstick again calls excitedly "mark three," the captain again gesticulates, the crew follow the captain's lead, and the *Victoria* runs hard upon a sand bank, whereon the boy jumps on the starboard paddle-box, and calls aloud to the *John Mullins* "Hi! jalliboatoo."

We reverse the engines and resort to every possible means of getting off, but at last accept the fact of shipwreck and take, as the boy at first suggested, to the "jalliboatoo" or jolly-boat, and make for the *John*

Mullins which was puffing backwards and forwards in momentary expectation of grounding like ourselves. It was of no use to be established safely on board the *John Mullins* without our kitchen-boat, which was attached to the *Victoria.* So we tried to get her off, and finally did, though we were within an ace of losing her in the rapid current. But we did not desert the *Victoria* in her troubles, and waited till some 200 coolies with infinite chattering and impossible delay came and pulled her off the bank. Then our flotilla again proceeded on its way, but all hope of getting up to the gorge, nearly 50 miles from Rajamundry, within the day, had to be abandoned. Luckily for us a camp had been arranged, at which we were to have halted on the way back, some six miles beyond the scene of our shipwreck. We spent the night there, and shipwrecked mariners never fared so well before. The fact is the shoals change almost hourly, and we were lost in a passage that had been explored and pronounced safe the day before.

Next morning we rose at cockcrow, at junglecock crow,—a very pleasant sound to hear all around your camp—and started, this time in the *John Mullins*, for the gorge, which we commenced to enter directly after leaving the camp. The river here winds through low hills rising to a maximum height of 2,800 feet and clothed from top to bottom in green and feathery forests of bamboo. When you have rounded a conical hill you find in front of you a long low range of mountains from which seemingly there is no outlet. The scenery consequently resembles a succession of peaceful mountain lakes, at such times as this at any rate when the river is not in flood. Sir Charles Trevelyan has likened it to the Rhine, and Sir Mountstuart Grant Duff compares the gorge to the iron gates of the Danube,—a comparison the felicity of which is attested by Lord Connemara. One of our passengers suggests the English lakes, and it certainly seems to resemble them rather than the Rhine. The complete solitude of the surroundings is of such a character as to make the 'castled crags' of the Rhine appear quite populous. As to the English lakes, the presence of palms and bamboos seems to me to give the scenery an unmistakably tropical appearance. I do not know why any one river should necessarily be compared with some other river, or some other scene in which water plays a part, but to follow the example of the distinguished personages named above, and to institute a comparison, I would say that each successive reach of the river as you approach the gorge resembles the solitary mountain lakes of Japan in general, and that of Chiuzenjee in particular. From Sirawaka to Kolur, a distance of four miles more or less, the channel is not more than 300 yards wide and the waters of the Godavari collected in an area of upwards of 115,000 square miles, and swollen on their course of 800 miles by innumerable affluents, roll down this narrow mountain gorge between two walls of hills rising, but not precipitously, to nearly 3,000 feet in height and clothed from top to bottom in bamboos and scrub jungle, the vegetation reaching right down to the high water-mark of the river, visible some 30 feet above us on the rocks.

Even here, however, there is nothing grand or stupendous in the scene, nothing at all resembling the cañons of the Rocky Mountains, or even approaching in beauty and effect the gorge of bare white marble rocks through which the Nerbudda rushes, near Meer Gunj, about 400 miles north as the crow flies. The scenery is beautiful and its solitude most striking; but those who want a grand effect should visit it, as I believe they cannot well do, when the great river is in flood. Beyond the gorge the Godavari enters an open country again, and an effort was made at a cost of £700,000 to make it navigable during its course through the Central Provinces,—a project which has been finally abandoned.

On the way back we got a shot at some crocodiles sunning themselves on one of the islands, and we accomplished the whole distance, of 50 miles more or less, from the top of the gorge to Rajamundry in a pleasant and at times somewhat exciting voyage of eleven hours. We had become so callous to shipwreck that we eat breakfast in the barge we were towing, while the hapless *Victoria* behind us was again being taken off a bank by crowds of chattering coolies.

During the greater part of this journey we were in the Agency tracts of the Godavari, a wild uncivilized region, in which the ordinary Civil Courts are not established, and where penal fiscal laws are not in force. On the left bank of the river stretches the Rumpa country where a little local mismanagement was magnified in 1879, into an 'interesting little rebellion' for so it was described at the time in the

English newspapers. The fact is that the disturbance was one with which a strong body of Police could have coped, and the Agent to the Governor in the Godavari of that day—a great scholar and mathematician—was reported in the neighbouring hill tracts of Vizagapatam, where I was serving at the time, to have ridden through the disturbed country alone on his elephant, clothed in a black frockcoat and wearing a black silk hat. This was his usual wear in all weathers. However that may be, the country is perfectly quiet and the people are quite contented now. The leader in this little war was finally caught, owing to his faithful attendance at a trysting place, where like other warriors he was welcomed by a fair, but I believe in this case not faithless, one, for she did not betray him. Mr. Martindale, or Lord Guillamore, or some other officer employed in pacifying Rumpa at the time, should write a popular account of this little rebellion, for it has been dignified with the name. The country is superlatively interesting, and, like the people, little known. Nor I believe has any narrative of the disturbance been published. That of Mr. Carmichael is confidential.

We heard many things, official and unofficial, of Rumpa and the surrounding regions from the Collector. It is well known that in past times human sacrifices were annually offered in these hill tracts to Kali, the goddess of evil, and it is within the Collector's own experience that, not long since, in one of the largest towns the people kept a man for a week in a cage before a temple where a festival was being celebrated. On the seventh day they shaved the head of a sheep, dressed it up in man's clothing, took the man out of the cage before the goddess, and then offered the sheep as a sacrifice saying, "Receive O! Kali! such an offering as in these times we are able to make to thee." At the same time it must be remembered that this tale is only characteristic of a particular wild and uncivilized tract, the people of which would be described now by the neighbouring inhabitants of the plains, very much as they are in the national Indian epics, as demons, monkeys and monsters. Yet are the hill-people, in spite of their former leaning towards human sacrifices, and their readiness to kill their enemies, in other respects by no means a blood-thirsty or savage race. They must, outside of courts at any rate, be judged by their own standard, and no judicial officer who has had to try them for the murders which they not infrequently commit, has not felt that the law which he applies, was created in, and is applicable to, another world than that of the simple and primitive hillmen. It is not long since the priest of one of their temples sat out in the jungle for a week, and coming back with a cane, of which many grew in the forest, alleged that he had been in communication with the deity, who had given him the stick. The production of the wand proved the truth of his assertion, and as he prophesied a good time for the hillmen, who would soon have the country for themselves, he was speedily joined by a little band of adherents, who plundered and burnt the police station, and spent a week in a state of pygmy rebellion, and at the expiry of that time quietly handed themselves over to the authorities.

These people are in every way the greatest possible

contrast to the inhabitants of the plains. They have no caste, and they worship the spirits of the mountains, and a tutelary god who protects them from the ravages of tigers. They revere, nay worship their ancestors, like the Chinese. They believe in one Supreme God, like the Christian. They regard heaven as a large and strong fort where there is an abundance of rice that defies the vicissitudes of seasons, and they picture hell to themselves as a place where an iron crow ever gnaws away the flesh of the sinner. Meanwhile at Rajahmundry, within a day's journey, the people are highly educated, take the most complex and metaphysical views of religion and philosophy, and boycott on all sides, one or two people, who are endeavouring to promote the remarriage of Hindu widows. There are 50 miles between Rajahmundry and Rumpa, and a whole world between the inhabitants of either locality. When travelling in these hill tracts myself some years ago, I remember hearing of the murder, by a hillman, of his child, to which he had been much attached. The man was brought down to the coast for trial, and in his defence, said he had lived and cultivated for some forty years. The day after that child was born, he had met a tiger, but thought little of it. The next day he met the tiger again, which disturbed his mind. On the third day he saw the tiger a third time. Then he knew that the child was at the bottom of it, and sorely against his will, he was obliged to put it out of the way. Far away in the Andaman Isles, this poor man expiates his offence, and speculates vaguely as to the reasons which induced the Englishman to view his misfortune as a crime. Witchcraft flourishes in these jungles, and but for the Police, witches' teeth would be extracted, and witches would be ducked in ponds, according to the approved prescriptions observed in such cases alike in East and West.

Travelling by steamer on the Godavari, we are reminded of another incident of the so-called "Rumpa rebellion." A band of "rebels" took one of the little river steamers from the Police, who fled for reinforcements, but on going back found that the victorious hillmen had been scared by the whistle, which they took for the devil, when one of them with the curiosity of ignorance had pulled the string, and let loose the steam fiend.

These steamers belong to the Irrigation Department, but fleets of private boats ply on river and canal, and carry passengers at ridiculously low rates. Competition has reached such a pitch that rival carriers are said to take passengers occasionally, not only for nothing, but also to give them bananas to eat on the way. Nothing like this has yet been exhibited in England, though occasionally you can go from San Francisco to New York for the price of a journey from London to Edinburgh, from causes similar to those which operate here.

Next morning, drums were beaten at 4 o'clock in a neighbouring temple, in honour of the deity, the noise also serving as an unwelcome *reveille* to ourselves. There was plenty to do in the day, but no need to get up so early. The Governor visited the jail in the morning, discussed with the Doctor and the Superintendent, the recent report on its health, and saw carpenters, smiths, potters, weavers, carpet, cloth and boot-makers, tailors, dyers, washermen, sawyers, wool-spinners, and oil-pressers, all engaged in their several occupations, and looking, for convicts, tolerably contented and comfortable.

The hospital too was not as full as we had expected. The winds, which blow over the feverish hills between the coast and the Central Provinces, are laden apparently with fever germs, and counteract and combat, sometimes only too successfully, the health-giving breezes from the coast. There were only 18 sick in jail, however, out of a population of 530. After the jail, the banks of the river had to be inspected at a point where a retaining wall is considered necessary, and sundry defects in the ferry steamer were investigated from her decks.

A visit was also paid to the girls' school founded by the Maharajah of Vizianagrum, but now maintained partly by Government, and partly by the very small fees paid for tuition. These children were, somewhat absurdly, made by their masters to petition for higher education, the continual articulate cry of the masters and the few pupils, as against the inarticulate and real want of the masses.

The excise system, under which a duty is collected upon every gallon of spirits passed into consumption, and which is the only satisfactory method of raising the duty and restricting the consumption, has not yet been introduced into the Godavari district. The effect of the introduction of the excise system in those parts of the Presidency in which it is in force, has been to increase taxation, and to obtain trustworthy statistics of consumption, which were never available under the previously existing farming system. In this district, however, it has been the custom to distil country spirits from toddy, which is furnished by every palmyra and date tree in the country. Speaking generally, a similar state of things only exists in four districts of the Presidency, and in such, the consumption is believed to have been larger than in the others, the difficulty of regulating it being obviously enormous, when the materials for distillation exist in every tree. For the present it is intended to collect the revenue by a tax upon every tree from which toddy is drawn, to reduce the number of stills and by thus concentrating manufacture, to pave the way for the introduction of the excise system into this and the few other districts, in which the right of manufacturing spirits is still farmed out.

Next morning, Friday, we passed the headworks of the Eastern Delta, and down the canal to Ellore. The banks are not very high, and on either side we could see a flat country covered with the stubble of reaped crops, and dotted with strawricks. Here and there, a herd of cattle crossing the canal would get entangled in our convoy, but they seemed to go under the boats, or between them and the steam tug, and we believed that we killed or injured not one head of cattle. Between Ellore and the sea, is the Colair Lake, a great depression between the higher deltas of the Kistna and the Godavari, which may yet be filled up in the course of ages by their surplus silt.

At Ellore His Excellency experienced a very enthusiastic reception, this remote town once the capital of the Northern Circars being seldom visited by Governors. A chorus of cholera horns on the banks of the canal had a very startling effect, and an extraordinary number of drums were collected.

The address as usual expressed gratitude for irrigation received, and for railroads to come, praised His Excellency for investigating the Ganjam famine on the spot in the height of the hot weather, and made sundry requests concerning local matters, all of which were investigated, but none of which need be further referred to here. In reply to an application for another high school, the Governor took the opportunity to commend to the attention of the Municipal Council, primary education as being of far greater importance, and to urge on their attention the necessity of educating their women. Carpet-making, for which other towns in the south of India are now famed, was originally introduced into Ellore by Persians who came there from the Court of the Mussulman Kings of Golconda, whither they had migrated from Persia. We went to see a carpet being made, and admired the lightning celerity with which the long lean fingers of the manufacturers inserted the warp of many colours between the multitudinous threads of the stationary woof. These carpets sell for sums varying from 8 to 12 rupees a yard, according to quality, and are still largely exported to London. The Mussulmans told me that the honour and glory of this manufacture was Persian, that they were poor men, and did not make more than a bare sufficiency by their labour.

We slept in the boats and made next day our last canal journey, from Ellore to Bezwada. This mode of travelling is extremely comfortable. You have a good-sized room in which to read, write or sleep, you can travel along sidewalks to the bow of your boat, and then jump, probably across the *batterie de cuisine*, into the next boat where you find an excellent breakfast or luncheon, as the case may be. You can stop the boats and get out and walk under shady avenues whenever you like. In fact, it is a luxurious but very lazy life. A constant amusement is to watch the native captain, the chief engineer, and the boy of the steam tug. The captain calls out 'half a spade' (half speed) or 'stap her' (stop her) or 'eaz or' (ease her), and the little boy repeats it all in a shrill tenor through the speaking tube to the chief engineer, these nautical terms getting very much modified and altered as they are repeated from mouth to mouth. All the crew are clothed in blue serge with red handkerchiefs tied round their waists and on their heads, and they look extremely smart.

At midday we could see the low hills through which the Kistna winds to the head of the delta. It is in this hilly country that the Pitt and Regent diamonds were found, and it is believed that it was here that Sindbad the Sailor saw the Hindus cast lumps of flesh into a valley, which the eagles and vultures might bear back encrusted with diamonds.

This myth, as Mr. Mackenzie tells us in his District Manual, has been repeated by Marco Polo in the thirteenth, and Nicolo Conti in the fifteenth, centuries, and it has been supposed that the Hindu custom of sacrificing animals to propitiate malevolent spirits gave rise to the story. The same region abounds in marble. We learnt that the agents of the Deccan Mining Company were examining the ground for diamonds, and the Governor received a petition from some ryots begging that the marble might be removed to places where the people are "much fond of stones" for building.

After luncheon we got out and walked along the shore of the canal, which is flanked by avenues of banyans and groves of gigantic tamarinds. Within six miles of Bezwada we came upon a tom-tom telephone. This is a long succession of drums at intervals of a quarter of a mile. As soon as the Governor's boat appears, the first man strikes a drum, and the next man carries it on, and so it goes from drum to drum, till the sound at last reaches Bezwada. On this occasion, however, one link in the telephone was either deaf or sleepy, and we came upon the Collector before he knew that we were near. As you approach Bezwada, several navigable irrigation canals take off from the main, and just within sight of the town, we turned down the Masulipatam canal to the charming camp in which Mrs. Arundel received the party.

Next morning we all visited the anicut. Bezwada is the head of the Kistna, as Dowlaishweram is the head of the Godavari, delta. In both cases a high alluvial tract stretches away, for a distance varying from 40 to 60 miles, to the sea, but the anicut of the Kistna is situated in a more picturesque and beautiful spot than that of the Godavari. The river here is three-quarters of a mile wide, and it passes between two barren conical hills which rise on either side of the stream like abutment piers, from which the great dam takes off on either side. Water is just now, of course, low in the river, but looking up the stream the effect is that of an immense lake bounded on all sides, except that whence you look, by low picturesque hills. At sunset when the red light is fading from the sky, these distant hills are hardly distinguishable from low-lying clouds, and the expanse of water before you seems almost illimitable. It is broken, however, at a distance of three-quarters of a mile from the dam, by a round little islet covered with forest, the Innisfallen, to continue my comparison, of the lake. We crossed the river above the anicut in the steam-tug *Alexandra*, walked a short distance and then ran along a material line in a trolly to Tadipalle, where the temporary terminus of the Bellary-Kistna State Railway is for the present hung up in a jungle. We hear on all sides complaints on this score. Doubtless there is objection to building a permanent station near the river bank now, when it has not been decided at what point the bridge shall be made, but it must be three or four years before the bridge can be completed, and meanwhile the temporary tin station *

* This has been done. See Chapter XIII.

might as easily be placed near the bank of the river, where produce is unladen, as three miles away. As produce has now to be unshipped and put into carts to get to the station, traders think it just as well to let the carts to go on to Guntur, 17 miles, and this they do, whereby the railway loses much business, and gains much abuse. A crowd of traders that followed us as we walked along, loudly protested. Meanwhile we learnt at the station that they had no goods traffic, but that an average of 150 passengers a day left Bezwada to travel down the line, which at present is open only so far as Cumbum, whence there is a gap * of 66 miles to Nandyal, whence again communication is complete with the Madras Railway at Guntakal. The Governor was anxious not only that a temporary station should be made on the river bank, but also that if possible a tram line might be continued to a place below the anicut where the ferry boats ply. Paddle boats they are, worked by men and not by steam. Goods and produce of course necessarily pass the river above the anicut, where the canals on either side take off.

Near the railway station we saw for the first time Singareni coal, which had a dull shaley appearance, and none of the sparkle of Welsh black diamonds.

Over the anicut of Bezwada the Kistna rolls in flood far more rapidly than does its sister stream at Dowlaishweram. Its flood discharge is 761,000 cubic feet per second containing enough solid matter to

---

* Communication is now open all through to Guntakal.

deposit silt of one foot over five square miles. The anicut was chiefly built by Colonel Orr, a lieutenant of Sir Arthur Cotton of Godavari fame, and here, as there, forced labour was largely used. The dam is 1,300 yards in length, and 20 feet above the bed of the stream, 348 miles of navigable and 800 miles of unnavigable canals distribute its waters, and over these canals goods valued at £740,000 annually pass. The total cost of dam and distribution works is about £834,000, and the number of acres irrigated is 400,000. Here as in the Godavari, a large extent of land belonging to zemindars is irrigated gratis. Such lands are those which obtained water from the river prior to the construction of the new works. They had consequently an equitable claim not to be placed in a worse position, than that in which they were before, and as a matter of fact, they are placed in a much better position. There is consequently a disposition to class as 'ancient customary cultivation' as much irrigated land as possible. We asked the Superintending Engineer what was the amount of these lands, to which that officer replied that 'the amount of ancient cultivation was annually increasing.' Before going home to breakfast, we drove round the town, and saw various improvements which Mr. Arundel has been carrying out with funds partly supplied by Government and partly by the Municipality, with a view to providing for the future requirements of this important town, which surely has a great future before it.

Arrived at camp, we found the makers of toys and

chintzes parading their wares. No muslins, however, were brought up for inspection. Since the publication of "Hobson Jobson," we know that the fabric took its name from Mosul, the modern site of ancient Nineveh, and not from Maisolia, or the country about Masulipatam. However, Masulipatam is no longer famous for muslins, and the exports of chintzes and coloured cloths, which still are made, have fallen from £50,000 to £5,000. Such muslins as are now produced are moreover coarse in texture. The trade in chintzes is steady, but owing to their high cost, the purely hand-painted cloths are seldom made now. A cheaper description is manufactured, the outlines of the designs being stamped by blocks and the intermediate colours filled in by hand. I do not know what are the "best and most delicate buckrams" of which Marco Polo says "in sooth they look like the tissue of a spider's web, there is no king or queen in the world but might be glad to wear them;" but pretty silk handkerchiefs are made at Jaggammapet, where the raw silk is worked up.

Among the exports of this district is one of small importance, which, none the less, commands attention. We often read of halcyon weather, and sometimes, for instance in 'Marius the Epicurean,' the beautiful tale that hangs thereby, but we seldom hear of halcyon's feather as an article of commerce. None the less, are kingfishers destroyed in this district for their plumage, destined, it is believed, to take part in the triumphs of London and Parisian milliners.

On Sunday we rested and went to church, and in

the evening, the dew rained very hard in the canal, so that some of us were more or less drenched in the house-boats, which we inhabit just below the tents. Before we could get up, Lord Marsham and I were interviewed from the banks by a woman of Bourbon, who explained in fluent French that she was shipwrecked, and, in short, wanted her passage paid back to the Isle of France.

On Monday morning the Governor received and answered no less than four addresses from the Hindus and Mussulmans of Bezwada, and from the inhabitants of Guntur and Masulipatam. Speaking within sound of the water rippling over the great Kistna dam, the reader of each address in turn expressed gratitude to the British Government for the construction of that great irrigation work.

The chief subject however referred to was railway communication. The inhabitants of the district who have an earnest and able advocate in Mr. Arundel, urged that a branch of the new East Coast line should be made from Masulipatam to Bezwada, through the rich country of the delta, and from Guntur through the cotton country to meet the Cuddapah-Nellore famine protective line at the last mentioned town. His Excellency in reply urged the necessity of any extension from Bezwada to Madras being broad gauge, in order that eventually a through broad-gauge communication along the coast, might be established between Madras and Calcutta. The Kistna bridge, sanction for the commencement of which by an happy accident was communicated at Bezwada, is to be made so as to allow of its carrying a broad-gauge line, and the East Coast Railway thence through the Northern Circars to Cuttack, and by the Bengal-Nagpur line to Calcutta, will, it is hoped, be completed upon the same gauge.

Opportunity was taken by the Governor to praise one municipality, and to admonish another. Several engineering questions were raised, which had been considered *in situ*, and were now to stand over till after the visit of the Chief Engineer for Irrigation. His Excellency dwelt upon the great future there was before this town which already shows signs of great commercial activity, and is being brought up by Mr. Arundel and his assistants, so as to be able to take the position which it is expected to fill in the world, situated as it is at the head of the rice-producing delta with a country rich in minerals at its back, and coal, gold, marble and diamonds around it awaiting the successful *exploiteur*. More than this ; to the list may be added garnets, agate, iron, mica and chalcedony.

The afternoon was taken up by a reception at which were present, besides the European officers and zemindars, Mr. Furdonjee Jamshedjee and Mr. Stevens who came as a deputation from the Minister of Hyderabad on behalf of His Highness the Nizam, to conduct His Excellency to Hyderabad territory, 20 miles up the railway. The levée over, the Governor and Mr. Arundel climbed up a high hill to visit Mr. Harrison, the clergyman, who comes from King's Lynn, and to see Bezwada from a high place. Close to Mr. Harrison's house, is an ancient Buddhist cave temple. Lord Marsham, Mr. Wolfe-Murray, and I climbed up the still higher telegraph hill on the left bank of the river, from which the anicut takes off. Half-way up is a temple of Kali, the goddess of evil before the outer portico of which we were not allowed to pass. The Brahmin priest spoke very apologetically of the slaughter of cocks, of which there was ample evidence on the steps leading to the temple. In the south of the Madras Presidency, you would not, I think, find a Brahmin priest in a Kali temple, or a Brahmin connected with any bloody sacrifice. From the top of the hill, you see that all the houses of the town are tiled. This in India is a token at once of prosperity and security. Only comparatively rich people build tiled houses, and in former days a tiled house, which was the exception, was always the one that was chosen to loot. Now-a-days in the Kistna people can not only be rich, but can afford to appear so.

From the top of the hill, telegraph wires start on a long and unsupported journey to the summit of the hill on the other side of the dam across the river. Besides the telegraph wires a thick cable spans the stream. I know nothing about the theory of strains, or the behaviour of a mile of wire, but when Mr. Wolfe-Murray and I sat upon this cable and tried with all our united strengths to shake it, we failed. After giving up all hope of moving it several minutes later we found that we had produced an impression, for we were nearly shaken off the wire by a violent and irregular vibration, returning we supposed from the other side. Descending the hill we found two religious devotees sitting on the dam surrounded by an admiring crowd. They were squatting on the ground with their backs against the wall, and singing hymns with immense energy and infinite gesticulation. One was fair and one was dark. The dark man was simple and serious, the fair man was a born comedian, and as he called on the gods in a prolonged breathless rhapsody he seemed quite pleased when we were unable to restrain an occasional smile, and delighted when all his audience laughed outright. Then we sculled down stream, in the canal of course, to camp, dined there for the last time, and left it by steamer to attend a native entertainment before joining the special train in which we were to sleep.

The illuminations in the evening were singularly beautiful. The canal here is not a dull stagnant water-way, but a broad and flowing stream of fresh water 100 yards wide flanked on either side by green banks on which are avenues of trees, whose shade at night made dark and unreflecting two lateral streaks of water-way, and caused the remaining moon-silvered middle streak to appear the brighter by contrast. Turning the corner before the bridge at the dam is reached, we saw up stream a town of lights hanging over its left bank, and perched in part upon a hill, lighted up in contour behind it. Along the wharves hundreds of barges and house-boats literally 'burnt on the water' and as you neared the end of the canal, and approached the terminal lock and bridge of the water-way, it seemed that the steam launch entered an aqueous passage roofed with fiery stalactites, which as you approached them more nearly, were broken into tremulous sections across the launch's bow. Then as red and blue lights burned, the banks crowded with dense masses of natives were revealed, and now and again the towers of the temple stood out in lurid light against the dark and precipitous hill.

Before leaving Bezwada, it may be as well to briefly notice one or two subjects of public interest connected with the administration. The liquor licensing system resembles, throughout half the district, that of the Godavari, that is to say, country spirits are distilled from toddy, and arrangements have been made by which a fee will be levied on every palm tree tapped, the privilege of selling such country spirits being sold by auction. In half the district the excise system is in force and it will be extended during this year over a still larger area. Under this system a distillery is established at Bezwada, and the distiller has the exclusive right of manufacture, and wholesale sale of country spirits which are distilled from coarse sugar. The liquor is taxed before it leaves the distillery, and it must be recorded, that it is generally drunk undiluted, as is believed to be the rule with the Indian dram-drinker.

Turning now to the Agricultural Loans Act. In the whole of this large district it has been brought into use in less than a dozen cases. Various reasons are assigned for this abstention, but it is quite sufficient that natives hate the preciseness and punctuality of our arrangements for repayment. They are not peculiar in this respect; for everywhere a sense of benefit derived from a past loan is apt to be dissipated by the annoyance of present repayment. It is said that the Russian Government by no means gained any popularity with the serfs, on whose behalf it carried out the great measure of emancipation.

In the Kistna district the house-tax has been gradually introduced into seventeen village unions, at rates as low as ½ or ¼ of the maximum. The tax does not appear to have met with much opposition. The Collector reports, regarding self-government in general, that a keen interest is felt in the subject, and that taxes are paid with greater readiness, when imposed by the Municipal Council, or the District Board, or the local Punchayets, than they would be if imposed by any single official. He observes, however, that the persevering gratuitous work given to such matters in England is wanting here. Mr. Arundel also informed the Governor that the value of the services of midwives attached to the district dispensaries was being recognized and appreciated, one proof among many of progress in this rapidly advancing district.

We slept in His Highness the Nizam's beautiful and comfortable railway saloons, and after sunrise travelled through scrub jungle of cassia and acacia, and past fields of sorghum and castor-oil, to Kummumett, the capital of the most eastern district of the Nizam's dominions. The villages and the villagers here are just like those of our Telugu country. The houses are thatched, and you do not see the flat mud roofs which are characteristic of other parts of the Deccan. At eleven o'clock we reached Yellandupad, the next station beyond Singareni, from which the mines take their name. Here we were met by Nawab Badr-ud-Dowlah, whose particular business it is, on behalf of the Nizam, to meet on the frontier all distinguished visitors. Here too were Mr. Lowinski, the Agent of the Deccan Mining Company, and other officials and employés of the mines. Close to the platform was an archway raised on two buttresses of Singareni coal, ornamented with sprigs of yellow-flowering cassia.

It is difficult to travel from British into native territory without speculating and enquiring as to the relative condition of the ryots in either case, and on all occasions there seems much reason to believe that the difference between their economic and social condition is probably very small. An official who has lived on the frontier of several Native States will notice that it hardly occurs to the inhabitants on either side to compare the conditions of British and native rule, and that migrations from one to the other are not very frequent, nor are they all by any means immigrations into British territory. The fact is that it is the condition of the country that determines the condition of the ryot, and he is probably not more taxed on the whole in the native than in the British territory. He may pay a higher land tax, but he does not pay various cesses for the different services of civilization. In one respect, however,—and that the most important—there is a great difference. The British Government spends a large proportion of its revenues in developing the districts, in making roads, railways and irrigation works. Thus indirectly, if not directly, its ryots are infinitely better off than those of Native States.

The mines at Singareni are situated in a vast, but not thick, jungle of teak and satinwood. At present there are seven workings and the output amounts to 600 tons a day. The Governor and his party went down one incline. They work here by inclines and not by shafts, chiefly because the seams are so near the surface. We descended 650 feet to get to a depth of 100 feet, and struck the seam very soon after entering the tunnel. The extraction of coal is comparatively easy and inexpensive, the roof is very good and does not require to be timbered, there is very little water, and the coal is so slightly gaseous that naked lights are used all over the works. The coal is very clean and of extremely good quality, and burns better than that of the Bengal coal-fields. It fetches from Rs. 3/8 to Rs. 6 a ton at the pit's mouth or rather at the incline head; but the cost of carriage is so enormous that it cannot be sold in Bombay under Rs. 22, and so cannot at present compete there with English coal. It is expected and hoped that the rates will soon be lowered, after which it is anticipated that the expensive and effective machinery will be fully occupied. Just now the direction have to refuse large contracts.

An article in the London *Times* of Friday, December 6th, quotes largely from reports by Mr. William Morgans, kindly furnished to us, who says that the Singareni mines produce an excellent steam coal, hard, and possessed of fairly good qualities for withstanding exposure to weather. Had the coal mines stood alone so as to be under the obligation to pay interest on the £61,000 expended upon their individual needs only, they would at the present moment be paying over 20 per cent. supposing that the expenditure has not exceeded £61,000 and that the output is 600 tons a day. Even if the latest expenditure on machinery be included, at the present rate of output it is probable that the return from the coal mine is not less than 18 per cent., but this calculation is only given for what it may be worth. As it is, however, the produce of the mines have to provide interest on one million pounds sterling, the whole capital of the Company. The diamondiferous and auriferous regions of the State have, however, yet to be worked, and in regard to gold, at any rate, the Company is very hopeful. Mr. Lowinski, its experienced Agent, is convinced that diamonds will pay. It is reported, however, that the manner and circumstances of the distribution of these precious stones have yet to be ascertained. They have been found quite lately in a formation of a derivative character and search is being prosecuted for original diamond-bearing strata. Mr. Morgans hazards an interesting conjecture *apropos* of the much discussed question whether the natives exhausted the old works or not, before they left them. He discovered unmistakable evidence that in old workings the ancients depended largely on the use of underground fires for loosening the quartz in their drives. He thinks the expense of fuel might have stopped the mines, but on the whole believes that the wars with which the Deccán has been continuously afflicted in times past, have chiefly brought about this effect. That is very likely, but probably in the fact that the labourers were seldom paid for their labour lies the most likely explanation. They were driven to work and rigorously searched to see they took nothing away, and had no interest in finding gold or diamonds, in the profits of which they would not participate, and the labour of finding which they alone had unrequited to experience. Mr. Morgans found the country between the Kistna and Tungabadra riddled with ancient diggings and superficial mines, and considers these fields to be of the same geological character as, but of far greater extent than, the gold fields of Kolar, whose star apparently is now in the ascendant. Meanwhile the assays of Raichore quartz are said to be encouraging, while Oregaum crushings are altogether phenomenal. British India generally and Madras more particularly cannot but profit by the development of the industrial resources of the Deccan, as Lord Connemara said in answering the Nizam's toast proposing his health. It is somewhat extraordinary how little interest is taken in Southern India in the gold mining and other industries of Mysore and the Deccan, a passing reference to which may be allowed.

We awoke on New Year's day to find ourselves climbing up the grassy uplands of the Deccan plateau in a frosty misty morning. Three blankets and a sheet were just enough to keep you warm in bed.

At the station at Hyderabad the Resident, Mr.

Fitzpatrick, the Minister Nawab Sir Asman Jah, the Amir-i-Kabir Sir Khursheed Jah, the General Commanding the Division, and many other officers and sirdars assembled to meet the Governor, who presently drove off with the Minister through streets lined with troops, Hindu and Mussulman, Abyssinian and Arab, reformed and unreformed. The morning was spent in receiving visits from His Highness the Nizam and His Excellency the Minister, and in returning the Nizam's visit.

Every one knows Hyderabad and every one knows that the drive to the palace is very interesting, through Chudderghaut, over the river, the dry bed of which is now cultivated with melons, under the archway, down the long street to the Char Minar, and on down the narrow passage, and into the palace, a quadrangle of pillared halls surrounding a raised masonry lake of water. In the evening at the banquet the palace looked even better than in the day. The pillared halls were filled with countless lights reflected in glass chandeliers, and the gardens and courtyards were lit up by thousands of oil-tumblers, as also was the long narrow street bounded by two high windowless walls, through which you drive to gain access to the courtyard. The houses and gardens of the Nizam, and of the great Hyderabad nobles are of enormous extent and consist of many squares and quadrangles all surrounded by high walls. Besides the two squares we saw on either side of the Banqueting Hall, and many others of the like character, there is a park within the precincts of the Char Mahala in which no less than

200 deer live. Many of the great nobles were present at dinner. In the familiar use of their titles we forget as a rule their meanings, which, however, are full of interest. One is "the equal of the sun in state, the great noble"; another is "the best of the nobles"; a third "the ornament of the peerage"; a fourth "the light of the State"; a fifth "its full moon"; and so on. In "the Benefactor" we recognize a more familiar appellation, and in the "crown of battle" we discover an old friend.

His Highness the Nizam himself was "the Director" or "Administrator" of the country under the Great Mogul, and so enjoys the privilege of possessing a title held by no other Prince or King. Had he been originally an independent Prince and not a Viceroy he would probably have been "The Shadow of God" like the Shah, or the "Son of Heaven" like the Emperor of China. After dinner there were fireworks and illuminations. They understand this sort of thing infinitely well at Hyderabad, which certainly is one of the greatest cities for entertainments in the world. Many of the great cities of the East have second names in which their more characteristic features are brought out. For instance, Ispahan is 'half the world,' Shiraz is 'the seat of learning,' Baghdad 'is the abode of (heavenly) peace,' and Hyderabad should be Dar-ul-Ziyafat, the city of entertainments. The best illuminations are produced by the simplest means, and nothing equals the mudpie and earthen saucer system, whereby at the installation of the present Nizam, the road and the prominent features of the landscape, on either side of it, were marked out for many miles in little lights producing an extremely beautiful effect. Just now the oil-tumbler process appears to be in greater favour, but it is not nearly so effective.

Next morning we rode with Nawab Afsar Jung, the Commander of the Golconda Brigade, to that ancient fortress where within an outer wall, seven miles in extent, six other lines of fortifications succeed one another, the last forming the citadel, which crowns the low rocky hill in the centre of the fortified post. A garrison of 5,000 troops still occupies Golconda, but while the art of war is encouraged, the arts of peace are not neglected, and Nawab Afsar Jung has introduced the manufacture of shawls with the aid of instructors imported from Cashmere. His little son, aged 10 years, rode a big horse at good hard gallop from Hyderabad to Golconda and back, and also acted as galloper to his father whenever any messages had to be carried, or there was any duty to be done. He rides wonderfully well, and promises to be as good a horseman, if possible, as his father. Most of the Mussulman nobles of the Nizam's Court are accomplished horsemen, and few of them are more at home in the saddle than His Highness himself.

The newspapers to-day bring Mr. Bradlaugh's Congress speech, and this recalls the fact that the people of Ellore, who informed us that they took no interest in politics, have according to the *Hindu* decreed an address and a casket to the "Member for India," just as in another town visited during this tour a member of the Municipality, who did not agree with his colleagues, desired to present an address on behalf of a 'sabha' or assembly. These sabhas are generally local congress agencies and very often consist of the founder himself, assisted by one or two of his friends. A not unusual combination is a schoolmaster with his assistants, and a few boys. Of course there are sabhas, which doubtless are much more representative institutions. Meanwhile those who are interested in the congress will be interested in sidelights upon its constitution, and these must be sought outside of large towns.

Owing to indisposition, Lord Connemara unfortunately was not able to take part in the many entertainments which were held, or proposed to be held in his honour. Among these was a morning's sport in His Highness the Nizam's reserves at Srinagar, where a most enjoyable morning can be spent, shooting black buck in an undulating rocky country affording good cover to the stalker. Breakfast with the Nawab Vicar-ul-Omrah in his splendid new palace of Falaknumah was also an entertainment His Excellency had to forego. This immense edifice is situated on the top of a rocky hill, whence you obtain a magnificent view of the Mir Alam tank on your left, and of the fortress of Golconda beyond it. Before the palace and below it, spreads the city of Hyderabad, like one huge garden whence minarets and palaces emerge at intervals. Beyond, in the distance, the blue waters of the Hoosain Saugor tank are just visible, and beyond that again the rocky hillocks of Secunderabad, the barracks of Trimulgherry, and the gleaming walls of distant Bolarum. On the right is another lake, and beyond it the preserves of Srinagar. This view is one of great beauty, and the undulating plain, broken by little hills and big boulders, is covered as far as the eye can range with the Hyderabad of the present, and the ruins and remains of Golconda, and its suburbs, of the past.

A curious feature of the Vicar-ul-Omrah's breakfast recalled the four and twenty black birds that were baked in a pie, of which we have all read in our childhood. Some rather, but not suspiciously, large cakes were handed round,' and as they were opened a little amaduvad or wax-bill flew chirping out of each, alighted on the flowers and shrubs with which the table was covered, or flew about the ceiling and room. As there were sixty guests, no less than five dozen birds suddenly appeared and began to sing, when the pies were opened.

The Governor obtained leave from the Minister, to bring down to Madras for a while, two modellers to teach their craft to a class in the School of Arts. These men are descendants of some pupils of an Italian, who came long ago to Lucknow, to decorate the palace of the King. They are extremely clever, but the art is said to be dying out in Northern India and has yet to be introduced into the South.

Lord Connemara's visit to Hyderabad concluded with calls upon His Highness the Nizam and the Resident, and on the evening of the 4th January we regretfully left the capital of the Deccan, and after crossing the Tungabadra found ourselves once more in Madras territories, where a Collector was waiting with representations concerning the approaching settlement of his district.

The chief features of the present tour were irrigation, railway communications, and a consideration of the future wants of the Kistna district, the most urgent requirements of which are, the East Coast Railway, with its proposed feeder lines from Bezwada to Masulipatam and to Guntur and Nellore, the early construction of the Kistna bridge, and immediate provision for the requirements of traffic pending its construction. Singareni coal mines, and the traffic of His Highness the Nizam's State Railway, are most important factors in the future of the Kistna district, and a return journey through Hyderabad—the most direct route from Singareni to Madras—also afforded an opportunity of accepting the invitation of His Highness the Nizam to spend a few days at his capital.

We travelled in all 1,370 miles,—upwards of 300 by sea, upwards of 700 by rail, and upwards of 200 by river and canal. The canal travelling was an agreeable novelty, and a most comfortable shipwreck merely added zest to our adventures.

CHAPTER XII.

THE EURASIAN SETTLEMENTS OF WHITEFIELD AND SAUSMOND.

Eurasian problem—Whitefield and Sausmond—History of settlements—Mr. D. S. White—His "Guide Book" and project—Maharajah of Mysore—Mr. Glenny's report on Colonies—Sir Dennis Fitzpatrick's opinion—Mr. Gantz—Governor's arrival at Kadgoodi—To Whitefield—Settlers interviewed—Sir Oliver St. John—Address—Characteristic holdings—Sergeant Crooks—Leases of holdings—Sausmond—Results of inspections.

A WELL-KNOWN writer has humourously described the difficulties of the Eurasian problem and the failure of various projects for the employment of the race of mixed blood, which has resulted from our occupation of India. He represents a personage high in authority as "looking round the windy hills of Simla and wondering why somebody does not make the East Indian a high farmer."

It might be said of many of Alberigh Mackay's sketches "*ridentem dicere verum quid vetat*" and somebody has tried to accomplish this supposed impossibility, for on the table land of Mysore, 200 miles from Madras and 15 from Bangalore are situated the Eurasian Colonies of Whitefield and Sausmond, living memorials of the energy and enterprise of the late Mr. D. S. White, who desired to make his brother East Indians ordinary agriculturists, if not high farmers. The Governor had long been anxious to visit these settle-

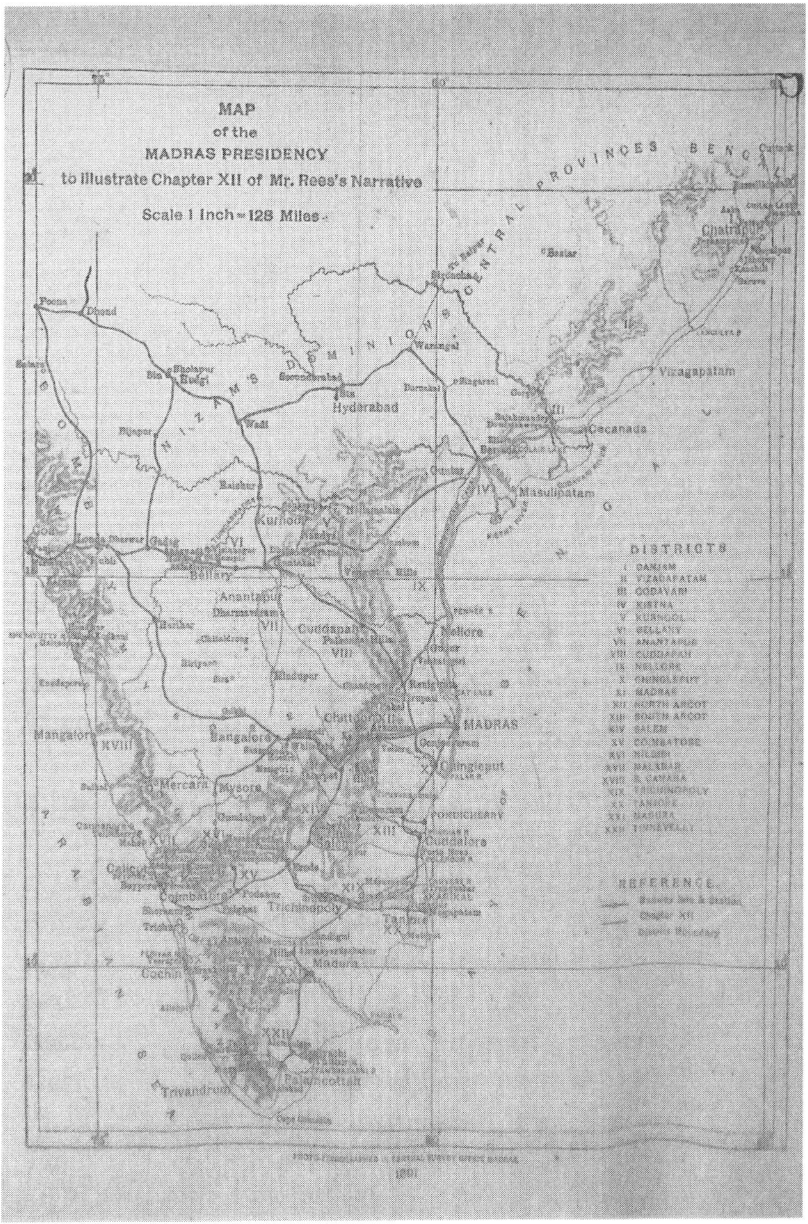
MAP
of the
MADRAS PRESIDENCY
to illustrate Chapter XII of Mr. Rees's Narrative
Scale 1 Inch = 128 Miles
CENTRAL PROVINCES
NIZAM'S DOMINIONS
Poona
Dhond
Hyderabad
Warangal
Vizagapatam
Cocanada
Masulipatam
Kurnool
Bellary
Anantapur
Cuddapah
Nellore
MADRAS
Chingleput
Chittoor
Bangalore
Mangalore
Mercara
Mysore
PONDICHERRY
Cuddalore
Salem
Calicut
Coimbatore
Trichinopoly
KARIKAL
Negapatam
Tanjore
Madura
Cochin
Trivandrum
Palamcottah
Chatrapur
DISTRICTS
I GANJAM
II VIZAGAPATAM
III GODAVARI
IV KISTNA
V KURNOOL
VI BELLARY
VII ANANTAPUR
VIII CUDDAPAH
IX NELLORE
X CHINGLEPUT
XI MADRAS
XII NORTH ARCOT
XIII SOUTH ARCOT
XIV SALEM
XV COIMBATORE
XVI NILGIRI
XVII MALABAR
XVIII S. CANARA
XIX TRICHINOPOLY
XX TANJORE
XXI MADURA
XXII TINNEVELLY
REFERENCE.

ments, which were last year described by the President Mr. Gantz as 'the *magnum opus* of the Eurasian and Anglo-Indian Association,' but no opportunity offered until the spring of the present year. The President-founder, Mr. D. S. White, in 1879 in his "Guide to the Eurasian and Anglo-Indian Villages," described, as the chief work of the Association, that "of settling "Eurasians and Anglo-Indians on the soil, to lead "them into agricultural and industrial pursuits, and "to remove for ever the feeling of anxiety as regards "their own future and that of their children." Mr. White was of opinion "that the true field of Indian "agriculture was still open and awaited the intro-"duction of capital, energy, intelligence, improved "methods, and new industries." He held that in laying the foundation of the first settlement, the Association was but "laying the foundation of thousands of others," and in a monograph upon the land scheme contained in the above mentioned Guide, it is boldly asserted that of all callings "that of the farmer "is least exposed to the vicissitudes of fortune, and "that a few acres, with the help of a small capital, "will feed a family generation after generation without "ever being exhausted." A further perusal of the "Guide" shows that pisciculture, sericulture, viticulture and agriculture were considered industries suitable to the colonists, who were further to eke out their incomes by keeping goats, pigs, sheep, by breeding horses, ponies, and mules, and by raising vanilla, tobacco, coffee, mushrooms, and arrowroot.

His Highness the Maharajah of Mysore granted to

the Association upwards of 3,000 acres of land in his territories upon extremely favourable terms in regard to the payment of assessment, and, in reply to its address of thanks, warned its members that "they "could never hope for anything more than the very "moderate return with which the industry of the "ryot is rewarded, except as the result of increased "labour, greater intelligence, and the application of "science and machinery."

Mr. White's "Guide" contains monographs on all the professions, trades, and occupations which it was considered the colonists might pursue, together with plans of the villages and much miscellaneous information.

In 1886 Mr. White again stated the main principles of his scheme, which were these:—"To send the "able-bodied *destitute*, old and young, only as labour-"ers to be fed and paid, leaving it to them by good "conduct to rise to the level of settlers; to send persons "of slender means to carry on trades of various kinds, "giving them each one acre of land; to send persons "of sufficient, yet moderate, means to farm, giving "them allotments of land extending to 20 acres; to "build houses and allow all settlers to purchase them "by rent for a stated period; to open libraries and "schools and allow children to acquire a knowledge of "various mechanical arts."

The experiments made with paupers proved unsuccessful, but grants of lots of 20 acres were made to several settlers possessed of independent means. In Mr. White's opinion the experiment in such cases turned out well and showed "that industrious individuals, by the expenditure of one or two thousand rupees, would lose nothing and gain a good deal by going into the land and by personally superintending their agricultural operations." It is to this latter expression of Mr. White's views that attention is chiefly directed, as it is obvious that he himself, when he wrote this in 1886, was conscious that he had been too sanguine in the views he originally entertained of the future of these settlements. In his pamphlet of 1886, Mr. White further stated that his scheme contemplated the constitution of a self-contained village community on the lines of an Indian village. He believed that only under such a constitution could the descendants of Eurasians in India live by ordinary manual labour, and he observed that the exclusion of cheap competition, though objectionable in the abstract, was the vital principle of his scheme. In the same year (1886) the then Director of Revenue Settlement and Agriculture, Mr. Glenny, was directed by the Madras Government at the request of Mr. White to visit the Eurasian settlements and report upon their condition and prospects. In making this request Mr. White again stated his plans for the working of the settlements. It was laid down "that land was only to be given to persons possessing means sufficient to enable them to supply their own cattle and implements and carry on cultivation with their own labour and that of their children, though small plots of land—an acre in extent—might be given to persons of less means desiring to live in the settle-

"ments and to carry on trades of various kinds neces-
"sary to the village community, while poor and
"destitute persons were to be encouraged by the
"Association to engage themselves as agricultural
"labourers and domestic helps to the settlers."

Mr. Glenny in his report observed that it would be very easy for a pedantic critic to find much in these settlements to criticise, but he has himself adopted a somewhat optimistic tone and has dwelt chiefly, as any one would wish to do in regard to such a novel experiment, upon the satisfactory features of the case. He described the operations of different settlers, and found that individuals had succeeded in selling pork, ham and bacon, jam and flour at a profit. In regard to the agricultural holdings he generally remarks : "they are doing well." He does not touch on the financial aspects of these holdings. He observes that the children of these people, having been provided with healthy homes, are saved from the temptations incidental to residence in large towns. After a perusal of this report, the Madras Government expressed itself gratified that the settlements of Whitefield and Sausmond were in a creditable and promising condition.

Subsequently to this, the President, Mr. White, petitioned the Government of India for a grant of Rs. 150 a month for five years for the school at Whitefield and a similar sum for the school at Sausmond, in order that technical and agricultural instruction might be imparted to the children of the colonists. This request led to an inspection of the settlements by Mr., now Sir Dennis, Fitzpatrick, then Resident in

Mysore, who desired to form an opinion as to what assistance could be given to these schools with due regard to the grant-in-aid rules of the Governments of Madras and Mysore. Mr. Fitzpatrick doubted whether the cultivation of ordinary crops would ever become an important source of profit to the colonists, and held that their main hope of success lay in the breeding of poultry and pigs, in the manufacture of ragi flour and of preserves, and possibly, after a lapse of time, in dairy-farming, in which however he observed only one colonist had succeeded. He was, however, of opinion that *for pensioners, and others having small independent means of their own*, an opportunity here offered of settling down in a healthy place possessing a good climate, with the prospect of obtaining by industry and good management a considerable accession to their incomes. As regards the settlement of artisans and agricultural labourers in the colony he did not think that such men could compete with natives. He observed on the whole that, though the colonies were not likely to effect all that was originally hoped, they had made a good beginning and had already served, to some extent, a useful purpose, which, within certain limits, might be improved and extended. While he considered that the Governments of Madras and Mysore might properly aid the cause of education in these villages, he was strongly of opinion that a grant for the purpose of affording *technical* instruction was altogether inadvisable. Those who wanted agricultural instruction might, he thought, be given scholarships at the Saidápet College at Madras, the Governments of Madras or Mysore endowing one or two scholarships for this purpose. As regards the teaching of individual trades, he thought the colonists would have to pick up such knowledge for themselves, as they do elsewhere. He observed that Mr. White's project of forming a self-contained community, possessing its own artisans and excluding competition, was altogether chimerical.

The Government of India, on perusal of Mr. Fitzpatrick's report, expressed a hope that the Government of Madras would see its way to devise some reasonable measure of help consistent with the requirements of the case, but observed that the amount of monthly grant applied for in the memorial seemed to be quite disproportionate to any results which were likely to be secured by the adoption of arrangements of the nature of those advocated by the Association, the settlements in question not being large enough to support expensive technical schools. Subsequently to the receipt of this letter, the schools were brought under the inspection of the Madras Educational Department, and are at present receiving grants from the Madras Government.

In 1889 the Anglo-Indian Association suffered a great loss by the death of Mr. White, to whose energy its existence was due. Mr. Gantz, Mr. White's successor, adopted that gentleman's later and more matured views as regards the objects and prospects of these colonies, and, as lately as October 1889, said that it was one of the main features of the land-scheme *that settlers should be capitalists*, and that the question of settling on the land persons without any means whatsoever, was one with which the Association at present had no concern. This brings the history of these settlements up to the time of Lord Connemara's visit.

His Excellency, accompanied by myself, left Madras at ¼ to 6 in the evening, of a blazing April day and reached Kadgoodi Station at ¼ to 6 next morning. We rode the two miles intervening between the station and the settlement, passing the kaolin hills, from which great things were anticipated. The settlers have made no effort to work this clay, but the Association leased it out to Messrs. Arbuthnot and Co., who, presumably, have not found it a paying business, as all operations have ceased. From the top of the kaolin hill a good view is obtained of Whitefield. You see the village school, the church, and a dozen cottages more or less, well laid out upon a plan somewhat too ambitious for the actual circumstances of the case. It was intended that from a central circus, different avenues should radiate, these avenues being connected by parallel lines of streets made up of houses, each standing in its own walled garden. A small church is almost completed, and the largest building is the now unused storehouse constructed by Messrs. Arbuthnot and Co. for the abandoned business of working the kaolin clay. An undulating country stretches all around the settlement. In the trifling depressions the soil is good; on the higher ground it is sandy, rocky, and more than indifferent. Here and there are groves of casuarinas and orchards of fruit trees. There were no crops on the ground, and abundant evidence was forthcoming that crops are sparsely raised. The settlement had not a very flourishing appearance. Some of the cottages were moderately neat, but in no case apparently had any settler the time or inclination to sacrifice to the Graces. In the neighbouring town of Bangalore, the bungalows and verandahs are generally covered with orange bignonia, violet petræa, various tunbergias and a wealth of convolvulus. All these beautiful creepers grow profusely in this favoured climate, but the Whitefield settler has not called them to his aid, and the village has a somewhat bare and unattractive appearance. The houses do not look like homes, and many of the settlers in fact live in Bangalore.

His Excellency began by interviewing individual settlers. On one point they were unanimous. They wanted a pound and a village headman. The Resident in Mysore, Sir Oliver St. John, who had met the Governor at the railway station, promised to bring this matter to the notice of the Government of His Highness the Maharajah, and also to arrange, if possible, that the lands belonging to the two native villages, of which Whitefield consists, should be clubbed together as a separate village. The first settler to speak, who was also the oldest, stated that the water-supply was bad, and asked that the standard of the school should be raised. He said that his lands had never paid him, that he had some capital, and had come there expecting to make a living. He had hoped for help from the Association funds. He found that the cattle were not strong enough for improved ploughs, and that the ground was not good enough for large crops. Another and a more recent settler said that he also had depended upon getting external aid from the funds of the Association, which had been granted in some measure to the earliest settlers. He hoped that the Government of Mysore would reduce the assessment and cut a canal. Another non-resident settler from Madras, however, was thoroughly satisfied with the existing assessment of one rupee an acre, had cultivated his land without assistance, and did not want any external help. The Secretary for the Mysore Branch of the Association observed that everything that was possible had been given to the settlers, and that the land had never been intended for colonisation by paupers. The Secretary for the Madras Branch expressed the same opinion, observing that the Association had done all it could.

The most characteristic holdings were afterwards visited in company with their owners. In no case did it appear that the cultivation of the land had paid the cultivators, though it seemed almost certain that orchards and casuarina groves in the lowlying and better lands would eventually pay fairly well. Several settlers had dug wells at considerable expense, having to go down as far as 60 feet in some cases for water.

The site of the settlement is open to the same objection as that of Bangalore. It is higher than everything around it, and consequently, though extremely healthy and pleasant as a place of residence, possesses a bad water-supply, while the rain washes off the surface soil and leaves little but rock and sand.

One of the settlers, Sergeant Crooks, had planted in his orchard graft mangoes, which were doing well, apples, oranges, limes, citrons, peaches, plums, guavas, figs, loquats, cherries, lichees, custard apples, pears, pine apples and pomegranates. He had also a flourishing casuarina plantation. There were a few miserable vines in one or two orchards, but no real effort is being made in viticulture. A jeweller from Bangalore also had, like Sergeant Crooks, planted a very promising orchard in lowlying ground. Both these settlers are comparative capitalists, and just as no settler can do any good at Whitefield without capital, so do those who have most capital occupy the best land and do most good with it. In the neighbouring town of Bangalore with 160,000 inhabitants, and in the prosperous gold fields of Kolar, Whitefield and Sausmond possess unfailing markets for more than all the fuel they can raise. Already has the growing output of the Mysore, Oregaum, Nundidroog, Balaghaut and other mines produced a rise in the local price of fuel, which offers an additional inducement to neighbouring landholders to enter into what previously was a sufficiently profitable investment.

One of the settlers' wives made very good ragi flour, which was said to sell well at Bangalore, but at a price higher than that of wheat flour.

The *puttahs* or leases for their holdings had only just been granted to the Whitefield colonists. They hold directly under the Government of Mysore, the leases merely containing a stipulation that they are not to sell, mortgage or alienate their lands except to members of the community. In the neighbouring settlement of Sausmond the Association is the tenant of the Government, and is responsible for the payment of the assessment, which it collects from individual holders. Owing to the liberality of the Maharajah, no assessments have yet been paid. His Highness' Government gave the lands free for a period of five years, which was subsequently extended, I believe, to the end of last year.

In the afternoon, Lord Connemara, Sir Oliver St. John and I visited Sausmond, a more prepossessing colony than Whitefield, situated on the margin of a large tank and close to a flourishing native village. The settlers looked contented and happy, but they were very few, and each individual settler stated that, like his brethren at Whitefield, he had not been able to make his land pay. The conditions here are precisely the same as those which obtain in the larger settlement.

The conclusions at which we arrived may be summed up as follows: firstly, that the present aid which is given to education in these colonies by the Madras Government may be continued, and even extended, should occasion require; secondly, that these colonies are worthy of support and encouragement, inasmuch as they afford an opportunity to European or East Indian pensioners of obtaining land on favourable terms in a village where they can cultivate it amongst their fellow countrymen; thirdly, that it is most improbable that any but capitalists can work these holdings at a profit; fourthly, that such profits are to be expected chiefly from fruit-growing, fuel raising, arboriculture and the like pursuits, while in respect of crops it is most improbable that these settlers will ever be able to compete with ordinary native ryots; fifthly, that there is little or no hope that the children of these settlers will ever make their living on these lands in the absence of capital such as their fathers possessed; and, sixthly, that the idea of a self-contained European and Eurasian village, possessing its own artisans, tradesmen, and agriculturists, independent of all outside help, must be abandoned as altogether chimerical.

It follows from these conclusions, however, that the Government of Madras should give a sympathetic ear to any requests proceeding from these colonies. At present it is believed that nothing is before Government, but the suggestion, which has been made that the name of the Kadgoodi Station may be * altered to Whitefield, might possibly be considered by the Railway Company if brought to its notice. The Dewan of Mysore says that no objection to the change exists on the part of his Government.

So novel an experiment as that described above has necessarily been as unduly lauded, as it has been unfairly disparaged. Mr. White's sanguine disposition led him in the beginning to express views and entertain hopes, which he had to abandon before his scheme was launched. Certainly a perusal of his "Guide" of 1879 would give the impression that an ideal colonist would leave the model village in the

---

* The alteration has since been made.

morning with the Georgics in one hand and a spade in the other, would live laborious days, and spend his evenings probably in comparing Whitefield with Plato's Republic in the public library, the central point in the settlement from which all streets were to radiate. All was pitched in the "*Fortunatos nimium*" key. Yet it required no small influence and the possession of no little energy to persuade thirty-two individuals with their wives and families to accept his assurances and to embark in a business of which they knew nothing, a business for which their previous lives and training in no way fitted them.

The case is one for kindly criticism and a helping hand, which the Madras Government is prepared to give, and whether the existence of these colonies be or be not prolonged to adolescence and old age, useful lessons may be learnt by observing their success or failure, and evidence collected which cannot but be of use to a Government, which has set before it the solution of the Eurasian problem, and the provision of a diversity of occupations for a *clientèle*, which at present for the most part cannot or will not dig, which of begging should be brought to be ashamed.

CHAPTER XIII.

TANJCRE, TRIVALUR, CHINGLEPUT, CONJEEVERAM, BEZWADA AND CUMBUM, SOUTH ARCOT.

MAYAVERAM-MUTTUPETT AND EAST COAST RAILWAYS.

Dispute at Courtallum—Railway tour—Our party—Departure from Ootacamund—Mangosteen—Burliar—Nilgiri Railway—At Mettapolliem—Karur—Amravati—Trichinopoly—Srirangam—Orloff diamond—Czarewitch's approaching visit—Wages in district—Price of rice—Jesuit Mission—Ex-Mahant of Tirupati—Raja of Puducottah—Ayanar temples—Arrival at Tanjore—District officials—Oleander—Palace troopers—Vallam—Ranees—Sivajee—Serfojee—Missionary Schwartz—Ekojee—Late Princess—Jail—Hospital—Curious petitions—Palace—Armoury—Durbar hall—Library—Late Dr. Burnell—Marco Polo—Lord Napier—Bishop Heber—Flaxman's statue of Serfojee—Oriental luxury—Capital of Cholas—Country of Sholas—Line from Tiruvarur to Muttupett—Mayaveram-Muttupett Railway—Ceremony of cutting first sod—Lord Connemara's speech—Tanjore settlement—Bernier and Tavernier—Sir Charles Trevelyan—Tamil cooly—Local water-supply—English-speaking power—Local officials—Arrival at Chingleput—Visit to Reformatory—Tamil lyric—Conjeeveram—Dr. Buchanan—Sankara Charriar—Ramanuja Charriar—Sanctity of town—Vishnu temple—Address from Sanscrit school—Prince of Wales—Professor Max Müller—Imperial Institute—Hieun Thsang—Weaving operations—Ancient customs—Hindu mother-in-law—Vegavati—Jain temple—Customs of Jains—Theatre notice—Wages of agricultural labourer—Bishop Heber—Free Church Mission Girls' school—State interference in marriage customs—Ktesias—Megasthenes—Local self-government—Female medical aid—Countess of Dufferin's fund—Departure from Conjeeveram—Colonel Baillie's defeat at Pullalur—Ghosts—Guntakal—Deputation of Bellary citizens—Corruption in district—Maddikera—Sir Thomas Munro—"Stony wolds of Deccan"—Hindu myth—Ramalcotta—Diamond prospecting—Nawab of Banganapalle—Wajra Karur—Tree-tapping system—Mr. Caine—Nandyal lacquer fans—Nallamalai Hills—Highest viaduct—Longest tunnel—Tigers at railway stations—Forest Bismarck—Aborigines of South India—Their early migration—Story of a Police

MAP
of the
MADRAS PRESIDENCY
to illustrate Chapter I of Mr. Rees's Narrative
Scale 1 Inch = 128 Miles
CENTRAL PROVINCES
NIZAM'S DOMINIONS
Hyderabad
Chatrapur
Vizagapatam
Cocanada
Masulipatam
Kurnool
Bellary
Anantapur
Cuddapah
Nellore
Chittoor
MADRAS
Bangalore
Mangalore
Mercara
Mysore
Chingleput
Calicut
Trichinopoly
Madura
Cochin
Palamcottah
Trivandrum
DISTRICTS
I GANJAM
II VIZAGAPATAM
III GODAVARI
IV KISTNA
V KURNOOL
VI BELLARY
VII ANANTAPUR
VIII CUDDAPAH
IX NELLORE
X CHINGLEPUT
XI MADRAS
XII NORTH ARCOT
XIII SOUTH ARCOT
XIV SALEM
XV COIMBATORE
XVI NILGIRI
XVII MALABAR
XVIII S. CANARA
XIX TRICHINOPOLY
XX TANJORE
XXI MADURA
XXII TINNEVELLY
REFERENCE.

officer—Congress in Kurnool—Cumbum—American Lutheran Mission—"Three Cheers" on paper—Railway stories—Kondavid fortress—Indian Beth Gelert—Feringipuram—Amravati tope—Bellamkonda—Guntur—Adulteration of Indian cotton—Sacrilege—Mangalagiri—Mr. Streynsham Master—At Beswada—Cutting first sod of East Coast Railway—Mr. Spring's address—Bridge over Kistna—Lord Cross—Lord Lansdowne—Mr. H. G. Turner—Alignment of line—Arrangements at ceremony—Addresses—Undavilli caves—Mr. Fergusson—Politeness of Telugus—Local self-government—Departure from Beswada—Cumbum—Tank—Savage-cattle—Railway extensions—Ruins of Bijapore—Railway administration during last four years—Opening of Tirvanamalai line—These narratives.

The summer season of 1890 was quite uneventful. Of all the business that came before the Government in all its departments, perhaps nothing excited more interest than the dispute at Courtallum, as to the right of bathing in the sacred waterfall. A disagreement arose concerning the hours at which Europeans, and Indians respectively, should use the bath, and though little or no force was used, the matter came before the Magistrates of the Tinnevelly district, and the conviction of certain Hindus, for using violence in support of their alleged right to use the falls at a particular hour, was reversed by the High Court on appeal. The Government interfered at no stage in these proceedings beyond instructing its law officers to watch the case, and to state that, in the event of the conviction being upheld, it was its opinion that the justice of the case would be met by a small fine. The Government also directed its local law officer in the Tinnevelly district to apply for bail on behalf of the prisoners, as it seemed very doubtful, whether the conviction by the local Magistrate would be upheld.

Railway extensions occupied much of the attention of the Government during the summer months, and when the time came to leave the Hills, the Governor determined to make a Railway Tour for the purpose of cutting the first sod of the Mayaveram-Muttupett, and the first sod of the East Coast, railways. We* left Ootacamund on the afternoon of 22nd September 1890.

* His Excellency The Lord Connemara, G.C.I.E.
J. D. Rees, Esq., C.I.E.
Captain Lovelace Stamer, 16th Lancers, A.D.C.

The passage down the mountain side presented no unusual features. We passed through alternate sun and shadow, as the winding road descended in zigzags, through the beautiful forest which clothes the slopes of Nilgiris, down to the stony bed of the river, in the valley below. At Coonoor were wild roses and well-grown oak trees, a little further down pomegranates, and bamboos bending under the weight of their feathers, on the lower slopes we passed through Burliar Gardens, where cinnamon, nutmegs and mangosteens were exposed for sale, the latter fruit costing about 4 shillings a dozen. In India, however, it is believed only to grow here, and at Courtallum mentioned above, as the scene of the waterfall dispute. Nor has the Indian mangosteen the flavour of its fellow in the Straits Settlements.

On the way we passed the spot where, in May last year, the carriage in which Lord Connemara was driving,* upset when turning a corner, and we looked down the abyss, masked with vegetation, into which His Excellency's servant was shot. When the acci-

* See Chapter VIII.

dent happened, in answer to an inquiry as to what had become of him, he called up from below, that he was "killed"; but the dead man looked cheerfully to-day upon the scene of his former dissolution.

Soon after leaving Burliar, we got into a country of plantain and areca palms, the air grew hotter, we saw fire-flies dancing in the bamboos, and once again were in the tropics. The rapid changes in the character of the vegetation, as you descend the ghaut, are very interesting to mark. The Nilgiri Railway survey had not got far beyond Coonoor. The Company has raised the necessary capital, and commenced operations, and it is calculated, that the line should be open for traffic in about 2½ years.

At Mettapollium we met the Collector of Coimbatore, Mr. Sturrock, and Colonel Pickance, Superintendent of the Central Jail. Colonel Pickance had to report that cholera no longer threatened the inmates of his jail. The medical officer in charge has been trying salol, or salicylate of phenol, as a cholera antidote and considers the results as more than satisfactory. The French Government, is believed to have sent a commission to Tonquin to investigate the merits of the remedy. It would be interesting to know the results. The Collector, amongst other matters, reported that Sir Oliver St. John, and Mr. Sanderson, had carried off the tusks of a rogue elephant which they had followed up into British territory, after wounding the animal in Mysore. Sir Oliver had written to inform us of what, he called, 'this unintentional poaching,' where, of course, of poaching there was none, but public service.

We travelled through the night to Erode, at 5 o'clock in the morning changed on to the South Indian Railway, and at 9 o'clock were safely landed in Trichinopoly. The railroad runs alongside the Cauvery, through a sea of rice-fields, dotted with little islands of sugarcane, and broken here and there by high conical hills of crystalline rock, such as that of Ratnagiri, the temperature upon whose summit is 10 degrees less than that of the surrounding plains. At Karur, where we had tea, the Amaravati joins the Cauvery. The former river is not more famed for its sanctity, than for its prawns and other excellent fish.

Trichinopoly which comprises 3,560 square miles, with a population of 1,215,000 souls, is one of the smallest of Madras districts; but the town of Trichinopoly, with Srirangam, which is practically a part of it, is among the twenty greatest cities in India, its population amounting to upwards of 104,000 inhabitants, with a municipal income of upwards of £10,000. Much of the land of the district is extremely fertile and not a few of the richest villages belong to the temples. I do not know what truth there may be, in the tradition, that the celebrated Orloff diamond, was one of the eyes of an idol at Srirangam, till stolen by a French deserter in the last century. The Czarewitch, who will visit Trichinopoly this winter, will probably know the true history of the matchless gem, that figures as the chief ornament in the Imperial sceptre of the Czar. The population of the district is generally well-to-do, and wages, within the municipal towns of Trichinopoly and Srirangam, are as high as annas 6 or 9*d*. a day, that is, a labourer in Trichinopoly in the present day gets nine times as much as a diamond miner in the Deccan did in the 17th century. Assuming that the purchasing power of money is not now more than one quarter of what it was then, the balance remains very much in favour of the 19th century. I am not at all sure that we can safely assume anything as to the relative values of money in different centuries in India, and in regard to rates of wages such assumptions are particularly to be deprecated, for in rural tracts to this day wages are generally paid in what money, if given, would buy, viz., grain. From a Despatch of the Court of Directors, dated 1733, we learn that paddy, or unhusked rice at 38 seers the rupee was considered cheap, in the early part of the 18th, while now in the latter part of the 19th century the average price is about 27½ seers per rupee, the Madras seer being slightly under 2 lb. Cleaned rice just now sells in Madras at about 12 seers, or roughly 22 lb. per rupee.

In this district Christians are 5 per cent. of the population, and are nearly all Roman Catholics. The head-quarters of the great Jesuit Mission of Madura, which was founded in the 17th century, are situated at Trichinopoly, and the Jesuit Fathers are most successful in their traditional occupation of educating the youth of the country. Two days before leaving Ootacamund, we had seen some of the pupils of this institution acting Moliere's *L'Avare*, and on a previous visit * to Trichinopoly, in 1887, we had heard most

* See Chapter III.

interesting dialogues and recitations in the hall of St. Joseph's College. The Collector, Mr. Fawcett, had information to impart, concerning the health of the Mahant, or High Priest of Tirupati, who was then a prisoner in the jail, convicted of having misappropriated the funds of the great mutt or monastery, which were entrusted to his care. Grief and shame have weighed heavily on this unfortunate man, whose physique is so much affected thereby, that the Governor called for a report as to his condition, and Government subsequently removed him to Vellore jail, a change which has proved beneficial to his health. The affairs of the neighbouring State of Pudukottah also demanded some attention, and it was reported that the young Raja was becoming very expert in the use of the gun.

From Trichinopoly to Tanjore is a short run of an hour through a level country,—indeed, the whole district does not boast a hill. The line frequently passes groves of trees, beneath which are herds of stucco horses. These are temples of Ayanar, a local Dravidian deity, who, with his followers, is supposed to ride about at night, and to entertain a kindly feeling towards those who furnish him with a mount. Childless women are in the habit of vowing a horse to Ayanar, so the long rows of these animals, beneath the tamarind trees, correspond in some respects to the votive tablets of a Catholic church.

On his arrival at Tanjore, the Governor was received by the Collector, Mr. Thomson, the Judge, Mr. Davies, and by other officials. The railway station was decorated with strings of oleanders. This flower, which is sacred to the gods, is largely cultivated, but it is marvellous how a whole district can supply the myriads of blossoms required for a single ceremonial, when the entire reception room, ceiling, walls and doors, will be one mass of its blossoms, strung upon invisible threads. The same flower is sacred alike in Hindu idolatry, and Christian hymnology. Oleanders flourish "where the heathen inflame themselves with idols under every green tree," and clothe the western bank of the lake of Gennasaret down to the water's edge.

> "All through the summer night
> Those blossoms red and bright
> Spread their soft breasts, unheeding, to the breeze,
> Like hermits watching still
> Around the sacred hill,
> Where erst our Saviour watch'd upon His knees."

I use the word 'idolatry,' without offence, and in its literal sense. The flowers are devoted to 'the service of an idol,' are reverently strewn before its feet, scattered over its head, or garlanded about its neck.

The troopers of the Senior Ranee of Tanjore formed an escort, as we drove to Vallam, seven miles distant, where the Collector resides. They still wear the picturesque, if somewhat irregular, uniforms of a hundred years ago, and the sentry, who presented arms, had stuffed the barrels of his musket full of flowers.

Next morning we left Vallam early, and rode to Tanjore to visit the jail and the hospital. The country through which we passed consists of a jungle of cashewnut and acacia trees, and it occurred to

His Excellency that this embryo forest might with advantage be rented from the Ranees to whom it belongs. These ladies, now nine in number, are the remaining widows of the last Raja of Tanjore, who died in 1855 leaving sixteen widows, and two daughters. The two latter were married successively to the same individual, who survives them, and the widows are now maintained by pensions granted by the British Government. They never leave the palace, we were told, 'except to bathe in the river, and worship god.' The last Raja, Sivajee, was the son of Serfojee Maharaja, the friend of the Missionary Schwartz, and his youngest daughter, who died in 1885 was the last direct descendant of Ekojee, the brother of the great Sivajee, the founder of the Mahratta dynasty. Ekojee obtained possession of the country in consequence of a quarrel between the Naik rulers of Madura and Tanjore. The latter Prince, who was worsted by his neighbour, called in the help of the Mussulmans, who despatched Ekojee with an army to help him, but the Mahratta General, having first placed his protégé in possession subsequently deposed him, and in 1676, took for himself the throne of Tanjore, which his descendants continued to occupy until, in 1799, Raja Serfojee ceded the sovereignty to the East India Company. The late Princess of Tanjore, the second and last surviving daughter of Raja Sivajee, the adopted son of Serfojee, was a lady of a dignified, but withal kindly, demeanour, and of a disposition which made friends of all those, who, like myself, had the privilege to have official relations with Her Highness.

The jail of Tanjore is an extremely well-managed institution. The Superintendent, Mr. McCready, since our last visit, in 1887, has introduced the manufacture of capital paper. We saw torn-up scraps going through every stage, from pulping to pressing, and were initiated into the mysteries of the making of that red tape, of which in another stage we all know so much. Excellent cloth is manufactured, and good bell-metal utensils. The Government has commended Mr. McCready alike for the institution of manufactures, and for reducing the cost per head for dieting prisoners, a reduction which, from their appearance, has obviously been carried out without diminution in the quantity of their food, and without damage to their health. Indeed, the condition of the inmates of the jail receives the greatest possible attention. They are regularly weighed, and whenever an individual is going down, the fact is reported to the Doctor. Though this is but a District Jail, the prisoners number no less than 322. We went into the kitchen and saw very good mutton and raggi cake. Then the civil debtors were paraded. The longest period for which they can be kept in confinement is six months, and the Superintendent informs us, that they rarely stay so long, as the judgment-creditors seldom continue to pay the expenses of their keep, when once they have discovered that incarceration fails to secure a prompt settlement of debt. Mr. McCready informs us too that respectable men, as a rule, go down in weight very much, when they first come to jail, as the shame preys upon their minds, and thus affects their bodies, while, habitual criminals, on the other hand, take very kindly to prison life. We had just received striking proof of the correctness of these views, in the case of the unfortunate High Priest at Trichinopoly. After inquiring how various suggestions made on the occasion of the last visit had been carried out, we proceeded to the Hospital, a very large and well managed institution, though His Excellency did receive an anonymous petition, stating that "the Surgeon in charge had not even got the pity to condescend to look at the miserable invalids, whose sight would shake any desperate and strong-hearted stranger." The petitioners expressed the opinion that this medical officer "had a string loose over his subordinates, and would never secure heaven." "Quite the contrary," said they, "will surely be his fate." Thus, though angry, they approached the subject of the doctor's future, with some reserve. Another petition, for an interview, received at Tanjore, set out, that the writer would have been at the station to receive His Excellency "had he not had the pleasure of a scorpion in his left leg, which rendered him unable to come." The same gentleman concluded his letter by saying "shall I bring my invaluable lute to play before Your Excellency as an indulgent son."

It is much to be regretted that the midwifery training school, established in connection with the Tanjore hospital, had to be closed for want of pupils, and the District Surgeon was exhorted to give the subject his earnest attention. The establishment of the school, now closed, was due in a great measure to the personal efforts of one of his predecessors. Midwives are, however, attached to no less than nine hospitals in the district.

Afterwards some of our party visited the Palace, which has often been described. In the great durbar hall, in a prominent position, is what appears to be a skeleton. A closer examination discloses the fact, that it is made of ivory, and on enquiry, we learnt that it was made for the penultimate Raja Serfojee, who desired to learn anatomy, without incurring the pollution, which results from handling bones. The hall which is open on one side to the air, contains a fine statue of the same Raja Serfojee, by Flaxman, and a bust of Maharaja Sivajee by the Honourable Anne Seymour Damer, a sculptrix of great repute, whose former home at Twickenham, has since been inhabited successively by a Prince of the House of Orleans, and an ex-Governor of Madras. The armoury contains many beautiful specimens of inlaid arms, bell-mouthed steel blunderbusses, flint lock pistols and the like, and an extraordinary ensign of rank granted to the kings of Tanjore by the Court of Delhi. It consists of the head of monster, half tiger, half fish, possessed of goggle ivory eyes and long rows of sword-shaped sharp-edged teeth. Within its palate depends from a string a kind of rolling-pin, covered with red velvet, which wags fatuously to and fro, tongue fashion, in its yawning cavernous mouth.

The durbar hall of the late Princess contains many most curious articles. Images dressed up in the uniforms of the early part of this century, and of the last, stand about on the floor, and the picture galleries are of the most comprehensive character. One of our party discovered the counterfeit presentment of his brother acting at Cambridge in "the Birds," of Aristophanes; pictures of prize-fighters, and an autographed photograph of the Princess of Wales, divided the honours with framed extracts from the *Illustrated London News*, photographs of the present Lords Lytton and Harris, and very interesting prints of historical battles. A beautiful painting on ivory of Raja Sivajee, hung by the side of an advertisement of Gulliver, tied up in the meshes of a particularly strong cotton, and fired at by a crowd of Lilliputian bowmen.

The Tanjore Palace library contains 25,000 volumes, of which 20,000 are written in Sanscrit. The latter were catalogued by Dr. Burnell, the late District Judge of Tanjore, the well known oriental scholar. The Sanscrit books include copies of the Vedas, and of the Puranas, with innumerable commentaries upon these works, and an infinite number of treatises on philosophy, logic, poetry and many other subjects. To the uninstructed most of these are sealed books. One poem of 6,000 verses teaches the science of horseflesh, and illustrations show what are lucky, and what are unlucky, equine marks. Amongst other prescriptions for sick animals is meat broth, and Dr. Burnell in his catalogue expresses his astonishment, that the world should be so incredulous, as to horses being nourished, to some extent, upon a meat diet in India. The veracity of Marco Polo has been hotly assailed on account of his reference to, what is well known to be, a not uncommon incident of horses' diet in this country.

A volume of 6,500 stanzas teaches the science of cookery. In this comprehensive treatise, the effect upon food of the different metals of which cooking utensils are manufactured, is thoroughly investigated, and the medical effects of different coloured cloths are discussed. Dr. Burnell, however, observes that the work is neither of any great culinary, nor philological merit. Books upon ritual naturally abound. Lustrations, for instance, are prescribed on the occasion of a child being born in a wrong position, and for the expiation of sin incurred by having killed a snake in a former state of existence, while dire and divers misfortunes are predicted for kings who do not support Brahmins—a crime of which the Rajas of Tanjore have never been guilty.

Dr. Burnell was appointed by Lord Napier and Ettrick in 1871 to examine the Tanjore library, and catalogue its contents; and, as he remarks, "it is due entirely to the scholarlike and lively interest taken in the past of India by Lord Napier that this invaluable collection has been saved." On the death of the last survivor of the widows of the late Raja, the library will, it is believed, escheat to Government, and Dr. Burnell estimates its money value at not less than £50,000. There is too much reason to believe that this distinguished scholar's early death was in no small measure due to his having spent the extremely little leisure available to the District Judge of Tanjore, in examining and cataloguing the contents of the Palace library. I remember his worn and jaded appearance in the heat of Tanjore and the worry of his judicial work. It is sad that his time was not exclusively devoted to pursuits, in which few indeed, can succeed him. At the same time he was no mere orientalist, but a man of great general culture and ability, whose researches would have been of value in any line.

Among the English books are many most interesting works. Bishop Heber described Raja Serfojee, who made the collection, as 'an extraordinary man, who quoted Lavoisier, Linnæus, Buffon and Shakespeare, and wrote fair English poetry.' His books reflect his varied tastes. There are the novels of Fielding and Le Sage, works on Anatomy and Philology, a very full collection of the writings of early travellers in India, and all the works of Morier, the best novels ever produced by a European, about the East. The Raja owed his cultivated tastes to Schwartz, whose hand he holds, in the monument by Flaxman, on the walls of the church within the Fort, representing the death of 'one of the best of Missionaries since the Twelve Apostles.'

In the library of the Palace of Tanjore, no one is ever likely to forget the friendship of the two men so honourable to both. The place and its associations are alike interesting. Seated in a large vaulted room, at a table littered with valuable works, with a Sanskrit curator on one side, and an English librarian on the other, fanned by two peons, while noiseless servants pour splashing water over the steps, that lead down to the quadrangle, which is shaded by big trees, and sweetened with the fragrance of roses and oleanders, one realises a most attractive ideal of oriental luxury.

Grateful as are these unsought attentions, flattering as it is to the undistinguished, to receive the consideration due to the learning of Burnell, or the position of a Raja, sensible as I am of the charm of historic association, I would have willingly bartered all the luxuries of the ancient capital of the Cholas, 'the best, and noblest province of India,' * for one breath of the cool breezes of the country of the † Sholas. It is on the morrow of leaving the Nilgiris, that one agrees most heartily with a late Governor of Madras, who said "their climate is probably one of the best in the world."

On the afternoon of the 25th September we travelled, by special train, from Tanjore to Trivalur, where the head officials of the South Indian Railway, the members of the Local Fund Board, and a vast concourse of the inhabitants, awaited His Excellency, on the side of the railway, in and about the rice-fields. The journey from Tanjore to Trivalur was uneventful, the deltaic country being as level as a billiard table, and as green as its cloth, for the young seedlings of rice had just been planted; and little else was visible from the railway windows, except the boundary hedge of aloes, which protects the permanent-way, and orchards of mango trees, groves of cocoanuts, and huge solitary banyans.

At Trivalur, a guard of honour of the South Indian

---

* Marco Polo (*Yule*), Vol. II, p. 299.

† The small self-contained woods of the Nilgiri plateau are so called.

Railway Volunteers was drawn up under the command of Colonel Crighton. An address was presented, and a sod of turf was cut, and wheeled away by His Excellency, who then made a speech highly commending the enterprise of the Local Boards of Negapatam and Tanjore, which have been, it is believed, the first in India to tax themselves for the purpose of constructing a railway. The southern section of the new line, from Trivalur to Muttupett, will first be constructed, and eventually a northern extension will join the main line at Mayaveram. The whole will then be 53½ miles long, and will cost, it is estimated, Rs. 28,94,000, the money being provided by the Tanjore Local Board, and the Government of Madras in equal proportions. The line is to be constructed, and worked by the South Indian Railway, which has now, in the last half-year, for the first time in the railway history of Southern India, earned a sum exceeding (by £10,000) the interest guaranteed by Government to the shareholders. It is hoped and expected that the first section of the Mayaveram-Muttupett Railway will be completed by the 31st December 1891.

Turning to another, and not less important subject, it has been decided, after much discussion, to introduce a new settlement of revenue into the Tanjore district, one of the most fertile in Southern India, which is held to pay less than its fair share towards the expenses of the administration. It has been recently asserted in Parliament, by a member who is not unacquainted with India, that the British Government takes, by way of assessment, the lion's share of the gross outturn of the land. It will not be superfluous, therefore, to state that, throughout the Madras Presidency, the Government assessment very rarely exceeds 20°/₀ of the gross produce, and generally amounts to something *considerably* under that figure. The proportion, in the case of unirrigated lands varies from 5 to 10 per cent. In the case of irrigated and unirrigated land alike, the holder profits by the considerable difference which exists between the rate at which the Government share of the produce is commuted into a money assessment, and the far higher rates which actually rule in the market. The market prices indeed are very often double those on which the commutation was based. It may safely be concluded that the Crown rarely indeed gets more than a quarter of the gross; and I think Megasthenes found that this was the usual proportion more than two thousand years ago.

The scheme for the settlement of Tanjore has not yet been submitted, but in revising the rough settlement made in 1832 the Government of Madras is not likely to disregard the injunction of the Government of India, to the effect that care should be taken not to raise too greatly the revenues of lands, which have long been subject to lenient assessment.

In connection with this question, enquiries were also made as to the income of an ordinary cultivator for hire. No advantage would result from quoting the details of what appears a simple, but is really an exceedingly complex and difficult subject; but it would appear that, in the rich districts of the South of India, the family of the ordinary cultivator, who is possessed of no occupancy right, enjoys an income of about Rs. 50 a year. This amount is made up of wages, which are generally paid in grain to the man and his wife, of presents of clothing, of harvest fees, of presents on domestic occasions, and on festival days. The fact that the wages of the agricultural labourer are for the most part paid now, as they were long ago, in grain, makes it extremely difficult to compare the position of the cultivators in the 19th century, with that of their predecessors in the days of Bernier and Tavernier, who expressed their wages in money form. In 1860 Sir Charles Trevelyan visited Tanjore and remarked in his minute, that the mirasidars or landholders of the district, asked that something should be done to prevent the Pallans, or agricultural labourers, from emigrating to Mauritius and Ceylon. Sir Charles replied that there was no such thing as slavery in the Queen's dominions, and that, with the high rate of wages then obtaining, it was necessary that they should pay their labourers better, if they wished to keep them. It now appears that Pallans, when dissatisfied, freely emigrate, and that mirasidars are frequently at a loss for labour wherewith to cultivate their lands. No one who has seen the Tamil cooly, and the Tamil cultivator in Singapore, can wonder that he freely emigrates. His condition there is most prosperous, and, as Sir Frederick Weld, the Governor, remarked to me when I was studying the emigration question there, "You might as well try to keep flies from honey as the Tamil man from the Straits Settlements." He is only a little less well off in Ceylon. The Tamil man is a capital colonist, and needs very little, if any, "protection" on the part of Government. In this district the majority of the ryots are well-to-do and do not need to have recourse to loans under the Land Improvement, and Agricultural Loans Acts, while the poor prefer the local money-lender, who gives unlimited credit whatever he may exact for the indulgence. The agricultural labourer is not quite so well off elsewhere as in Tanjore, but there are few places, where he and his family have not an income of Rs. 50 a year between them. Small landholders of course, are better off than labourers. Mr. Clerk, who is preparing the Tanjore settlement scheme, estimates the income of the ryots, of the smallest holdings, as not less than Rs. 200 a year. This may be true of Tanjore, but in many districts there certainly exists a much poorer class of ryot.

The water-supply of Tanjore, like that of Trichinopoly, is under the consideration of the Madras Government, which is prepared to devote no inconsiderable share of the surplus of its revenues, to assisting the large towns of the Presidency to provide themselves with good water. Enquiries were made here as to the attitude of the people of the district in regard to legislative interference with marriage laws, and it appears that such interference would be unwelcome. As regards the Congress, no public opinion has apparently been formed, though, as a branch of the Madras Committee exists in the district it is inferable, that some persons are interested in the subject.

It was reported that Local and Taluk Boards showed great interest in that portion of their duties which relates to the up-keep of communications, but that the elective system had not proved a success in municipal towns.

On the afternoon of the 26th of September riding into Tanjore, and having to discover my way to the house of a friend, of the location of which I was altogether ignorant, I found, that of half a dozen people picked out at random on the road, all were able to direct me in excellent English. Had Sir Charles Trevelyan visited Tanjore in 1890, he would not have said, as he did in 1860, "we ought not to forget that English is a difficult foreign language to the natives of India, and that their acquisition of it should commence at the earliest age at which children go to school, while the memory is tenacious and the organs of speech are supple." The increase in the English-speaking power of the people is absolutely extraordinary, and in this there is political as well as educational gain.

We spent the night of the 26th in the train after dining at the Tanjore Club, an institution maintained in a high state of efficiency by its members, who number about eight souls in all! The few European officials at Tanjore are as cheerful, as they are hospitable, and the fact that life there is literally 'all work and no play,' seems very far from producing the proverbial consequences.

At half past 5 o'clock next morning, the train stopped at Chingleput, where the Governor halted for two hours to inspect the Reformatory. Magistrates are empowered to direct, that boys under 16, sentenced to imprisonment, should be sent to this institution, in which, however, youths above 18, are not detained. It is only within the last $2\frac{1}{2}$ years that the Madras Government has established a Reformatory, of the absence of which Judges and Magistrates had for many years complained. On the day of inspection, the inmates included 121 boys of all ages from 8 to 18. They were nicely dressed in clean white clothing, and wore conical caps, each of which bore the badge of the trade, its wearer was learning. For instance, the carpenter had his chisel, the smith his anvil, the weaver his shuttle, the tailor displayed a scissors, and the gardener was proud of his spade. They all said that they were happy and comfortable, and it appears that they only "ask for more" on fish and mutton days—a fare they prefer to the alternate days' diet of vegetarian food. Only one boy had a complaint to make. He said he did not like raggi, which makes a most nutritious pudding, and having lately seen his mother, he was anxious to get back home. All the boys sang "God save the Queen," accompanied by a fiddle, the proprietor of which teaches some of them to play the kettle-drum, their fingers being rendered supple by constant practice on the inevitable kerosine oil tin. They also sang other songs, some of them accompanied by action. For instance, the smallest boy in the school, a desperate offender of 8 years, who stole a cloth, as he says at the dictation of his uncle, went down on all fours, and groped about in the sand, while a ring of others standing around pointed at him, and described in shrill and thrilling strains, how "this mouse" was the most evil of living creatures, because he was always stealing something. This referred to the natural disposition of mice, and not to the actual offence of this very little boy, in whose case no application of the maxim *malitia supplet ætatem* could well lie. A recent proposal to remove the Reformatory to larger quarters, has been under consideration; but it appears that there is room at Chingleput, for 20 more boys, than the school contains. It was decided to investigate this point, to amend the constitution of the controlling board by the inclusion of the District Magistrate, and to take into very serious consideration the possible occurrence of fire, and the disastrous effect in such a contingency, of the existence of a large number of locked-up separate cells, which could not be quickly opened, for the liberation of their occupants.

I have done into English one of the simple Tamil lyrics of the Reformatory. My translation is free, but it reproduces the sense, and I daresay the quality, of the original.

Before the sun has lit the skies
With rosy light, we early rise,
And first we supplicate the Lord
That he may health and help afford.

When thus prepared with thankful heart
To run our course, the day we start,
Each to his labour to address
Himself, nor lie in idleness.

Some, happy they, 'neath plantain shade
Delve in the yielding earth with spade,
While many more unceasingly
The weaver's shuttle deftly ply.

Others the molten iron know
To fashion with unerring blow,
And nimble pairs of hands are made
To learn the useful tailor's trade.

We all are busy, all confess
That sin begins with idleness,
That those who work with all their might,
At least in that, are doing right.

Thus when our sojourn here is o'er,
And we, reformed, are free once more,
In after life we always mean
To be good boys, and bless the Queen.

While everybody was occupied in devising schemes for their comfort and improvement, one of the boys was so ungrateful, as to take the opportunity to escape.

On the morning of the 27th at 8-30 we arrived at Conjeeveram, where the Governor was the guest of the Collector, Mr. Murray Hammick. This ancient and sacred city may be described now, in the terms used by Dr. Buchanan, who has left such a valuable record of his travels, in 1800. He said "Conjeeveram is a type of the Hindu cities of the Peninsula. The streets are broad, and lined with cocoanut trees, and cross one another, at right angles. The houses are built in the form of a square, with a courtyard in the centre."

The great divines of Hinduism, Sankaracharíar and Ramanujuchariar, both lived, and lectured here. The first was the pillar of the Sivite, and the latter of the Vishnuvite faith. Years of study merely increase the difficulty of understanding Hinduism; but it may suffice for a rough division to separate all the orthodox Hindus of the south into three sects, the Smartha, the

Madava, and the Vishnava. The Smartha sect, which includes the Sivites, holds that the creature is not separate from the creator but possesses '*partem divinæ mentis et haustus, Ætherios.*' The Madava sect believes that the creator and his creatures are separate, while the Vishnuvites maintain, that the creature is separate from the creator during life, but becomes absorbed in him after death. How strongly do these differences remind us of the causes which led to the earlier œcumenical councils of the Christian Church. The Hindus, however, unlike ourselves, are far from having reached that tolerant frame of mind, born of indifference, which regards these doctrinal disputes as possessing a mere academic interest.

The sanctity of Conjeeveram or Kanchi is unsurpassed. Siva addressing his wife said "Kanchi is the best. Its inhabitants, those that have seen it, heard and spoken of it, meditated upon it, and the birds and beasts that inhabit it, obtain salvation. Even in the deluge I will raise Kanchi on the point of my lance. It is to be without destruction for ever." Nevertheless its temples, though quite of the first class, are not so grand and imposing, as those of Tanjore and Madura. They were constructed in the 16th century, during the rule of the temple-building dynasty of Vizianagar, the ruins of whose capital are described in the second chapter. The Vishnu temple is the richer, and contains a hundred pillared hall of great architectural merit, seated in which the Governor received an address from the trustees, and from a Sanscrit school, established in connection with the temple. In replying to this address His Excellency impressed upon the trustees, the necessity for enforcing sanitary measures during the great festivals of the year; and urged the Sanscrit school, to contribute, from its stores of learning, to the new oriental school lately founded in London under the illustrious patronage of the Prince of Wales, and under the auspices of that distinguished scholar, Professor Max Müller, whose interest in India is inexhaustible. We do not know how far the idea of establishing a school for modern oriental studies, in connection with the Imperial Institute, has been developed, but we can all agree with the learned Professor, when he says that no one can so well understand the people of India, can sympathise with them, and can influence them, as those who know their religion and can read their sacred works. The new school should be of great assistance to learning, science, and diplomacy, to the arts, and to administration, and one cannot but echo the wish expressed by the Prince of Wales to the effect, that those whose future duties will involve an intimate acquaintance with oriental languages should avail themselves freely of the resources for study and practice, which the Imperial Institute will place at their disposal.

In the year 640 A.D. the Chinese traveller Hieun Thsang mentions Conjeeveram as a Buddhist town, and though the followers of Buddha have been expelled hence, as indeed, with few exceptions, they have been from the whole of India a thousand years ago, a small Buddhist temple still exists near the town. In order to visit it, it is necessary to pass through the weavers' quarters. The town has for ages been the head-quarters of a large community of weavers, who have of late suffered grievously owing to the competition of Manchester goods. Coarse country cloths however are still manufactured, and excellent silk can be bought for less than six shillings a yard, while the price of a dozen very good silk handkerchiefs does not exceed 16 shillings. Weaving operations are carried on for the most part in the open air, either in the broad streets, or preferably under shady groves of tamarind trees, which abound in and about the town. As you enter a weavers' grove, it appears at first sight as if those occupied in this industry were engaged in a pretty game or * in a

* Country life in India often suggests comparisons with the customs of the youth of the world. These women at their "soft tasks" unconsciously recalled the scene referred to in the text. I have tried to translate the passage, which begins Ἐν δὲ χορὸν ποίκιλλε.

"And next the godlike cripple worked out upon the shield,
"A village dance, the like till then had never been revealed,
"Save once when Dædalus himself had fashioned one as fair
"For love of Ariadne with the glorious locks of hair.
"And men and much-wooed maidens, each worth a herd of kine,
"All holding one another's hands danced deftly up the line.
"The maids wore soft white linen, and as oil shines in the sun,
"So shone the woven tunics, which the men wore, everyone.
"Twined round their shapely foreheads, the maids wore beauteous wreaths,
"And the men bore golden scimitars encased in silver sheaths.
"So tripped they lightly, knowing well the figures of the dance,
"As potters twirl the new-made wheel, to see if it perchance
"Runs true and fair. And now they part, and now again join hands,
"Each with the other intertwined, as in a rope its strands."

These lines written and forgotten long ago, I chanced lately to remember in a happy hour, in recollection of which, as well as because they illustrate my subject, I reproduce them here.

"To give an instance of the survival at the present day in India of customs of great antiquity. Not long since the daughter of a rich country village dance, such as Homer describes, as portrayed on one compartment of Achilles' shield. Rows of women walk up and down the shady aisles, each holding aloft in the left hand a spindle, and in the right a bamboo wand, through a hook at the end of which, the thread is passed. Alongside are straight upstanding rows of split bamboos reaching as high as their hips, and as they pass, they unwind the thread from the spindle, by means of the wand, and pass it over each alternate upright. The threads, thus separated, are subsequently lifted, with their bamboo uprights, from the ground, and while extended from tree to tree, in a horizontal position, are washed with rice water, and carefully brushed. The threads are now ready to be made into cloth, and the actual weaving is carried on by means of primitive hand-looms, inside the houses. In this manner are manufactured men and women's ordinary clothing, as well

---

gentleman, I know, was given in marriage to a Rajput princeling. The lady had received an English education, and had adopted to a great extent English habits and customs, but her mother-in-law was a dame of a proud stomach and of the olden school. She insisted that her new daughter should grind at the mill, and take her share in other household duties, which, though in their case of merely symbolical efficacy, were considered the proper occupations of a gentlewoman in a family belonging to the proudest caste in India. The younger lady, I believe carried the day, but it need hardly be pointed out that in the heroic ages ladies of rank were engaged in such homely occupations, while Briseis in her tent idly awaited her Achilles, just as the beauties of Vijianagar, as Barbosa tells us, trifled away the hours in silken pavilions, till the battle was over, and the bravest claimed the fairest, as valour's best reward.

"I would tell yet another tale that rather recalls, however, the atmosphere of mediæval Italy. An Indian chief, who had lost many of his near relations, lately went to England to study medicine and walk the hospitals. Some surprise thereat was expressed by an English neighbour, but a follower of the doctor-chief explained, that it was as well that he should know as much about poisons, as those around him in his home!"

as the red pocket handkerchiefs dear to the Tamil man, which he takes with him to Singapore, or any other distant place, to which he may migrate.

Leaving the weavers' village behind you, and crossing the sandy bed of the Vegavati or 'Swift-flower,' which, however, contained not a drop of water, you reach the ancient Jain temple. To the uninstructed eye it does not widely differ from a Hindu fane. The images, however, are those of deified saints, or just men made perfect, who are worshipped by the few descendants of the Indian Buddhists. I was shown over the temple by a so-called Jain Brahmin, but the Brahmins of Chingleput do not recognize these sectaries as belonging to that caste. This, of course, is quite natural, since Hinduism is not merely a caste organization, but also a religious society.

The house of the chief priest is supported by beams of wood resting on transverse ploughshares, which again are supported on stone pillars, a most agricultural style of architecture. The Jains here as in other parts of India are extremely scrupulous about taking life; so much so that they will not touch food after 6 o'clock, lest in the failing light, the life of any insect be sacrificed during the preparation of their food. They carefully strain their water too through cloths, lest peradventure any animalculæ be swallowed, and this they do for the sake of such animalculæ, and not for their own good. On returning, I saw upon the walls of a small Hindu temple a diglott notice in English and Tamil, the former portion of which ran thus:—

LONG LIFE TO H.H. THE MAHARAJA OF MYSORE,

whose Dramatic Company will act

"THE NUNNERY."

No rival, no equal.

Attractive night.

Worth hearing, worth seeing.

Enacted in a refined style.

Short and sweet.

Chairs for 1	..	..	Annas	8 (or 1 shilling).
Bench for 2	..	..	,,	4 (,, 6 pence).
Mat for males	..	..	,,	2 (,, 3 pence).
Mat for females	..	..	,,	2 (,, ,,).

In Chingleput as in Tanjore, efforts were made to discover the money value of the wages, *plus* perquisites, of the agricultural labourer, with the result that, as in that district, so in this, it appears, that the income of the poorest class in India, amounts to something between 40 and 50 rupees a year. It must not be imagined for a moment, that this necessarily implies, want of food. I have never seen signs of want in any ordinary year, in any part of the Madras Presidency: and Mr. Crole, an excellent authority, who takes by no means rosy views of the condition of the cultivator, says in his district manual of Chingleput that "in the majority of years the lot of the ryot is far from a hard one." The agricultural labourer comes below the poorest ryot in social position, but I am not sure that the material condition of the latter is much more favourable. I am much of the same opinion as that shrewd observer, Bishop Heber, who said in 1824 : "I do not apprehend that the peasantry are ill off, though they cannot of course afford to live luxuriously."

It should not be forgotten that in this stronghold of Hinduism no less than 500 boys and 300 girls are being educated by the Free Church of Scotland Mission. We saw all the girls. As they were mostly Sudras, few of them were married, though many approached the years of maturity. It may be remarked, that neither political nor social reform excites any sort of interest, either here, or anywhere in the district. Indeed I have been told that such native papers as are advocating legislative interference with Hindu marriage, and other reforms, are experiencing a large falling off in their circulation. By the way for the benefit of those who hold that infant marriage is a new thing, and a characteristic of a late, and iron age, I may refer to the writings of Ktesias, and Megasthenes, who upwards of 2,200 years ago, said "that in India women bore children at 7 and were old at 40."

In the Chingleput district generally there seems to be no desire, that the State should interfere in any of the marriage customs, rights and disabilities of the people. The question of reform chiefly affects the Brahmins, who set an example, not so largely followed by other castes, as is generally supposed, of marrying their girls, before they reach maturity. All are agreed that the Brahmins and the castes who follow them, would strongly resent any legislative interference. Indeed, doubts were expressed, whether Government would be justified, in the face of their pledges to the people, in amending the law, so as to provide that a widow, who remarries, should retain the property she inherited from her deceased husband.

Though the Chingleput district is not a rich one, and possesses no great works of irrigation, very few applications have been made by its ryots for loans under the Land Improvement and Agricultural Loans Acts. An improvement in this respect has, however, been manifested in the last two years.

There seems some reason to doubt, whether the extension of local self-government to village unions, has not been more unpopular, than has been represented.

During Lord Connemara's tours enquiries are made in each district concerning the supply of female medical aid to the women of the country. The Madras Branch of the Countess of Dufferin's Fund arranges for the training and supervision at Madras of scholars, who are supported by Local Boards, and are bound, when qualified, to serve such Boards. Midwives are attached to no less than nine hospitals in the district, and it is considered that no further advance is, at present, feasible.

Soon after leaving Conjeeveram, the train passed Pullalur, where Colonel Baillie was defeated by Hyder Ali, in the memorable engagement, so * graphically depicted upon the walls of the Daria Dowlat, at Seringapatam. The peasants in the neighbourhood say that spectres are frequently seen upon the battle-

---

* See Chapter VI.

field, where cannon balls, arms, and other accessories of warfare are constantly turned up by the plough. Such superstitions are common in England, as in India. On the site of Edgehill, a similar belief has existed, since the days of the battle, soon after which it was currently reported that—

> " Fierce fiery warriors fought upon the clouds
> In ranks and squadrons and right form of war.
> The noise of battle hurled in the air,
> Horses did neigh, and dying men did groan."

It may not be generally known that a Commission was appointed by King Charles I to report upon this circumstance, and that 'three officers, men of honour and distinction, and three other gentlemen of credit, testified to the appearance on the field of battle of the strange and portentous apparition of two jarring and contrary armies.'

At Arconam we met the district officers of North Arcot, and after the Governor had held brief conference with them, we proceeded through the night to Guntakal. The heat was stifling, and at Renigunta station we encountered 300 of the noisiest pilgrims that ever prayed, many of whom were taken on by the train.

We awoke in a more finely tempered clime at Guntakal, where Mr. Laffan, the Collector of Bellary, awaited His Excellency, and introduced a deputation of citizens, headed by Mr. Sabapathy Mudelliar, who asked for the intervention of Government to save, from prosecution, certain bribe-givers, on whose evidence bribe-takers had been convicted. The law of India, under which both parties to the transaction are punishable, is no doubt a great obstacle to the punishment of offenders. The difficulties arising alike from its enforcement, and from its evasion, by the grant of indemnities or pardons, have proved infinite. There is no doubt, however, that the giver of a bribe shares the moral obliquity of the receiver, and whether or not the law be expedient as it stands, it is at least intelligible.

Our party, which had received welcome additions in Mr. Price at Arconam, and in Colonels Lindsay and Gracey at Guntakal, thus augmented, proceeded on its way to the Kistna, passing first of all Maddikera, not far from which Sir Thomas Munro died of cholera. This scourge is seldom altogether absent from the Kurnool district, and deaths resulting from it had been reported just before our arrival at Cumbum. On either side of the aloe hedge that bounds the permanent-way, were tall glistening crops of cholum (sorghum), and dark green fields of castor oil. Rocky hills occurred at intervals and big boulders of rock, on which generally smaller rocks are nicely balanced. You would say, in many cases, that this phenomenon must have been due to human action, but geologists tell us that such combinations are the usual result of the action of the weather on gneissic formations. They are eminently characteristic of what Sir Alfred Lyall happily calls, "the wide stony wolds of the Deccan." The imaginative Hindu does not, of course, accept a geological explanation, and sees on these, "stony wolds," the rocks dropped by Hanuman's monkey warriors, when carrying material down from the Himalayas for the construction of the bridge from Ramnad, in Madura, to Ceylon, an engineering work, which was essential to the recovery of Rama's wife, from the clutches of Ravana, Ruler of the Golden Isle.* The great fortress of Gooty, which we passed at 6 o'clock in the morning, continued to dominate the country we travelled over, till noon. The crops looked very well, and the natural prosperity of this unirrigated dry cultivation, explains in a great measure the financial failure of the adjacent Kurnool canal,† the water of which the ryots will not use.

At Kurnool Road, formerly called Dhone, Mr. Kough, the Collector, joined us, and the question of connecting Kurnool town with Kurnool road naturally arose, the capital of the district being situated 32 miles from the railway. The Local Board is willing to find the money for a branch line, and just now the only question at issue appears to be, who shall pay for the cost of a survey, in case such survey proves abortive, and does not end in an accomplished line. It is believed, however, that early action is contemplated. Within twenty miles of this station is Ramalcotta, the site of the diamond-fields described by the jeweller-traveller Tavernier, who tells us that the miners of the 17th century used small irons crooked at the ends, which they thrust into the veins of rocks, to draw from them the sand in which they found the diamonds. No systematic effort is now made to work

---

* Ceylon in Hindu literature is termed Serandip, or the Golden Isle.

† See Chapter II.

these ancient and renowned fields. Diamonds are, however, still found from time to time, and after rain, women and children may be seen hunting for gems in the sands washed down from the hills. A mine is worked by the Nawab of Banganapalle, whose small jaghire is situated in the district, and only the other day, an Armenian merchant was wandering about Kurnool, carrying with him a bag full of models of all the principal diamonds in the world. Meanwhile, however, a company formed to work the fields of Wajra (or Diamond)—Karur in the neighbouring district of Anantapur, has quite lately had to suspend operations, though a mining expert's report on the character of the rock and soil, was very favourable. On the other hand, diamonds are certainly being found by the Deccan Mining Company on the banks of the Krishna river, near the site of the mines of Kollur, which like Ramalcotta, was one of the most prolific sources in the 17th century of the so-called Golconda diamonds.

We halted awhile at Nandyal, where we met Mr. Crole, the Commissioner of Salt and Excise Revenue, engaged, as the Madras Government has been for years past, in trying to perfect our excise arrangements. A new system called the tree-tapping license system has lately been introduced in many parts of the Presidency, and it is expected that it will bring the consumption of the fermented juice of the toddy-palm under better control. The change causes infinite trouble, of which no one thinks anything, yet Government in India gets no credit for its new experiments, and its past improvements in excise. Mr. Caine, however, allows, that Madras makes very conscientious efforts to carry out the avowed policy alike of England, and of India.

Beautiful lacquer fans are manufactured near Nandyal, but this art, and that of making inlaid weapons, are both dying away, and the lacquer manufactures have, it is said, dwindled down to one man. The Collector calculates that agricultural labourers in the rural tracts get as much as Rs. 4-10-0 per mensem, and in towns a rupee more, while artizans earn from Rs. 13 to Rs. 18, a month. In 1824 Bishop Heber calculated that an agricultural labourer in Bengal got slightly under Rs. 4 a month. This is a striking confirmation of the accuracy of the estimate I have made in an earlier part of this chapter.

After leaving Nandyal, the Bellary-Krishna Railway winds its way up into the heart of the Nallamallai hills, through many a cutting, and around many a sharp curve, in which the train takes an alarming cant to starboard. The scenery in these solitary hills is very beautiful. On either side, as far as the eye can reach, are undulating woodlands, and here and there hills rise to a maximum height of 3,000 feet. Teak, bamboo, yepi (*hardwickia*) and many other trees spring from a thick under-growth of coarse grass. The Government attaches great importance to these forests, which have been constituted reserves, and are being carefully developed. The railway, on this section, burns as fuel, the local timber, which is supplied at the rate of Rs. 5-8-0 a ton. Assuming

$3\frac{1}{2}$ tons to be equal to one ton of coal, the consumption of wood remains cheaper, than that of Singareni coal, though the latter can be bought at the pits' mouth at Rs. 7-8-0 per ton. This is only another proof of the prohibitive nature of the railway freight paid for coal in India. Reverting for a moment to the important subject of wages, the coal miners at Singareni, who work by the piece, make from Rs. 25 to Rs. 30,—rates which, for India, are about equal to the Rondda valley rates of 20 years ago—while ordinary labourers get from 6 to 8 annas, or from 9*d.* to 1*s.*, per day.

Shortly before descending from the hills on the Krishna side, the line crosses a valley, which has been bridged by a viaduct, at an altitude of about 200 feet above the level of the ground, the highest, it was said, in India, as the tunnel of half a mile which immediately follows, is, it is believed, the longest. The length of the girder, 250 feet, detracts in effect from the height of the piers of the viaduct, upon which we halted to enjoy the prospect of mountain scenery.

All along the railway, at every station, dancing girls danced, tom-toms were beaten, Indian flutes were played, and every kind of noisy welcome was offered. The arrival of a train is still a great event in these districts, into which the railway has been newly introduced, and when the train contains the Governor, the whole place is convulsed with excitement. The antelope have not yet got accustomed to the steam-engine, and you may see them bounding away as it invades their solitude. Tigers take more kindly to civilization, and one of these brutes quite lately killed a buffalo in the station-yard at Gazzulapilli on the Krishna-Kurnool frontier, in high noon. Another was observed examining the line a little further on, and scratching the ballast, from under the rails.

The Nallamallais will form a great reserve, and everywhere we are now providing the fuel of the future. Sir D. Brandis, a Forest Bismarck, has brought home to Indian administrations the real danger of supineness in conserving our forests. Yet we have hope, reflecting that from the Indus to the Mediterranean, there is little more than camelthorn, while in Bengal in the 17th century fuel was so scarce, "that * widows begged for wood out of charity, to burn themselves withal, beside the dead bodies of their husbands." The wild tribes, who inhabit these hills, live on forest produce, and fearlessly gather honey, hanging by bamboo ropes over dizzy precipices. They are the descendants of the aboriginal inhabitants of Southern India,—men who were described by the Northern invaders as monkeys or goblins. I say Northern, and not Aryan advisedly, for the one thing we do know is that such invaders came from the North. The complacent theories of the Aryan family upon the Pamir steppe, have been subjected to several rude shocks, and now we are told on far more satisfactory grounds than have hitherto

---

* Tavernier (*Ball*), Vol. II, p. 213.

been forthcoming, that the original home of the so called Aryan family was in Southern Russia. It is not a little absurd to hear the supposed common descent of Englishmen and Hindus from this source, gravely urged in Madras as a ground, on which similar laws and customs might be applied to and followed by both races alike in the present day.

I quote one description of the aborigines which sounds like 'a fine piece of invective.' 'The aboriginal inhabitant is of the complexion of a charred stake, with flattened features, of dwarfish stature, with short arms and legs, large ears, protuberant belly, black as a crow, with a projecting chin, a flat nose, red eyes and tawny hair.' In spite of all this the Chentsu is a very inoffensive creature, though shy, as savages ever are. It is not safe, to presume on his docility. An English Police officer of Kurnool, after a long hunt, once captured a Chentsu offender, and as the day was hot, gave him his sword to carry! This proved too strong a temptation to the robber, who cut the policeman down, and made his escape.

It is reported that Kurnool district takes little interest in the Congress, and contributes little or nothing to the cause, in the shape of money. It appears too, that in this backward district, the non-official element, proves lukewarm in its love of local self-government.

At nightfall, we reached Cumbum where we saw several members of the American Lutheran Mission. Here we dined and slept, and next day passed on through a cultivated plain, broken in all directions by low picturesque hills. Yesterday we had passed through country, where even domestic cattle, escaped from their owners, had reverted to the savage state, and were a terror to the few inhabitants. To-day we saw nothing less domestic than ploughing bullocks, as we passed through several villages of the Nellore District, belonging to the Rajah of Vencatagiri. His people, too, danced and made music. It is curious to see "three cheers" put on paper, but here they were, or rather on cloth, in letters of gold, "Cheers, Cheers, Cheers." Not that the people wanted such a lead. They were most hearty, and clapped their hands in a way that was almost British.

During this long railway journey we naturally heard many railway stories. Of these, one was of a railway employé, up in the hills, whose platform was invaded by a panther. He reported the circumstance, and said that he had met the attack by shutting himself in his office, and ringing the station bell. Another, a station master, whose meaning has never been discovered, reported to his superior, that "serpents were percolating in streams through his office." Yet another official telegraphed to the agent of the line "whole goods train passed over one gang cooly;" but thinking this needed some comment on his part, supplemented the sad intelligence with another telegram to the effect that the "cooly was dead." There was no cause for wonder in that, but considering the agency that is enlisted for the working of a new line in India, it is wonderful that trains run at all.

After passing Vinukonda and Narasaraupett—both,

places of some importance—the line passed through Feringipuram, or Franks' Town, a great missionary centre, where the French Jesuits settled in the 18th century, while a French garrison was quartered at the neighbouring fortress of Kondavid. This celebrated hill fort is situated on a range of hills, the highest of which reaches an elevation of 1,700 feet above the sea. The works are of great extent, and the place was the seat of a Telugu race of kings of Kondavid, who flourished in the 14th century. It subsequently passed by conquest under the Mussulman kings of Golconda, and under the French; and it continued to be strongly garrisoned, until it was made over to the East India Company in 1788. Near here is a town called 'Kukka' or Dogs' Kakani, where a stone, on which is graven a rude presentment of a horseman and his hound, commemorates the death of an Indian Beth Gelert. A gentleman of the olden time lived here, and lived well, and ran in debt. Being unable to pay, he gave his creditor, a money-lender, his best hound. The trader said he thought the dog would return to his master, but the laird replied, that the dog had never disobeyed his orders, which now were that he should stay with his new owner. That night, thieves broke into the house, and had possessed themselves of all the trader's wealth, but for the hound, which gave the alarm. Thankful for his money saved, the trader told the faithful dog he might go home to his old master, but when the latter saw him returning, he slew him with an arrow, for his disobedience. Soon afterwards, a letter explained it all, but the hound was dead, and naught remained, but unavailing grief.

From one of the stations near here, a station master reported two of his pointsmen for fighting. He said the aggressor "threw a stone at Ram Buksh, which fortunately hit Ram Buksh's wife, and unless both these men are scattered in different directions by opposing trains, there will be murder and suicide, including to myself." Asked why he considered it fortunate that the stone hit Ram Buksh's wife, this chivalrous controller of trains explained "that otherwise it would have hurt Ram Buksh."

Feringipuram is in the district of Satanapalli, in which also are situated the celebrated Amaravati tope, and the unworked marble quarry of Bellamkonda. The last halt in the long railway journey was made at Guntur, one of the largest towns in the district, where much cotton is pressed, for despatch to the port of Cocanada. The chief business done here, is cotton broking and packing, and to a casual visitor, it would appear to be more remarkable for the number of dancing girls it contains, and for a plethora of red umbrellas, than for any other characteristics. Just as the Governor was answering a brief address presented, by the Municipality, down came the rain, and up went the umbrellas. Not only are these useful articles invariably red in Guntur, but the inhabitants affect the same colour for their clothing, to such an extent that the whole place is of an ensanguined hue. Mr. Gill drove us round the town, and a visit was paid to a school for Mahomedan women, belonging to the American Lutheran Mission. In this excellent institution, embroidery is taught in gold, silver, brass, and silk thread, and the patterns, be it said to Miss Dryden's eternal credit, are exclusively oriental. General education is also attended to; and there is a Kindergarten department. Several arches in the town bore the practical and original inscription of, 'Cotton's warmest welcome.' Oddly enough, while we were in the yard of a cotton pressing firm, a man came up with a Reuter's telegram, which reported that further measures were being taken by Cotton Associations at home to protect the trade against the adulteration of Indian cotton. Unfortunately the complaint is too well founded. The fault rests in Madras chiefly with the grower, and not so much with the packer, and with silver rising he had better look to it, lest he find his occupation gone.

Not long since, a complaint that a temple here, had been profaned by a European gentleman, was made to Government, which gave much attention to the matter, ordered the fullest inquiry, and gave complete satisfaction to the complainants. It is interesting to note how a similar complaint was disposed of under native rule in the 17th century. Tavernier, the traveller, intentionally entered the inner apartment of a temple in this district for the purpose of satisfying himself, as to what he believed to be an imposture. He got rid of the priest by sending him for water, but the latter returned, and found the Frank inside the temple. Says Tavernier, "He cursed me because I had profaned, as he said, his temple, but we soon became friends by means of two rupees, which I placed in his hands, and he at the same time offered me betel."

Between Guntur and Bezwada lies Mangalagiri, or the hill of happiness, at the foot of which, is situated a pagoda with a very high pyramidal tower, the god of which is said to be in the habit of drinking "just the half of any pot of sherbert bigge or little, that is given to him, and to refuse to drinke more of the same pot." So Mr. Streynsham Master reported, after his journey from Madraspatnam to Mechlipatam in 1679.

On the morning of the 1st October we travelled before breakfast from the site of the present Krishna terminus to the right bank of the river, to which the line has been extended since our visit* to Bezwada in December last. On that occasion representations were made to the Bombay Government, which controls the South Mahratta line, with the result that passengers, to their great convenience, and to that of trade, are now booked from the river bank, and not from a jungle station 3 miles distant.

The afternoon of Wednesday, the 1st October, was devoted to cutting the first sod of the East Coast Railway, the main object of this very hot tour, during which, the thermometer ranged in the railway stations, in which we encamped, from 95° to 107°, the higher figure being frequently exceeded in the train. On the metre gauge carriages rock a great deal, going

---

* See Chapter XI.

round corners they take a list to starboard or larboard as the case may be, and when the kitchen is ahead of you, and its culinary odours incessantly prevail, the illusion is complete, and you feel sea-sick. I constantly expected to see the fiddles on the table, and was always burning "to land."

The "opening ceremony" took place upon the approach to the right-hand abutment of the new Krishna bridge, the construction of which is entrusted to Mr. Spring, an engineer of long experience and high reputation, whose name is already honourably connected with several engineering works in India. This gentleman, in the absence of Mr. Walker, the Chief Engineer of the East Coast Railway, presented an address. The bridge will connect the Bellary-Krishna metre-gauge railway with His Highness the Nizam's guaranteed railway, a broad-guage line, and also with the East Coast Railway, now to be constructed on the broad gauge from Bezwada to Cuttack, and ultimately on to the Central Provinces or to Calcutta. At the site of the bridge the river is a mile and a quarter broad. It will, however, be guided by stone-faced embankments into a breadth of ¾ of a mile, which alone will be bridged, the system of narrowing the river being that which has been adopted in the case of the Chenab, and for the protection of Dehra Gazi Khan from the floods of the Indus. The bridge will consist of 12 spans of 307 feet; the iron work of each span weighing 460 tons. The girders will rest on piers 45 feet high, which themselves will rest on well foundations, sunk 83 feet below the lowest low-water. The girders will carry a metre-gauge, as well as a broad-gauge train, provision is made for ordinary cart traffic, and there will also be side-walks for foot-passengers.

As regards the construction of the bridge the first season will be mainly one of preparation ; the second will see well-sinking, and masonry in full swing, and training works established. The third will be a girder season, and the 1st of April 1893 will probably see the whole bridge finished. If anybody can complete it earlier Mr. Spring is probably the man.

The circumstances under which the East Coast Railway was first brought to notice, and the history of the project from its conception to the date of the inaugural ceremony of cutting the first sod, were fully given in Lord Connemara's speech. From first to last His Excellency has had the project much at heart, and nothing he has done during his tenure of office, has given him sincerer pleasure, than to be permitted to inaugurate a work so useful to the people of India, and of such supreme importance to the inhabitants of his own Presidency. The names of the Secretary of State, Lord Cross, of the Viceroy, Lord Lansdowne, and he hopes his own, will ever be associated with the construction of this great link in the communications of India.

Lord Connemara began his speech by paying a well-earned tribute to Mr. H. G. Turner with whom the idea of the East Coast Railway originated, and he quoted Mr. Turner's able monograph, to show how rich and populous is much of the country through which it will pass, how important it is to give the Central Provinces communication with the sea, and what a rich and promising country exists in the highlands of Vizagapatam-Jeypore, which the line will serve. He referred to the importance of this railway from a famine protective point of view, as a distributor of Singareni coal, as the parent line of future extensions, and the inevitable forerunner of direct communication between Madras and Calcutta.

It is of the highest importance that the alignment should be satisfactory from a geographical and commercial, as well as from an engineering point of view, and the Madras Government is most anxious, that every mile, that passes through the Krishna and Vizagapatam districts, in which work is to be commenced, should be carefully considered by the engineers in communication with the heads of these districts, who have received instructions to keep Government posted in their opinions, as to the route that should be followed, to the end, that no land shall be actually acquired until it is quite certain, that the alignment decided upon is the best possible.

Lord Connemara also expressed an earnest hope that the Government of India, by whom the East Coast Railway is being constructed as a State line, will decide to bridge the Godavari at once. Sooner or later, this must be done; it will not cost more, it appears, than will the Krishna bridge, and by beginning with a bridge, the considerable expense of the temporary ferry will be saved.

Very admirable arrangements were made for the

opening ceremony by Mr. Spring and Mr. Morse, and a large number of officials, and others from Hyderabad, Guntur, Masulipatam, and elsewhere attended. It goes without saying that crowds of people from the surrounding country flocked in to witness the first outward and visible sign of the commencement of this railway, in which they are sufficiently enlightened to be deeply interested.

An address from Masulipatam urged the claims of that port to an extension in its direction of the railway system. This is to found a good case on a bad argument. The Krishna delta from end to end should be traversed by the Bellary-Krishna line, which was constructed to bring its "golden grain" to the famine haunted area of the Ceded Districts. That line should, if possible, be extended down the delta to Masulipatam, not to restore to life, that once famous, but now decaying port, but to take away from its vicinity, its rice and other produce, which could thus be sent from the field, across the river to the market, without breaking bulk.

Masulipatam, famous of old for muslin, has in later days been an educational centre of some note, though it has not yet by any means become, as Sir Charles Trevelyan prophesied in 1859, "more to the Northern Circars, than Oxford and Cambridge have been to the United Kingdom."

There are some rock temples in a hill overlooking the Krishna at Undavilli, not far from our camp, and as in the weather we experienced, the middle of the moonlit night was the only tolerable time of day,

Mr. Campbell and I started after dinner to visit them. We rode along in comfort after causing the flaring and oil-exhaling torches of our attendants to be put out. When we got to a bad place, they were lighted again in a moment. The torch bearer, σπέρμα πυρὸς σώζων, is ever ready. Out of Cimmerian darkness, apparently without tinder, flint, or spark, he produces a light. Where he keeps 'the fire seed' is a mystery. We reached the village and aroused the curnam or accountant, who lived in a nice mud-house, the walls of which were painted in streaks of white and brick colour, and the roof of which was thatched. A baby was crying inside and I said I feared we had disturbed it. 'No matter,' said he, 'the child is not usually awakened at this time, but I am delighted to see your honours. All times are equally convenient, in which I can be of service.' Then he took us to the caves, making polite remarks at intervals, and apologising for every individual thorn that presumed to bar our way. In the hill at the back of his village are temples and rest-houses, hewn in the rock, small and unimportant, compared with those of Karli, for instance. Though these temples are of Hindu origin, as a great recumbent effigy of Vishnu proves, they are nevertheless, as Mr. Fergusson tells us, built in obvious imitation of the Buddhist monastery, in which, each in his own little rock-hewn cell, the Buddhist monks spent the rainy season studying the sacred books, and practising a temperate asceticism. The caves were full of loathly bats, which, dazzled by the torch-light, flew almost in our faces, hovered around us, or hung head downwards from the blackened roofs. In the winding stairs, and on the terraces, we lost our way, but soon regained the stone-steps, and exchanged, with pleasure, the atmosphere of a catacomb, for the now fairly cool air without, and a view of the glorious moon shining placidly down on the sacred river. Our friends escorted us some way and there was just a little petition before we parted. We knew the hill, they said. Well they lived below it, and their ancestors had pastured their flocks on it, 'ever since it was born,' it was a little hard that new forest rules prevented the exercise of this privilege; doubtless my companion, whose power was only equalled by his learning and sense of justice, would at once see this put right. They would send in a humble representation on the subject, and so good night.

The politeness and courtesy of the Telugu people are remarkable. Their speeches, done into literal English, sound somewhat subservient, but when the usual allowance is made for Eastern hyperbole, their language is not obnoxious to this charge. In fact, their manner and bearing are frank and independent, compared with those of the inhabitants of many parts of India.

The condition of local self-government, and the local affairs generally of the Krishna district, had been fully gone into on the occasion of our visit last October. It was now stated, that among others than Brahmins and traders, the age at which girls are married tends to rise beyond that of puberty to that of the attainment of full maturity. It was satisfactory too, to learn, that not one of the fifteen hospitals of this great and improving district, lacked the services of a trained midwife.

On the way back from Bezwada we halted at Cumbum to visit this fever-stricken station, once a place of greater importance. The town and neighbourhood have been reduced by malaria to very small proportions, the various public offices, that once existed here, have all been removed, and the sole remaining glory of the place is its tank, or lake, for a sheet of water of 15 square miles deserves the latter name. The country is traversed by low parallel offshoots of the Nallamalais, in which mountain streams have their origin. The outlets from the hills, around the Cumbum tank, have from time immemorial been closed by Titanic embankments, and the area within is thus flooded with water, which irrigates large tracts below. The embankment of this great work once breached, and the people sacrificed to the goddess of the water two shepherds, whose name both tank and town have ever since borne. Once, in warfare, it was wantonly cut, and once a Princess spent her dowry on its repairs. On one side of the water, the hills rise to an height of 3,000 feet, and in the centre of the lake are dotted little round islets, on which roam domestic cattle, which have reverted to the savage state. They escaped during the dry season when the island was accessible, having by some instinct learnt that the rising water would soon secure their continued liberty. On the embankment a petition was presented for the restoration of Cumbum 'to its former glorious condition,' and though all that the petitioners want cannot be done, it seems possible that a dam, advisedly demolished for sanitary reasons, may perhaps, without sanitary objection, be repaired. Less information is available about Kurnool than other districts, because one of its Nawabs finding the records in hopeless confusion, had them all thrown into the Tungabhadra river, when in flood. The district of Krishna boasts of a Hindu Beth Gelert, and the district of Kurnool has its St. Patrick, for there is a tradition that in the Yerramalai mountains snakes never bite. It appears that a serpent, there, once bit a Saint, but the snake died and the holy man lived, and forbade all snakes in that locality to bite, with fatal effect, ever afterwards.

On our return to Madras we had travelled 1,515 miles by rail in 12 days, had slept four nights in the train, and had experienced a temperature ranging between 95° and 107°. It was hotter and more exhausting altogether, than any of our previous journeys, and some of us felt the effects long afterwards. It is odd, that in Madras, the hottest of Indian provinces, the cold weather, which alone allows of travelling without danger and risk, should during the last few years have been spent at the capital, while in other parts of India, it is devoted to touring, which is done for the year before the annual visit to the Hills. There seems little advantage in making two months earlier a tour which perhaps so affects the Governor of a Presidency, that he has in consequence to leave India a year earlier, than he otherwise would have. Coming down from the European climate of the Nilgiri Hills the effects of sudden heat and continued exhaustion are very great. A month later this tour would have been quite pleasant and at the same time of equal profit from a public point of view.

The Bellary-Krishna State Railway is worked by the Southern Mahratta Railway Company, as a part of its system, which now serves the southern portion of the Mahratta country proper, and extends across the Peninsula to Bezwada, whence it is hoped it will ere long be prolonged to Masulipatam. Different branches take off from this line from sea to sea. One runs northwards to Poona, the Mahratta capital, another passes through Bijapore, one of the earliest Mahratta conquests, to join the Great Indian Peninsula Railway, near Sholapore, and a third branch runs southwards to Bangalore, and Mysore, whence it will soon run on to the foot of the Nilgiris.

The Southern Mahratta Railway thus serves much of the country which at one time or another was subject to the sway of the short-lived, but widely extended empire of the Mahrattas. The portion first constructed was, that which runs from Gadag, in Dharwar district, across the river Krishna, to Bijapore and on to Sholapore, a tract of country which has often been desolated by famine and other natural calamities. In 1791 the ground was covered with skulls, during what is known to this day, as the Skull famine. In the famine of 1876 and 1877, which led to so many railway extensions, the Bijapore district suffered more severely than any other part of the Bombay Presidency, and in 1879 its crops were devoured by rats, of which upwards of four millions were destroyed. Plague, pestilence and famine, have for ages seized upon these uplands as their own, but from the Mahratta country, whence hordes of robbers once sallied forth on their plundering expeditions, leaving ruin and want in their train, the beneficent railway now stretches forth its branches conveying food and succour to the Deccan, the Ceded Districts, and Mysore.

It is to their misfortunes that these tracts of country owe the early provision of railway communications. The Northern Circars, on the other hand, which until lately have been more remote from railways, than any other part of India, have generally been rich and prosperous. They were among our earliest acquisitions, and those who know these districts best, are most confident that the East Coast Railway, by which they will now be connected with other railway systems, will prove a more remunerative line, than any one that has hitherto been constructed within, or upon the confines of, the Madras Presidency.

The Governor had hoped to travel westwards by the South Mahratta Railway as far as Bijapore, but his engagements forbade the excursion. The ruins of the "Palmyra of the Deccan" are well worth a visit. They bring home to those who see them, the greatness of the Mussulman kingdoms of the Peninsula which were added to the empire of the Mogul, in the time of Aurangzebe. Since the Adil Shahi dynasty was founded in 1489, by a reputed son of the then Sultan of Turkey, at least two of its kings have been housed in death in such fashion, that their memories yet live. The beautiful proportions, profuse, yet graceful ornament, and lace-like carvings of the mausoleum of Ibrahim Adil Shah, excite the admiration of visitors familiar with the Taj, and other masterpieces of Saracenic architecture, while Sultan Mahmood reposes beneath the largest dome in the world, which crowns a suitably imposing mass of plain masonry. Architects have fully described this wondrous work, astonished at a covered area of upwards of 18,000 square feet, uninterrupted by supports. They compare it with the Pantheon, the next largest space covered by a single dome, and with St. Paul's, with which it is contemporary. The buildings are of a widely different character, and all technicalities apart, I would describe the Bijapore dome as resembling an inverted teacup, while that of the Pantheon favours the form of an inverted saucer. The Gothic arches of another incomplete mausoleum, notwithstanding the wholly different character of the surroundings, at once recall the ruins of Tintern Abbey. I should hesitate to say so, but that every visitor makes the same remark.

To return to the railways of the Madras Presidency.

As this has been *par excellence* a Railway Tour, it will be interesting to sum up the results of railway administration for the last four years, a term which synchronizes with Lord Connemara's tenure of office up to date.

The Bellary-Krishna and Tripati-Nellore lines have been opened, the Nizam's Railway has been extended to Bezwada, and the Madras Railway to Calicut, while a branch of the last-named line has also been made to Palghat.

The Villupuram-Tripati and Pakal-Guntakal lines are under construction, and approach completion.

The construction of the above-mentioned lines was of course sanctioned before 1886.

The East Coast, Trivalur-Muttupett, and Nilgiri Railways have just been commenced, and the Madras-Bezwada, and Mysore Frontier to Gudalur, lines are under survey.

To sum up, during the last four years 393 miles of railway have been opened, 366 miles are under construction and well advanced towards completion; operations which will eventually extend over 558 miles, have been commenced within the last few days, and the survey of 284 miles has just been sanctioned.

VILLUPURAM-TRIPATI RAILWAY.

Lord Connemara made one more tour before he left Madras, on the 7th December 1890, exactly four years after his arrival. He went to open the * Villupuram-Tirunomalei section of the Villupuram-Tripati

* Lord Wenlock has since opened a further extension to Tripati.

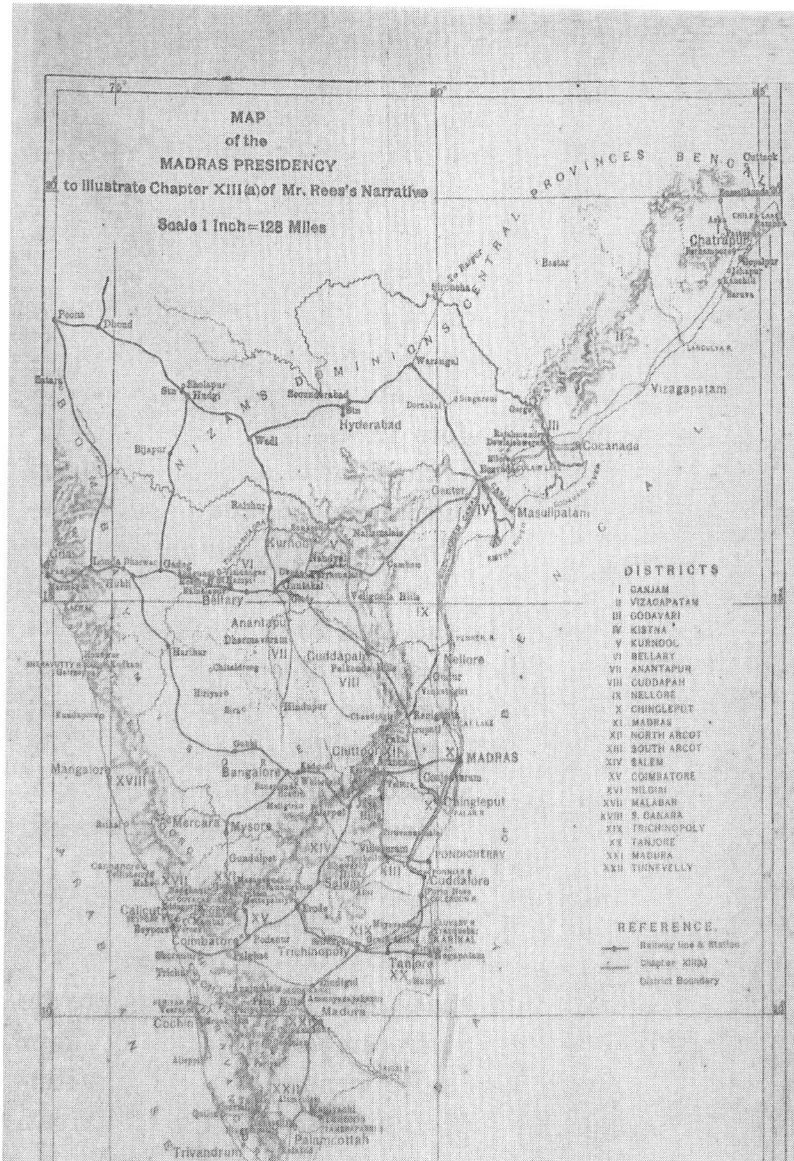
MAP
of the
MADRAS PRESIDENCY
to illustrate Chapter XIII (a) of Mr. Rees's Narrative
Scale 1 Inch = 128 Miles
DISTRICTS
I GANJAM
II VIZAGAPATAM
III GODAVARI
IV KISTNA
V KURNOOL
VI BELLARY
VII ANANTAPUR
VIII CUDDAPAH
IX NELLORE
X CHINGLEPUT
XI MADRAS
XII NORTH ARCOT
XIII SOUTH ARCOT
XIV SALEM
XV COIMBATORE
XVI NILGIRI
XVII MALABAR
XVIII S. CANARA
XIX TRICHINOPOLY
XX TANJORE
XXI MADURA
XXII TINNEVELLY
REFERENCE.
Railway line & Station
Chapter XIII(a)
District Boundary
NIZAM'S DOMINIONS
CENTRAL PROVINCES
Hyderabad
Vizagapatam
Cocanada
Masulipatam
Nellore
MADRAS
Chingleput
Cuddalore
Bangalore
Mysore
Mangalore
Calicut
Coimbatore
Trichinopoly
Tanjore
Madura
Cochin
Trivandrum
Palamcottah
Bellary
Anantapur
Chatrapur

line mentioned above, and Captain Stamer and I accompanied him. The tour merely consisted of a run to Tirunomalei, where there is a great Shivite temple, and back again to Madras. The inhabitants of a town on the new line complained of the situation of their station, and His Excellency, after a brief consultation with his colleague Mr. Garstin, and with the Consulting Engineer, and after visiting both sites, with characteristic readiness, resolved, upon the spot, to make the change desired.

Speaking at luncheon at Villupuram the same day he made an appreciative reference to the foregoing Narratives of his journeys in and around the Madras Presidency, which had given me the opportunity to lay down the pen of a "historiographer" in a happy hour, but for the regret I feel, that our frequent travels together are over, and our ever pleasant relations, ended.

FINIS.

INDEX.